# Creative Writing
## An Introduction to Poetry and Fiction

David Starkey

Santa Barbara City College

Bedford/St. Martin's    Boston ◆ New York

# For My Mother

**For Bedford/St. Martin's**
*Senior Executive Editor:* Stephen A. Scipione
*Production Editor:* Kerri A. Cardone
*Production Supervisor:* Victoria Anzalone
*Senior Marketing Manager:* Stacy Propps
*Editorial Assistant:* Laura Horton
*Copy Editor:* Beverly Miller
*Indexer:* Steve Csipke
*Senior Art Director:* Anna Palchik
*Cover Design and Art:* Billy Boardman
*Composition:* Cenveo Publisher Services
*Printing and Binding:* RR Donnelley and Sons

*President, Bedford/St. Martin's:* Denise B. Wydra
*Editor in Chief:* Karen S. Henry
*Director of Marketing:* Karen R. Soeltz
*Production Director:* Susan W. Brown
*Director of Rights and Permissions:* Hilary Newman

Manufactured in the United States of America.
8   7   6   5   4   3
f   e   d   c   b   a

*For information, write:* Bedford/St. Martin's, 75 Arlington Street, Boston, MA 02116 (617-399-4000)

ISBN 978-1-4576-6167-9

**Acknowledgments**

*Acknowledgments and copyrights are continued at the back of the book on pages 239–42, which constitute an extension of the copyright page. It is a violation of the law to reproduce these selections by any means whatsoever without the written permission of the copyright holder.*

# PREFACE: A few words to instructors

*Creative Writing: Four Genres in Brief*—the predecessor of the text you are reading, *Creative Writing: An Introduction to Poetry and Fiction*—came about because I found the available creative writing textbooks, while often excellent, didn't reflect two important realities of the four-genre course: the lack of sufficient time (how can an instructor effectively teach writing in multiple genres over the span of only a semester or a quarter?); and the range of students who take the class (not just creative writing majors, but students from a variety of disciplines just testing the creative writing waters).

Given the time constraints and diverse knowledge levels of students, it seemed to me that model pieces of creative writing in textbooks were generally far longer and more complex than the work we *really* expected students to write, while the craft instruction similarly assumed that students had practically unlimited time to complete their work. So for *Creative Writing: Four Genres in Brief* I chose model stories, poems, plays, and essays that were very short, and kept my own instruction relatively brief and punctuated with many quick-review checklists.

However, as soon as the four-genre book published, I began hearing from colleagues whose introductory creative writing courses cover only poetry and fiction. While these instructors liked the student-friendly tone and condensed format of *Creative Writing: Four Genres in Brief*, the inclusion of two additional genres they didn't plan to teach—creative nonfiction and drama—made the book, for their purposes, too long by half.

The people who contacted me weren't alone. Nearly a third of all creative writing classes taught in the United States and Canada focus only on the two main genres, and yet there are remarkably few options for instructors who would like a single craft textbook covering both genres that also includes a robust of sampling of contemporary work.

Enter *Creative Writing: An Introduction to Poetry and Fiction*. Above all, this book, like its four- genre predecessor, is intended to be pragmatic. If money and time were no object, an introductory course might include two craft books on the two different genres, as well as two separate anthologies packed with representative examples of each genre. But because money and time are important considerations, *Creative Writing: An Introduction to Poetry and Fiction* combines all the resources students will need in a single compact, affordable package.

The suggestions of several instructors who teach a two-genre course helped me shape the four-genre book into *Creative Writing: An Introduction to Poetry and Fiction*. Specifically:

▸ Because students in two-genre classes have more time to work on assignments than their counterparts in three- and four-genre classes, I have slightly adapted the craft discussion of fiction to include not just short stories but longer stories as well.

▸ Both the poetry and fiction anthologies include significantly more model stories and poems than in the four-genre book. The increased number and variety of stories allows instructors to highlight full-length stories, remain focused on short stories, or teach a combination of both. In the poetry anthology, more poems mean more opportunity for inspiration and emulation.

▸ Three new poetic forms are included in the popular Poetic Forms section. Students seem to be particularly enamored of short forms, so I have added the haiku, rondelet, and triolet.

## How the book is organized

That's the *why* of *Creative Writing: An Introduction to Poetry and Fiction*. Here's the *how*.

▸ The book begins with a general introduction to the differences and similarities between creative writing and the expository writing done in most college classes. The introduction orients students by suggesting what they already know that might be useful, and what they can expect to learn. A brief section following the introduction lays out some proven strategies for revision, and students can turn to the endpapers to find checklists of tips for revising in both genres.

▸ Following the introduction are the chapters focusing on poetry and fiction. Both chapters begin with a brief opening section that sketches out the broad parameters of the genre. Then, I analyze three model examples of work in the genre, focusing on their use of literary elements. After the discussion of each element, I summarize for students the main points about using the element in their own writing. Sprinkled throughout the chapter are key terms (called out in **boldface** the first time they appear in each chapter and collected in a glossary at the end of the book). The chapters culminate with a series of "Kick-Starts," exercises and strategies to help students generate ideas and begin the writing process.

▸ After the "Kick-Starts" are anthologies of work in each genre. Occasionally, I have included an important older work, but the focus is on excellent contemporary writers whom students probably have not encountered before. The anthology selections range from the more traditional—with work by such writers as Allegra Goodman, Ron Rash, Jane Kenyon, and Mary Oliver—to the experimental—including pieces by Rae Armantrout, Lynne Tillman, Joyce Carol Oates, and Matthew Zapruder.

▶ A section at the back of the book offers students practical suggestions for getting their creative work out into the world. The recommendations are detailed and realistically scaled to what beginning writers can hope to achieve in their first attempts at bringing their poems and stories to a larger public.

Ultimately, the instructor and the students make a great creative writing class, but most instructors will be glad for any help they can get in conveying basic information about poetry and fiction. A book like this one helps you focus your attention on the needs and talents and the fears and aspirations of your students. *Creative Writing: An Introduction to Poetry and Fiction* is here to help make the complicated business of teaching just a little bit easier.

## Thanks

My thanks to the many readers, reviewers, and adopters of the four-genre book, whose suggestions improved the first two editions, and whose advice is reflected in the pages of *Creative Writing: An Introduction to Poetry and Fiction*: M. Lee Alexander, College of William and Mary; John Belk, Pennsylvania State University; Jenny Box, East Mississippi Community College; Daryl W. Brown, University of North Alabama; Jeanne DeQuine, Miami-Dade College; Melvin Donalson, California State University, Los Angeles; Amie A. Doughty, SUNY-Oneonta; Laurie Lynn Drummond, University of Oregon; Marilyn Y. Ford, East Mississippi Community College; Pamela Gemin, University of Wisconsin, Oshkosh; Mary B. Graham, Cuyamaca College; Martha Greenwald, University of Louisville; Kevin Griffith, Capital University; Joseph D. Haske, South Texas College; Sonya Huber, Georgia Southern University; Claire Kageyama-Ramakrishnan, Houston Community College, Central Campus; Laura Kopchick, University of Texas at Arlington; Thomas Maltman, Normandale Community College; Michael Minassian, Broward Community College; Rebecca Mooney, Bakersfield College; Juan Morales, Colorado State University, Pueblo; Jim Peterson, Randolph-Macon College; Joyce Pesseroff, University of Massachusetts, Boston; Stuart Peterfreund, Northeastern University; Lauri Ramey, California State University, Los Angeles; Christopher Ransick, Arapahoe Community College; Brent Royster, Ball State University; Tom Schmidt, Rogue Community College; Jeremy Schraffenberger; Binghamton University; Pat Tyrer, West Texas A & M University; Vallie Lynn Watson, Southeast Missouri State University; Theresa Welford, Georgia Southern University; Jerry Wemple, Bloomsburg University; Robert Wiley, Oakland Community College; Paul Willis, Westmont College; Martha Witt, William Patterson University; and Angus Woodward, Our Lady of the Lake College. I am especially grateful to Jim Peterson of Randolph College, Thomas Schmidt of Rogue Community College, and Paul Willis of Westmont College, all of whom reviewed the longer book with an eye to adapting it for two-genre courses.

Thanks also to the good folks at Bedford/St. Martin's: Maureen Tomlin, who suggested that I submit my proposal; Leasa Burton and Ellen Darion, who saw its potential; and Joan Feinberg, Denise Wydra, and Karen Henry, who gave the book the green light. I'd like to thank Margaret Gorenstein and Kalina Ingham for their work on permissions, and Laura Horton for the editorial tasks she performed throughout the development process. Thanks to Stacey Propps for her marketing efforts. In the production department, I'm grateful to Susan Brown and Elise Kaiser; to Beverly Miller for her sensitive and tactful copyediting; and especially to the book's friendly and efficient production editor, Kerri Cardone. Above all, I appreciate the editorial contributions of Steve Scipione, who was there from the initial concept to the final product—and every step in between.

Finally, I would like to thank my parents, Frank and Betty; my children and stepchildren, Elizabeth, Carly, Stephen, Miranda, Serena, Andrea, Julia, and John; and especially my lovely, patient, and brilliant wife, Sandy.

—David Starkey

## Further resources for teaching and learning

*Creative Writing: An Introduction to Poetry and Fiction* doesn't end with a print book. Online you'll find resources to help students get even more out of this text and your course. To learn about or order any of the products below, contact your Bedford/St/Martins sales representative, email sales support (sales_support@ bfwpub.com), or visit **bedfordstmartins.com/starkeypoetryfiction/catalog**.

**This book is available as a Bedford e-Book to Go**    This PDF-style e-book matches our print book page for page, and is ready for your tablet, computer, phone, or e-reader device. You and your students gain access to the e-book through this book's catalog page (see below) and can take it with you wherever you go. To order the e-book for your course, use **ISBN 978-1-4576-6484-7**. At 50% the cost of the print book, the *Bedford e-Book To Go for Creative Writing: Introduction to Poetry and Fiction* is convenient and affordable.

**Download your instructor's resources.**    *Resources for Teaching Creative Writing: An Introduction to Poetry and Fiction,* written by David Starkey, offers commentaries on the poems and stories in the book's anthologies, along with a bibliography of useful resources for teaching creative writing. For the PDF, go to **bedfordstmartins.com/starkeypoetryfiction/catalog**.

## Packaging options

Take advantage of our collection of author videos—and an e-portfolio tool available at a discount with student copies of *Creative Writing: An Introduction to Poetry and Fiction*.

**This book comes with video**    Bring today's writers into your classroom. Hear from T.C. Boyle, Ha Jin, Jane Smiley, and others, on character, voice, plot, and more. Questions, biographies, and transcripts make each video an assignable module. To package this collection, free with new student copies of this book, use **ISBN 978-1-4576-8270-4** or visit **bedfordstmartins.com/videolit/catalog**.

**The Bedford e-Portfolio**   Select. Collect. Reflect. The Bedford e-Portfolio makes it easy for students to showcase their writing and other coursework—whether for their class, for their job, or even for their friends. With flexible assessment tools, the Bedford e-Portfolio lets you map learning outcomes or just invite students to start their collections. Use **ISBN 978-1-4576-8269-8** or visit **bedfordstmartins.com/eportfolio**.

## Get teaching ideas you can use today

Are you looking for free & open professional resources for teaching literature and writing? How about some help with planning classroom activities?

**LitBits**   Ideas for Teaching Literature & Creative Writing. Hosted by a team of instructors, poets, novelists, and scholars, our *LitBits* blog offers fresh, regularly updated ideas and assignments for teaching creative writing, including simple ways to teach with media. Check out posts on teaching literature and creative writing at **bedfordstmartins.com/litbits**.

**Teaching Central**   All of our professional resources, in one place. You'll find landmark reference works, sourcebooks on pedagogical issues, award-winning collections, and practical advice for the classroom—all free. **bedfordstmartins .com/teachingcentral**

## Add value to your course

Could your students use some help with style, grammar, and clarity? Have you ever wanted to put together your own custom anthology? Would you like to teach with longer works by adding a trade title or two to your course?

**Add a handbook & save your students 20%**   Package *EasyWriter* by Andrea Lunsford or *A Pocket Style Manual* by Diana Hacker and Nancy Sommers with this text and save your students 20%. Visit **bedfordstmartins.com/easywriter/ catalog** or **bedfordstmartins.com/pocket/catalog**.

**Create your own anthology of poetry and fiction**   *Creative Writing: An Introduction to Poetry and Fiction* includes anthologies of contemporary poetry and fiction, but are you looking for more? Choose your literature, select a cover, and publish at **bedfordstmartins.com/select**.

**Save 50% on hundreds of trade titles**   Package a trade book for half off with new student copies of *Creative Writing: An Introduction to Poetry and Fiction*. Visit **bedfordstmartins.com/tradeup**

# Contents

## 1  Writing Poetry  14

## An Anthology of Poems  74

## 2    Writing the Short Story  104

## An Anthology of Short Stories 156

# A Few Things You Should Know about Creative Writing

The first thing I say to my students once they have settled in their seats on the first day of class is, "Welcome to the best course in the college." I mean that, too. I can't imagine a better place to spend time as a student, or as a teacher, than in an introductory creative writing class.

The level of excitement and possibility in a class such as the one you're now part of is hard to match. You may already feel some of that exhilaration yourself as you begin reading this book. Are you the next great novelist? The next U.S. poet laureate? Of course, the chance of becoming famous is slim, especially in early-twenty-first-century America, where there are loads of writers and a lot of competition—but you never know. And even if your work doesn't receive wide critical acclaim, even if it's not published, there is no satisfaction quite like the satisfaction writers get from knowing they have written something they can be proud of.

If this class truly is the best in your college or university, what makes it so different from the others? In order to enroll in introductory creative writing, you probably have taken at least one college writing, or composition, course as a prerequisite. *Composition* is a word students tend to dread seeing on their course enrollment forms. But is composition, or expository writing, really so different from creative writing? Not as much as you might think, and that's a good thing, believe it or not. In your composition classes, you acquired a repertoire of writerly skills and strategies that will serve you well in this class.

Creative writing builds on these abilities, although it's sometimes difficult to convince students of this fact. Do you recognize yourself in the description of a student who "found composition a dreary, teacher-imposed task and creative writing something done to pass time, for fun"? This is how Wendy Bishop (one of the great creative writing teachers of the late twentieth century) described many of those who signed up for her courses. Another of Bishop's students said, "In creative writing, I feel that there are no set guidelines. It leaves room for experimentation, and you can go in any angle or direction. In expository prose [composition] you have set guidelines of what you must write and how you should write it."

Although experimentation is certainly a quality about creative writing that many writers find appealing, it is not true that the field has "no set guidelines." Once you begin thinking of publication, as most writers eventually do, more often than not, you will find that there are particular editors and agents who handle specific **genres**—that is, a particular category of literary work. Poetry goes to the poetry editor, this agent handles only mysteries, another specializes in romances, and so on. Even within the broad outlines of a genre, editors have "set guidelines"—whether or not they are articulated—about what's good and what's not. Otherwise, how would they decide which work to accept or reject?

In her book *Released into Language: Options for Teaching Creative Writing*, Bishop made a number of innovative connections between the teaching of expository and creative writing. Most of her contentions were adaptations of ideas that theorists in composition and rhetoric had developed through decades of research and discussion. Many of these discipline-wide values were spelled out in November 2004, when the National Council of Teachers of English issued a position statement, "Beliefs about the Teaching of Writing." Looking more closely at these beliefs will be useful to you as a new creative writing student because

▶ these beliefs underlie the **pedagogy**, or theory of teaching, behind this book;

▶ your instructor—the person who will be awarding your final grade—probably shares many of these assumptions about the teaching of creative writing;

▶ knowing *how* we learn something is a necessary prelude to actually doing the learning; and

▶ even if you find yourself disagreeing with one or more of these beliefs, thinking about *why* can be a critical stage in your development as a creative writer.

# "Beliefs about the teaching of writing" ▶

**1. Everyone has the capacity to write, writing can be taught, and teachers can help students become better writers.** This may sound like an obvious statement. After all, if your college or university didn't believe it, why would it be offering this course? But for a long time, creative writers themselves disagreed about whether creative writing *could* be taught. Some famous writers who also happened to be teachers contended that the ability to write well was a gift passed down from the gods. Either you had it or you didn't, and there wasn't much your teacher could do about it if you were in the have-not camp.

Fortunately, in recent years, these writers have tended to leave teaching to those people who truly love doing it. And although some students arrive in the class with more talent and experience than others, in general everyone in a creative writing class can learn quite a bit—not only from the teacher but also from one another.

**2. People learn to write by writing.** It's great to think about writing and to talk about it. It's wonderful to read the work of other writers. But the only way you will ever become a better writer is to sit down and write. "The first and most important thing you have to know about writing," according to Walter Mosley, "is that it is something you must do every day. Every morning or every night, whatever time it is you have. Hopefully," Mosley adds, "the time you decide on is when you do your best work."

For some people, finding that time can be a real problem. They have busy schedules—jobs, family obligations, other classes—that keep them from writing. Time management and sheer willpower are their allies. Other people have time but find they have difficulty focusing; they have enrolled in this class to force themselves into a writing schedule. Fear of receiving a poor grade is a motivating factor for this group.

Even if you're not disorganized or in a perpetual time crunch, you may find all those ideas that have been swirling around in your head for weeks or months or years have suddenly vanished now that you have been assigned to sit down and actually write something.

Don't panic. Listen to Mosley: Keep trying to write. Keep reading. Keep talking to people about what you're trying to do and why it suddenly seems so hard. Fortunately, writer's block is not fatal, and it doesn't last forever. In fact, it's fairly common. "Death and taxes. Writers and writer's block," Wendy Bishop said, suggesting that—like those other two inevitabilities—block is something no writer can avoid facing at one time or another. Writing theorist Robert Graves even argues that "blocking is a by-product of any creative endeavor." According to Graves, the problem and solutions represented by blocking allow us to grow as writers. If there wasn't a hurdle to overcome, our work would never get any better.

Writer's block usually comes when those writing hurdles are too great for our experience and skill to surmount. One of the rationales for beginning your creative writing experience with just two main genres, poetry and fiction, is that their parameters are more clearly defined, so your goal of completing each assignment will be more easily reached.

**3. Writing is a process.** Again, this may seem self-evident, but too often students feel that their first draft, written at a moment of heightened inspiration, is all the writing they need to do. If this description of the writing process sounds like your own, you should—in this class, at least—try to modify it. While it's true that every creative writer remembers a moment when a piece of outstanding work just came pouring out, almost perfect from the start, that's a rarity for most of us. Chances are that the story or poem that looked "perfect" the night you wrote it will turn out to have more than a few flaws the next morning.

Researchers have found that writing done well is usually a recursive process rather than a one-time effort. We start with an idea, or an image, or a phrase. We talk about it with friends, or we begin to make notes, or we simply jump in and start writing. We breeze through the first draft, or we get stuck but keep returning to it until it is finished. We share the piece with another writer, or we put it in a drawer for a week. But we always come back to it, look it over, and work at it again. We may tweak a few sentences, or we may save only the final passage and delete everything else. We make more notes. We talk to friends. We go at it yet again.

Revision is crucial in the writing process. Most writers have a small but trusted group of friends or editors to whom they can show their drafts without worrying that the comments they receive will be overly negative. The more ambition you have for your poetry and fiction, the greater you want it to be, the more likely your work will need not only some major surgery but also plenty of tinkering and polishing.

Even professional journalists working on a deadline, who appear to produce flawless first drafts, have a process of some sort. If they're reporters, they have taken notes. And the rare writer who takes no notes at all will have been silently thinking about an idea, talking it over with colleagues or friends, rehearsing mentally and verbally for the task of facing the page.

**4. Writing and reading are related.** In *Reading like a Writer*, Francine Prose reminds those who want to be creative writers that there is no substitute for reading. She claims that is how it has always been:

> Long before the idea of a writers' conference was a glimmer in anyone's eye, writers learned by reading the work of their predecessors. They studied meter with Ovid, plot construction with Homer, comedy with Aristophanes; they honed their prose style by absorbing the lucid sentences of Montaigne and Samuel Johnson. And who could have asked for better teachers: generous, uncritical, blessed with wisdom and genius, as endlessly forgiving as only the dead can be?

Growing up in a home where reading is valued is a common experience for creative writers, Meg Wolitzer says, "Reading was always something given great importance in my family, and becoming a writer seems to be a natural progression." Nicholasa Mohr adds, "I am always glad to express gratitude to the library. I spent my youth there, reading."

Even if reading was not a central part of your own youth, you can still acquire the habit. Learning to write well in a genre requires reading extensively in that genre. Your instructor may not assign all the work in this book, but I urge you to read it anyway. And when you're finished, go to the library or the bookstore and check out or buy anthologies of recent work. Read *The Pushcart Prize* and *Best American Poetry* and *Best American Short Stories* series. Visit literary clearinghouse Web sites such as the Council of Literary Magazine Publishers (www.clmp.org /directory/index.php) and Litline (www.litline.org), and read through sample issues of both print and online journals. What poems are being published in the *Kenyon Review*? What is the latest in avant-garde fiction according to the editors at *Conjunctions*?

The more committed you are to your own writing, the more likely you are to want to know what has been written before. Pulitzer Prize–winning poet Jorie Graham says, "Right from the beginning, I knew that I was going to be reading for the rest of my life, and I guess part of the act of writing poetry is involved with the enormous pleasures of reading a thousand years of poetry written in the English language and constantly feeling the people writing six, seven, eight hundred years ago are still bringing you the news."

Some students avoid reading because they worry about being overly influenced by another writer. Don't worry. Embrace the influence. *Try* to write the best Charles Bukowski imitation you can manage. You won't be able to pull it off, and sooner or later you will grow tired of sounding too much like the writer you adore. At that point, your own voice will begin to emerge.

Novelist Jeffrey Eugenides says it splendidly:

Influence isn't just a matter of copying someone or learning his or her tricks. You get influenced by writers whose work gives you hints about your own abilities and inclinations. Being influenced is largely a process of self-discovery. What you have to do is put all your influences into the blender and arrive at your own style and vision. That's the way it happens in music—you put a sitar in a rock song and you get a new sound. . . . Hybrid vigor. It operates in art, too. The idea that a writer is a born genius, endowed with blazing originality, is mostly a myth, I think. You have to work at your originality. You create it; it doesn't create you.

We learn from studying examples of good writing, but we also learn from the advice of other authors: those who have gone before us, faced similar struggles, and come up with strategies for overcoming the obstacles that are blocking our paths. As a result, this book is liberally sprinkled with quotes from writers, both obscure and renowned.

**5. Writing benefits from talking.** Just about any introductory creative writing course will include a significant amount of in-class discussion. Most instructors want to talk about both the model readings *and* the student work being produced for the class. Look at these discussions as a way to learn from your classmates as well as your instructor. If you're shy, try to participate at least once every class. If you're gregarious, look for ways not to dominate the conversation but to bring out those students who aren't lucky enough to have your confidence.

Talking about writing allows you to begin developing an **aesthetic**, a sense of what you want to see in a work of art. Becoming a creative writer means becoming articulate in your analysis and informed in your opinions of the writing of others. In fact, Brett Hall Jones believes that workshop participants grow "more by looking closely at another's work than they do when it is their turn to have their piece critiqued. The selfless attention to another writer's work is where the real learning takes place."

Moreover, if your own writing is suffering from block, talking about it can often help you see what you're doing wrong. Ideally, you can discuss your work with your instructor or another student in the class, but even if your conversation is with your mother, who knows nothing about creative writing, or your dog, Rusty, whose only qualifications as a listener are his big brown eyes, the act of dissecting your own work aloud is usually beneficial.

**6. Writing and reading are part of a matrix of complicated social relationships.** *How* you write depends on *who* your audience is. If, for instance, you are writing a story that only your best friend will read, you might include a number of **allusions**, or references, that only he or she would understand. That same story wouldn't work as well for a class of people who didn't already know the characters involved, and your classmates would probably recommend that you revise certain aspects of the story to make it more accessible. Your decision about whether to follow their advice might hinge on your ultimate goals for your story: Is it something personal and private, not meant to be shared? Or are you trying to reach a broader audience, which would mean that your responsibilities as a writer would change?

"If you want to write, or really create anything," Allegra Goodman says, "you have to risk falling on your face." Most writers would agree with Goodman, but do you really want to risk falling on your face when you're trying to get a good grade? Luckily, creative writing instructors tend to favor the portfolio method of assessment, which allows you to experiment and revise your work throughout the quarter or semester.

Writing is a social activity, and we don't all start writing from the same place. Some of us grew up in communities in which nonstandard English was spoken. Some of us come to English as our second language. The words you use and the way you use them depend largely on who you are and where you're from. In a traditional expository writing course, instructors sometimes try to minimize linguistic markers of class, race, gender, region, and so on. However, the same use of language that might worry a composition teacher can be the basis for outstanding creative writing. In her critically acclaimed work, *Borderlands/ La Frontera: The New Mestiza*, Gloria Anzaldúa embraces "the borderland dialect that I grew up with, talking both Spanish and English." Anzaldúa wants her readers "to start thinking about the myth of a monocultural U.S." Multicultural and even multilingual writing celebrates the author's heritage; it reaches out to different groups and expands our ideas of creativity.

If in your class you read writing that describes experiences outside the boundaries of your own life and that doesn't initially resonate with you, come back to it later and give it a second chance. Whether this work is by a student or a professional writer, it's sure to have some merit, and one of the great benefits of taking a creative writing course is the way it deepens, enriches, and complicates our understanding of other people.

**7. Conventions of finished and edited texts are important to readers and therefore to writers.** When you turn in a paper for a standard academic course, whether it is for English or Communication or Psychology, your instructor is likely to expect a clean copy of that paper—one that has been edited to eliminate spelling, punctuation, and grammar errors. If you hand in an essay that hasn't been carefully proofread, you will probably get it back with lots of red ink.

Some students enroll in a creative writing class with the idea that the conventions of written English are no longer applicable. It's true that you can write sentence fragments here. If your characters have poor grammar, you can mimic their mistakes. However, it's not true that everything you have ever learned about correct writing goes out the window in creative writing. Just look at the models of professional writing in this book. Even the majority of the poets, typically the most relentless experimenters with language, write in carefully wrought sentences. The fiction writers are, if anything, *hyper*conscious of issues of prose styles and conventions.

In short, don't turn in an unrevised first draft in the belief that all those mistakes won't really matter because your creativity will shine through. The best creative writers are the best *writers*. Period. Abstract painters know how to paint. Free jazz musicians know how to play. Language is your medium; use it with care.

**8. Assessment of writing involves complex, informed human judgment.** Like it or not, someone will grade your work, and that someone is your instructor. Evaluating writing does involve "human judgment." You can't feed a poem into a Scantron machine and get back a score. At least as of this moment, computers have serious difficulty in assessing expository writing, much less creative work. So to a large extent, you have to trust your instructor's considered opinion about your work.

Some instructors provide a checklist or a rubric that details exactly what they want and don't want you to do. Other instructors allow their guidelines to develop from class discussion. If you're not clear what your professor is looking for, ask. Normally instructors feel they have already made their expectations clear, but they're happy to reiterate what they're looking for in a particular genre.

Sometimes students find that an instructor doesn't have nearly as much enthusiasm for a poem or story as do the students in the class. The students *loved* it, but the teacher had a number of reservations. By all means, enjoy your classmates' compliments, but don't let them go to your head. The praise of one's peers, particularly when they are still in the process of finding their own voices, can be notoriously fickle. And the reservations of your instructor are likely based on his or her extensive experience in reading and assessing creative writing. What sounds like an incredibly innovative idea to a class of new writers—a story about a writer not being able to write a story, for instance—won't be nearly as fresh to your instructor, who has read many versions of the same idea in the past.

And let's face it: your teacher may have a very different aesthetic than you do. Some of us are more sympathetic to experimental work. Others are quite traditional in their tastes. Not every piece you turn in is going to get a perfect reading from your instructor. Nevertheless, your teacher is quite likely a published author and, at the very least, has been reading and writing considerably longer than you have. Ultimately, at least for the duration of this academic term, you will have to trust his or her judgment of your work.

## Final words

Finally, here are a few simple words before you jump into this book:

- ▶ Read.
- ▶ Write.
- ▶ Listen.
- ▶ Don't give up.
- ▶ Have fun!

# A Few Words about Revision

Although **revision**—the act of reconsidering and altering a piece of writing—may initially seem like a chore, most literary writers come to enjoy the process as much as, if not more than, the creation of the first draft. Indeed, finding yourself deep in a successful revision can become almost a mystical experience. "Revising makes a person aware of how vast imagination is," Baron Wormser writes. "One accesses something much larger than one's self."

While editing and proofreading may take place in the revision process, those tasks are not what most teachers mean by revision. *Editing* means eliminating sentence-level errors. *Proofreading* is simply making a final pass through your draft to ensure that you haven't left in any silly mistakes ("loose" for "lose," "it's" for "its," and so on).

Revision in creative writing is a much larger process. It involves what might be called global as much as local issues. A thorough revision might mean reconceptualizing both the protagonist and the plot of your story, or it might mean deleting the first three stanzas of your six-stanza poem. According to Todd Lubart, "The revision process involves comparing an existing text to a writer's goals or ideal text, diagnosing the differences, and deciding how to reduce or remove these differences to bring the text as close as possible to the desired status." Georgia Heard likes to remind her students that "revision doesn't necessarily take place after they've finished a piece of writing, but instead . . . will most likely occur throughout the writing process."

In an essay comparing the composing strategies of student writers and experienced adult writers, Nancy Sommers notes that "experienced writers describe their primary objective when revising as finding the form or shape of their argument." Sommers goes on to remark that experienced writers believe that "their first drafts are usually scattered attempts to define their territory," while the goal of second drafts "is to begin observing general patterns of development and deciding what should be included and what should be excluded." Ultimately Sommers finds two general elements common to the revision process of most experienced writers: "the adoption of a holistic perspective and the perception that revision is a recursive process."

That word "recursive" comes up frequently when writing teachers discuss revision. It has different meanings in different contexts, but in this case here usually refers to modifying the piece of writing repeatedly and in all stages of the composition process in order to discover the work's optimal form. Revision, as you probably already know, can be messy. Susan Osborn describes the composition process of fellow writer Florence Howe as "neither precise nor formulaic but rather ambiguous, complex, recursive, at times inefficient, bewildering." As Brock Dethier puts it, "Writing is almost never a linear process that starts with a title and marches directly to a conclusion, with never a backward glance. Instead, most writers take a few—or a few hundred—steps forward, then circle back and cut, expand, and revise."

If revision is such a challenging and unsystematic activity, you might ask yourself if it's even necessary. After all, John Keats famously wrote, "If poetry comes not so naturally as leaves to a tree, it had better not come at all." Similarly, Charles Olson contended, "From the moment [the poet] ventures into FIELD COMPOSITION . . . he can go by no other track than the one poem under hand declares, for itself." Aren't writers inspired by the Muses? Don't we know instinctively what to do? Doesn't the best writing just *happen*?

The answer to these questions is "Unfortunately not." While the "white-hot" process of unrevised composition may occasionally occur, every creative writer of any experience will acknowledge that redrafting nearly always comes into play before a work reaches its final state. Donald Murray observed, "The published writer knows it takes a great deal of practice to be spontaneous." More often than not, that first draft turns out, on closer inspection, to be considerably less wonderful than you initially thought. Usually a word or image or phrase can be salvaged from even the least successful effort, but that's not always the case. Isaac Bashevis Singer once remarked, "The wastepaper basket is the writer's best friend," and any number of writers have made similar observations: it's better to dispose of material that simply isn't working rather than remaining stubbornly attached to it.

Let's say, though, that like Nancy Welch, you find yourself driven to the revision process because you are "getting restless . . . with familiar scripts in [your] writing, recognizing their limits." Something is wrong, and you want to make it right. How do you know what to revise?

# Refer to your textbook ▶

The first place to turn is your textbook. Revision checklists punctuate every section of this book, and there are overall genre checklists on the end papers, inside the cover. These are good places to turn as you look into revising specific aspects of your work—making the dialogue in your story more believable, trimming unnecessary words from your poem.

# Work with your peers ▶

In *Acts of Revision*, Wendy Bishop writes, "You need others to revise wisely. You need to share your work with supportive readers (peers, friends, family) on the road to learning to share with more demanding critics. You need to learn to forgive yourself and play and to become your own most demanding reader." Much of the oral and written revision advice you receive in this class will be given in small peer groups and full-class workshops. In order to avoid sessions that amount to nothing more than an extended self-defense of the work, the author is normally asked not to speak while discussion of her manuscript is in progress. After the workshop, students return their marked copies to guide the writer's revisions. The workshop model suggests that writing, like carpentry, *can* be both learned and taught. While the qualities that make a master carpenter—a feel for wood, a knowledge of the appropriate tools, precision, perceptiveness—may be as elusive as those that make a master writer, the assumption is that just about anyone can become functional in the craft.

"Functional" is an important word here. Obviously the goal of your revision is to make your work as strong as it can be, but don't set your expectations too high. Donald Murray frequently told his writing students, "Great is the enemy of good." He wasn't discouraging students from aspiring toward greatness, but he was warning them against becoming so preoccupied with some unattainable goal that they didn't make the revisions necessary to make the work simply "good."

# Consult your teacher or a tutor ▶

Receiving advice in the classroom is important, but what other avenues do you have if you find that particular venue daunting or just embarrassing? Individual conferences with your teacher are among the most valuable time you can spend while in the midst of the revision process. Your instructor knows you and your work, and she or he has a good deal of experience, as both a writer and a teacher, in negotiating the writing problems you are facing. Ask brief questions before or after class, and take advantage of your professor's posted office hours to look closely with her or him at your revised work.

Your campus writing center is an important resource that many creative writing students forget to access. Granted, most tutors spend the majority of their time talking about academic prose, but many tutors are English majors and writers themselves, and they will jump at the chance to vary their workday and discuss poems and stories. Even if your writing center tutor isn't a creative writer, she or he will be trained to point out places in your text that need further modification.

# Read aloud, and read other writers' work ▶

What if you don't have time to visit your teacher or a tutor? Robert Graham notes, "A lot of writers swear by reading a work aloud—even better if it's to somebody else, because as you read you will see it through their eyes. In the absence of an audience, you will still find reading aloud to yourself an effective way of finding flaws in your writing. Read it to the wall." That advice may sound a bit odd, but generations of authors have found that simply hearing their work spoken makes it fresh and strange, allowing them to approach it from a new perspective.

Of course, there is no substitute for reading the work of other writers who have faced, and conquered, the very challenges confronting you. Reread the pieces in this book's mini-anthologies. Check out a new book from the library, or pick up an old favorite from your own shelves. Georgia Heard says, "Sometimes when I'm in the middle of writing, and I feel like I'm slogging through and the words just aren't flowing, I choose a book I like . . . that I know will sing with my own voice and help me write what I want to."

# Take a break ▶

For millennia, writers have counseled putting away material and coming back to it later on. The Roman poet Horace suggested placing a piece of writing in a drawer for nine years before returning to it with fresh eyes. Poet Donald Hall revised that number down to nine months for contemporary writers, but students enrolled in a class that may be as short as ten weeks don't have the luxury of time. Nevertheless, you will find, to use a culinary metaphor, that most writing is tastier if it is allowed to simmer rather than if it is always cooked at a full boil. At the very least, it's worth setting something aside overnight before attempting another draft.

Clearly, there is no single revision strategy suitable for every writer. Far from it. In their study "Analyzing Revision," Lester Faigley and Stephen Witte "found extreme diversity in the ways expert writers revise." Among the "situational variables" Faigley and Witte determined were "the reason why the text was being written, the format, the medium, the genre, the writer's familiarity with the writing task, the writer's familiarity with the subject, the writer's familiarity with the audience, the projected level of formality, and the length of the task and the projected text." In other words, the *context* of the situation dictates much of what can be done.

You already know that, though. You very likely have other classes and other responsibilities you need to address. Even if you hope to make creative writing your life's work, you can't devote every minute to it. You may decide that revision can wait, or be avoided altogether. Don't make that mistake. While the revision process may be chaotic and frustrating at times, in the words of Naomi Shihab Nye, "*Revision* is a beautiful word of hope. It's a new vision of something. It means you don't have to be perfect the first time. What a relief!"

# Writing Poetry

## ▶ A few things you should know about poetry

A poem, according to the dry language of the dictionary, is "a composition in verse," and verse is "metrical writing," that is, writing concerned with the number and variety of accented and unaccented syllables.

Perhaps a few hundred years ago, this might have made a barely passable definition (or perhaps not), but it certainly doesn't work well in the twenty-first century. Even many traditionalists now acknowledge that **poetry** can be made in **free verse**, a composition *not* in metrical writing. (The lines of free verse end where the poet feels they would be most effective ending, not when the required number of stressed and unstressed syllables are tallied up.) Experimental writers push free verse so far that sometimes it almost seems to become a language other than English. And if many American poets are still uncertain about the issue, just about every French poet would acknowledge that there is something called a **prose poem**, a composition that looks very much like the paragraph you are now reading but has all the heightened, compressed, and figurative language found in poetry. (**Prose** is the ordinary language of writing and speaking.)

So does "anything go" in poetry? Not exactly. If it did, there would be no need for this chapter. In his poem "A Course in Creative Writing," William Stafford says that most students "want a wilderness with a map," a diagram of how to do things. As we have just seen, it can be difficult even to define poetry, yet it makes sense that creative writing textbooks should neverthe-less attempt to sketch out the terrain. Consequently, in this chapter, you will learn about everything from the basics of the poetic line to a few of the many poetic forms that have evolved over the centuries. Because short poems are significantly shorter than even very brief stories, we have room to print quite a few examples in the anthology at the end of this chapter. For our model poems, we focus on three markedly different types of poetry: a sonnet by Gail White, a free verse poem by Ruth Stone, and an experimental piece by Rae Armantrout.

Although we'll be looking at poetry from various angles and breaking it down into its component parts, you should never lose sight of your ultimate goal for this chapter: to write good poems. If you write frequently, you'll be surprised how often you realize something you didn't know you knew, or say something you didn't think you could say. Even a master like Robert Frost found the process a constant adventure. "I have never started a poem yet whose end I knew," he said. "Writing a poem is discovering." Most good poems con-tain some element of the unexpected. A poem that's overdetermined from the start—one in which the poet can see the beginning, middle, and end before he sets down a word on paper—will probably arrive dead on the page. Nothing kills a poem faster than a **cliché**, whether it's an overused phrase or a formu-laic structure with a predictable conclusion. Novelists usually create an outline before they start to write, but poets rarely begin with more than an idea, a phrase, an image, or just a hunch. In fact, John Ashbery has said that "poetry is mostly hunches."

It may be that "hunch" is simply another word for "inspiration." John Keats famously wrote that "if poetry come not as naturally as the leaves to a tree, it had better not come at all." Even though we may ultimately spend a lot of time revising our best poems, often they are written quickly, in a burst of mental energy. Poems that *ought* to be wonderful are often a mess, while those dashed off in a moment of insight sometimes turn out to be far better. Ironi-cally, poets frequently spend much more time working on a bad poem than on a good one, and in large measure that's because the stronger work tends to emerge more fully formed right from the start. Often the hunch turns out to be a good one.

The problem with counting on the Muse, that Greek goddess presiding over the creation of poetry, is that she's notoriously fickle. "Inspiration" refers to the sacred revelation visited on a person by a god, and unfortunately that's not the sort of event that happens to most of us every day. Sometimes you'll find that the Muse is in the neighborhood, but you just don't know how to guide her to where you are: you may *want* to write a poem, but you don't have a wide enough repertoire of strategies to draw on to get started. Or you may simply feel distant from the act of writing altogether (this condition often occurs the night before poems are due in class). In either case, the kick-start prompts in this chapter will ease you into the writing process.

Another method of getting started when you're not sure where or how to begin is to write in traditional forms. For centuries, poets have been testing themselves not only against the "restrictions" imposed by elaborate rhyme and metrical schemes but also against those poets who have come before them. Consider the sonnet, for instance. Among those who have entered its "field of play" (to quote Phillis Levin) are some of the greatest poets writing in English—everyone from canonical authors such as Shakespeare, Donne, Milton, Wordsworth, Keats, and Frost to contemporary masters such as Marilyn Hacker and Molly Peacock. The "Poetic Forms" section in this chapter looks at the sonnet, the villanelle, the cinquain, and several other types of poetry. You will also read about non-Western patterns, such as the ghazal and the pantoum, which in recent decades have become staples for American poets.

For many students, entering the world of forms will be comforting. You may already be drawn to a certain type of formalism, the regular metrical rhythm and perfect rhyme that many people associate with poetry. For much of the history of poetry written in English, meter and, to a lesser extent, rhyme were considered fundamental. Whether or not poets such as Gail White would consider themselves "New Formalists"—a label given to those working in meter and rhyme in the 1980s—clearly they do value the traditional elements of verse. As the **etymology** (the derivation) of the word "poetry" suggests, a poet is one who arranges thoughts and images in an artful way. From this perspective, the poet is a kind of architect, an artisan. Like apprentice furniture makers, poets working in forms must study carefully, practice hard, and be prepared for their early efforts to be seriously flawed. A good chair, after all, is much harder to make than we might suspect—until we put our hands to the task.

Poetry can also be written in free verse, and poets such as Ruth Stone draw on a rich tradition. From the seventeenth-century translators of the King James Bible, many of whom were poets, to the nineteenth-century American innovator Walt Whitman, an effort has long been under way to capture the power of poetry without having to adhere to strict metrical patterns and rhyme schemes. Drawing on the examples of writers such as T. S. Eliot and William Carlos Williams, twentieth-century poets turned more and more frequently to free verse, and in today's creative writing classes, poetry written in free verse is the norm rather than the exception. As one of my colleagues tells his new poetry students, "If it doesn't rhyme, and you think it's a poem but aren't sure what to call it, it's probably free verse."

Like poets working in forms and in free verse, experimental (or avant-garde or postmodern) poets such as Rae Armantrout are themselves part of a long tradition, although that tradition may not be as easy to pin down. Armantrout's "Duration" is in free verse, yet with its rhythms, repetitions, and rhymes, it also contains elements of traditional verse. What *is* explicitly avant-garde about "Duration" is the way it challenges conventional expectations of what a poem should do. For most readers, the poem will initially resist interpretation or will open itself to a myriad of possible readings. Those who want their poetry straight and simple may be frustrated by Armantrout. Unlike Gail White's "My Personal Recollections of Not Being Asked to the Prom," for instance, which works hard to clearly convey a particular experience, Armantrout's poem seems to be a riddle with a number of equally plausible explanations.

Some beginning poetry students are drawn to experimental poetry because it seems to be an outsider's art: they imagine themselves as wild rebels like Allen Ginsberg, taunting the establishment, breaking all the rules, channeling the Muse, and never *ever* revising their work. "First thought, best thought," Ginsberg often said; nevertheless, he frequently revised his work, as do most other experimental writers. And as far as turning to poetry as a method of rebellion, it should be remembered that Ginsberg was a professor at both Brooklyn College and the Naropa Institute. Similarly, Rae Armantrout is a tenured professor at the University of California at San Diego. A glance at the résumés of most well-published experimental poets shows that they often make their livings as professors. Moreover, one need only think of T. S. Eliot's *The Waste Land*, once the cutting edge of experimental poetry, to realize that today's avant-garde is tomorrow's assigned reading.

Naturally, the varieties of poetry aren't limited to the three strands we have just discussed. If you have ever been to a poetry slam, you have been exposed to spoken-word or performance poetry. Although older audience members may sometimes feel they have wandered into a hip-hop show rather than a poetry reading, there's no doubt about the excitement generated by a talented performer and a ready, rowdy audience. However, because poetry intended primarily to be said aloud may differ drastically from poetry meant to be read on the page, some creative writing instructors have reservations about incorporating spoken-word poems into their curriculum. One creative writing instructor forbids his students from writing anything resembling rap lyrics; another *insists* that her students write "a rap poem" as one of the course assignments.

Whatever the policy in your class, Pamela Gemin reminds us that "the poet and the lyricist are two different creatures, though some lyrics may be 'poetic.'" Gemin notes that "the poet is a one-man band," while "songwriters have the benefit of a full range of mood-enhancing instruments, formulas and automatic cues." Therefore, if you are writing a poem that you plan to read aloud, remember that your work should be able to stand on the merits of its language. If it's full of clichés on the page, it's still full of clichés when you are belting it out in front of a crowd—even if you are charismatic enough to convince your listeners that what you are saying is fresh and new.

Ultimately, the only real way to become a poet is to keep writing poems—lots of them—most of which you'll end up throwing away. Some of those you show to other people; others are never read by anyone but you. Sooner or later, something worthwhile is bound to appear on the page, and once you train yourself to write consistently, you will begin to distinguish the good poems from the bad. Students who turn in the best poems at the end of the semester tend to be those who have been writing constantly. Not only do they rework their better poems—revising and revising them—but they also write new poems whenever they can. Their best work, they believe, is always just around the corner.

# The elements of poetry ▶

Poetry consists of a number of elements, which will be discussed more fully later in the chapter:

▶ **Lines and Stanzas** When we write prose, the sentence is our basic unit of composition. In a poem, however, we think in terms of lines—those entities that begin on the left side of the page and end somewhere on the right. Like a line of computer code, a line of poetry contains one or more usually implicit commands on how it is to be read. (An exception to this rule, the prose poem, is covered in the "Poetic Forms" section.) Stanzas are made by grouping lines together.

▶ **Meter and Rhythm** **Meter** is a regular pattern of accented and unaccented syllables. **Rhythm** refers to a variable but nevertheless recognizable pattern of strong and weak elements in a poem. Because the term "rhythm" is more flexible than "meter," we often use it when referring to free verse or experimental poetry. Even if a poem is not strictly metered, it will still have a rhythm.

▶ **The Music of Poetry** Readers and listeners often comment on the "music" of a poem: the sounds words make when coming together. The section on the music of poetry focuses on rhyme and alliteration as devices for creating musical effects in poetry.

▶ **Images, Symbols, and Figurative Language** Using concrete images, as opposed to abstractions, is a cornerstone of most contemporary poetry. Poetry also relies on **symbols**—acts, sounds, or objects that signify something other than themselves. Much of the strangeness of poetry, as opposed to everyday conversation and writing, results from the dense use of figures of speech such as metaphor, simile, metonymy, synecdoche, personification, puns, and irony.

▶ **Diction, Syntax, and the Language of Poetry** **Diction** refers to the choice of the words themselves, while **syntax** refers to the way that words are put together to form phrases in a sentence. Together, these two elements ultimately result in the creation of each individual poet's "language of poetry."

▶ **Poetic Forms** One of the pleasures of writing poetry is working in the forms handed down to us from previous generations of poets. Many of these structures have strict rules that must be followed, although we will embrace a certain amount of play and experimentation in the forms we work with. In addition to the sonnet, we will look at the villanelle, rondeau, rondelet, triolet, sestina, cinquain, haiku, pantoum, prose poetry, and ghazal.

# The short poem: Three models ▶

"What we term a long poem is in fact merely a succession of brief ones," Edgar Allan Poe writes in the *Philosophy of Composition*, "that is to say, brief poetical effects. It is needless to demonstrate that a poem is such only inasmuch as it intensely excites, by elevating the soul; and all intense excitements are, through a psychal [psychological] necessity, brief." Poe may be overstating the case, but in keeping with this chapter's focus on shorter work, the sections that follow—and the kick-starts and anthology of poems at the end of the chapter—are designed to show you a variety of ways of briefly yet "intensely exciting" your readers.

M. H. Abrams defines the **lyric poem** as "any fairly short, non-narrative poem presenting a single speaker who expresses a state of mind or a process of thought and feeling." Some of the poems you write may indeed fit neatly into this category. Others, however, will contain elements of **narrative** (that is, storytelling) or will be told from multiple points of view. Your instructor may have specific restrictions on length, but in general, if your poem begins to creep onto a third page, it probably can benefit from paring down. Rare is the poem—lyric or otherwise—that cannot be strengthened by judicious editing. If it takes you three lines to say something, see if you can say it instead in two lines, or one line, or one word.

The three model poems take very different approaches to the art of poetry, and it will pay to reread each one several times. Gail White's sonnet "My Personal Recollections of Not Being Asked to the Prom" foregrounds not just the meter and rhyme of formal verse but also the speaker's darkly comic voice. Ruth Stone's "Winter," written in densely imagistic free verse, uses the present to explore the power of memory. Rae Armantrout's elliptical "Duration" may be the least immediately accessible of the three; however, avant-garde poems like this one (and those in the anthology by Ben Lerner, and Matthew Zapruder) represent an important strand in contemporary poetry and another potential source of inspiration for new poets looking to follow Ezra Pound's famous command to "make it new."

## Gail White

# My Personal Recollections of Not Being Asked to the Prom

Gail White lives in Breaux Bridge, Louisiana, and is a regular contributor to journals specializing in traditional forms. White is known not only for her devotion to rhyme and meter but also for her dark sense of humor. She is the author of a number of **chapbooks** (a chapbook is a short book of poetry, usually fewer than thirty-two pages) and coeditor, with Katherine McAlpine, of *The Muse Strikes Back: A Poetic Response by Women to Men*.

Of the admixture of light and darkness in White's poetry, Julie Kane has written: "By refusing to create a victimized female persona as the target of her own wit, White claims a new authority for the woman light-verse writer: the right to assert herself as a satirist, as a clear-eyed critic of the world around her—a role that men have occupied almost exclusively for more than two millennia." We see that strong sense of self on display in "My Personal Recollections of Not Being Asked to the Prom," from her book *The Price of Everything*.

> I never minded my unpopularity
> in those days. Books were friends and poets (dead)
> were lovers. Brainy girls were still a rarity
> and boys preferred big bosoms to well-read
> and saucy wits. I look back now with pity
> on the young Me I didn't pity then.
> I didn't know that I was almost pretty
> and might have had a charm for older men.
> And my poor mom, who never bought a fluffy
> ball gown or showed me how to dress my hair—
> she must have wondered where she got this stuffy
> daughter. She didn't say it, but her stare
> asked whether genes or nurture were to blame.
> (But I got married, Mother, all the same.) ◄

# Ruth Stone

## Winter

Ruth Stone was born in Roanoke, Virginia, in 1915. Her husband, who may well be the man described in this poem, committed suicide in 1959. Widowed, with three daughters to support, Stone began teaching creative writing. According to critic Willis Barnstone, she worked "for nearly thirty years as a wandering professor at a new college or university almost each year, sometimes two in a year." Stone published her work widely but for many years was never given the credit her devoted readers believed she deserved. That began to change in 1999 when her book *Ordinary Words* received the National Book Critics Circle Award for Poetry. *In the Next Galaxy* won the National Book Award for Poetry in 2002. Stone died in 2011 at the age of ninety-six.

"Winter" is from Stone's book *Second-Hand Coat: Poems New and Selected* (1987). Here the speaker is someone who seems to be both on a train and yet waiting in a station; she is in the present, on an excursion to the city, but also in the past, remembering previous journeys with her late partner. With a tone as sharp as winter wind, the poem unrelentingly hurtles past an assortment of memorable images on the way to its astonishing conclusion.

> The ten o-clock train to New York,
> coaches like loaves of bread powdered with snow.
> Steam wheezes between the couplings.
> Stripped to plywood, the station's cement standing room
> imitates a Russian novel. It is now that I remember you.
> Your profile becomes the carved handle of a letter knife.
> Your heavy-lidded eyes slip under the seal of my widowhood.
> It is another raw winter. Stray cats are suffering.
> Starlings crowd the edges of chimneys.
> It is a drab misery that urges me to remember you.
> I think about the subjugation of women and horses;
> brutal exposure; weather that forces, that strips.
> In our time we met in ornate stations
> arching up with nineteenth-century optimism.
> I remember you running beside the train waving good-bye.
> I can produce a facsimile of you standing
> behind a column of polished oak to surprise me.
> Am I going toward you or away from you on this train?
> Discarded junk of other minds is strewn beside the tracks:

mounds of rusting wire, grotesque pop art of dead motors,
senile warehouses. The train passes a station;
fresh people standing on the platform,
their faces expecting something.
I feel their entire histories ravish me. ◀

# Rae Armantrout

## Duration

A native Californian, Rae Armantrout earned her bachelor's degree at the University of California at Berkeley and her master's degree at San Francisco State. She is frequently associated with the first generation of "language poets," (**language poetry** is defined as a loose affiliation of avant-garde writers whose poetry often foregrounds language itself, questions or rejects traditional forms and thinking about poetry, and requires the reader to engage actively in constructing the meaning of the text). Armantrout has served as a literature professor at the University of California at San Diego for two decades. Winner of the 2010 Pulitzer Prize and the National Book Critics Circle Award for her poetry collection *Versed*, Armantrout has published ten other books of poems, including *Money Shot* (2011), from which "Duration" is taken. *Publishers Weekly* notes that Armantrout builds her "wily, jumpy, intricately witty and wise poems from scraps of popular and high culture, overheard speech, and found text, as well as her own quirky observations."

This playful and "jumpy" eccentricity is very much on display in "Duration." The poem transitions quickly and without comment from the speaker's memory of her mother's quick "leaky faucet" kisses, to the afternoon sun on a power line outside her home, to a heaven in which blackbirds "needle" the air all day with their songs. There is no easy answer for what these seemingly disparate scenes have in common, although we may find a clue in the title, which comes from two Latin roots—"to last" (*durare*) and "hard" (*durus*)—and in the final lines, which seem to insist that readers stick with this "hard" poem if they are to appreciate it fully and tune in to the poet's airwaves.

Those flurries
of small pecks

my mother called
leaky faucet kisses.

Late sun winks
from a power line

beyond the neighbor's tree.
In heaven,

where repetition's
not boring—

Silver whistles
of blackbirds

needle
the daylong day.

We're still
on the air,

still on the air,
they say.  ◀

# Lines and stanzas ▶

The poetic line begins on the left side of the page (usually, but not always, at the left margin) and ends where the poet decides to "break" or wrap the line (usually, but not always, before the right margin). To illustrate (and to explain my parenthetical qualifications), here is the previous sentence broken into lines of poetry:

> The poetic line begins
> on the left side of the page (usually,
>       but not always,
> at the left margin)
> and ends where the poet decides to "break" or wrap the line
>       (usually, but not always, before the right margin).

The first line of this makeshift poem—"The poetic line begins"—is the way most lines of poetry look on the page. Sometimes, however, as in line 3, a line of poetry may be indented from the left margin and still be considered a line. Likewise, a very long line, like line 5, may continue *past* the right margin. To show the reader that the line is continuing on past the right margin, the poet flows some of the words to the next line and indents them five spaces. If you have read Walt Whitman, a devotee of long lines, you will recognize this convention. In his "Song of Occupations," for example, Whitman writes the following single line:

> Coal-mines and all that is down there, the lamps in the darkness, echoes,
>       songs, what meditations, what vast native thoughts looking through
>       smutch'd faces.

It would take a book with wide pages indeed to accommodate a line such as that one, so Whitman simply indents the overflow five spaces at the left margin and stops his free verse line only at the point where he thinks it makes sense to do so.

Whether the lines of a poem are long or short, in traditional meter or in free verse, there should be some logic or intuition governing the placement of a line break. Whitman was a master of using line length to reflect a poem's content. Consider, for example, his "A Noiseless, Patient Spider":

> A noiseless, patient spider,
> I mark'd, where, on a little promontory, it stood, isolated;
> Mark'd how, to explore the vacant, vast surrounding,
> It launch'd forth filament, filament, filament, out of itself;
> Ever reeling them—ever tirelessly speeding them.
>
> And you, O my soul, where you stand,
> Surrounded, surrounded in measureless oceans of space,
> Ceaselessly musing, venturing, throwing,—seeking the spheres, to connect
>     them;
> Till the bridge you will need, be form'd—till the ductile anchor hold;
> Till the gossamer thread you fling, catch somewhere, O my Soul.

The poem begins with a short four-word line announcing the presence of the spider; the subsequent longer lines seem to depict the spider spinning its web. In the second stanza, the lines become even longer, as Whitman imagines his soul engaged in the same process of sending out strands of filament, hoping that they, too, will latch on to something. The fact that a soul has to venture much farther than a spider to connect with a like-minded spirit makes these longer lines appropriate.

When you read, your eyes move back and forth across the page, and your sense of this forward and backward movement is often heightened in the process of reading a poem. Robert Pinsky reminds us that "*versus* in Latin, from which the word 'verse' derives, signifies the ploughman at the end of a furrow turning about to begin again, so that 'verse' and 'reverse' are closely related." If you haven't read many poems before this class, the experience can take a little getting used to. When we are reading prose, our eyes often skim across the surface, gleaning main ideas but not really pausing to linger over matters of style. However, that technique doesn't work well for readers of poetry, and it certainly won't work for you as a poet. Your reader expects more—word for word—from a poem. As you write and revise, you'll need to stop, think, slow down. Life might be hurtling around us faster and faster all the time, but poetry is an oasis in the midst of that rush.

In a poem properly written, every word receives its due, and every line begins and ends where it does for a reason. Fanny Howe has said that the rapid movement of prose across the page "indicates another thought process—one with a goal." Like drivers on a freeway, readers of prose usually want to get from one place to another as quickly as possible. Poetry, by contrast, puts up speed bumps. While poetry can also be said to have a goal, that objective is often to make the reader pause to reflect, to consider. According to Howe, the difference between prose and poetry is "the difference between taking a walk and sitting still."

Even the emptiness where a line ends, and the so-called white space begins, is important. Let's think for a moment about that white space. Suppose we were to take that last sentence and turn it into a short three-line poem:

Let's think
for a moment
about that white space.

If you were to see this "poem" in a book, it might be the only thing on the page, and readers used to paragraphs and paragraphs of prose might well ask: "What's the point of all that emptiness when we normally try to cram as much content as possible into every nook and cranny? Why all that 'unused' space?"

The answer, of course, is that the white space isn't unused. The expanse of blank paper gives those nine words real importance. If the poet felt he could condense everything he wanted to say into a single short sentence, perhaps the expression of that thought deserves our attention. Similarly, because there are so few lines, each line takes on more weight, and a reader is likely to go back over the piece a number of times, looking hard for clues as to what it might be about. Consequently, the shorter a poem is, the stronger it needs to be.

There is nothing more to find in our little "poem," so let's look at a real one by Barry Spacks:

Satie playing,
beloved cat on my lap—
what more could be desired?

Wait, wait . . .
raspberries and cream?

If you know the piano music of the French composer Erik Satie—brief pieces with titles such as "Jack in the Box" and "Le Flirt" that are by turns odd, warm, funny, and moody—you can imagine how those sounds inform the miniature world of this untitled poem. The notes in Satie's pieces are often soft and held until they almost diminish into silence. Spacks, too, seems to cherish empty space and quiet. After all, so much can happen in silence, just as so much can transpire in the white space of a poem. As Ted Kooser says, "The white space out there on the right is an opportunity, and you ought to take advantage of it." Spacks does this by including only the essentials of the experience he describes: the music, the cat, his feeling of near contentment, then the sudden desire for raspberries and cream. All the other wheres, whens, and whys of this moment are on the periphery; they have disappeared into the white space of the poem.

Because the last word of a poetic line—just before the white space—typically receives the most emphasis, poets delight in finding ways to exploit the line break. One way to do this is to let the end of the sentence coincide with the end of the line. A line that ends with any sort of punctuation (a period, semicolon, comma, or dash) is said to be **end-stopped**. Ruth Stone frequently employs this technique in "Winter":

> Your profile becomes the carved handle of a letter knife.
> Your heavy-lidded eyes slip under the seal of my widowhood.
> It is another raw winter. Stray cats are suffering.

In general, an end-stopped line slows the movement and rhythm of a poem; a poem in which many or all of its lines are end-stopped causes readers to pause and ponder during the act of reading. As Robert Wallace points out, "End-stopped free verse tends toward long lines because they permit internal pauses and greater internal rhythmic variation." The longish end-stopped lines in Stone's poem create the effect of a repeated halting, which emphasizes both the stop-and-start movement of a train and the finality of the speaker's loss: there is, after all, no more resounding "end-stop" than the one that Death insists on.

Unsure how to handle the freedom (or potential anarchy) represented by the line break, new poets often choose to end their lines on a mark of punctuation. That's a safe choice, but it can be a boring one. The impact of this "chopped prose," Wallace says, "is about as arresting, in its lack of variety, as a stack of lumber." Ezra Pound similarly warns: "Don't make each line stop dead at the end, and then begin every next line with a heave. Let the beginning of the next line catch the rise of the rhythm wave, unless you want a definite longish pause." Be sure to have a reason for ending your line where you do, but if you always settle for a mark of punctuation, the movement of the poem may become too predictable.

The alternative to breaking a line at a mark of punctuation is to wrap it in the middle of a sentence so that related words are in different poetic lines: this is called **enjambment**. In contrast to a poem that is heavily end-stopped, a poem with run-on or enjambed lines tends to move more quickly down the page. Take a look at this short poem, "Foothill Road," by Paul Willis:

> It happens in the slow light
> of December dawn, the waking
> of clouds, the acknowledgment
> of a long presence. The road
>
> gathers under your feet, the roughness
> of it felt, not seen. Too cold

for snakes, but a palm frond
blown to the ground can rake

your soles and spear your toes
straight through with thorns.
Crucifixion happens daily, just
like that, on the heels of triumphal entry.

The images in "Foothill Road" are clearly drawn; the subject is weighty. Yet because of Willis's skillful use of enjambment, there's barely a pause here, even between stanzas, as we race down the road in morning light toward the marvelous and unforeseen ending.

In their essay "The Line/The Form/The Music," David Baker and Ann Townsend have this to say about enjambment: "The line argues with the sentence, it disrupts the momentum of the sentence, but it also can heighten the interior meanings of a sentence. The line focuses on and magnifies the phrase, the piece, the fragment." The simple act of breaking a line causes a reader to pause, if only for a microsecond, in preparation for the next line. We digest what we have just read and ask ourselves, "What's coming next?" Then we move our eyes down the page to learn if our expectations will be confirmed or confounded.

Look how the skillful enjambment in the second stanza of Gail White's sonnet accents meaning and highlights irony:

And my poor mom, who never bought a fluffy
ball gown or showed me how to dress my hair—
she must have wondered where she got this stuffy
daughter. She didn't say it, but her stare
asked whether genes or nurture were to blame.
(But I got married, Mother, all the same.)

Enjambment allows White a small moment of surprise; she makes us wonder what exactly is "fluffy" (her ball gown) and what is "stuffy" (herself). That slight pause—when our eyes are moving back to the left margin and we have yet to discover what noun the adjective is modifying—is essential to the experience of poetry. This is the *versus*, the turning and returning to which Pinsky alludes. Similarly, the break between "stare" and "asked" causes us to linger over it momentarily, to stare—like the speaker's mother—at her socially inept daughter.

Knowing when to break a line, how to take advantage of these gaps, and when not to is part of the learning curve of becoming a poet. The fact that there are no definitively right or wrong ways to enjamb lines of poetry makes that process all the more difficult, especially for students accustomed to classes where there is only one correct answer. Practice, trial and error, conversations with peers and your instructor, reading lots and lots of other poems, and constant practice: these are the ways poets develop a sense of the integrity of their lines.

As you craft the lines of your poem, you will also want to think about how to group them into stanzas, a poem's equivalent to the paragraphs in prose. There are several ways to approach stanza formation. Poets who are drawn to symmetry may begin writing their poems and wait until the opening lines cohere into a single logical unit—five lines, for example. The poet then manipulates word choice and phrasing so that all subsequent stanzas are also five lines. Other poets allow each stanza to develop organically, based on the poem's content. The opening stanza may be a single line, the second stanza twenty lines, the third stanza five, and so on. Still other poets, especially those such as Gail White who are writing in forms, know beforehand the length of their stanzas; their efforts go toward writing lines that fit well into those preordained packages.

The important thing for you as a poet is to achieve the maximum impact from your stanzas. White space is both vertical and horizontal, and the pause between stanzas is even more pronounced than the one provided by a line break. If you want your reader to give extra weight to each grouping, you will, like Rae Armantrout in "Duration," want to have more stanzas with fewer lines. But if, like Ruth Stone in "Winter," you want to present your poem as a single propulsive thought, one that will tolerate no interruption, you will avoid stanza breaks.

The word "stanza" is derived from the Italian word for "room," and like the many rooms in a mansion, the range of stanza forms is daunting. We will discuss a few of these in more detail in the section on poetic forms. However, in an introductory course like this one, you don't need to become a stanza expert. You simply need to know the names of the most common stanza forms:

A **couplet** is two lines of verse
that are connected in some way.

A **tercet**
is a group
of three lines.

A **quatrain**
is a group
of four lines
of poetry.

Beyond these, the most common patterns are stanzas with

five lines: **quintet**
six lines: **sestet**
seven lines: **septet**
eight lines: **octet**

# CHECKLIST Lines and stanzas

☐ **Do your line endings make sense?** There are many rationales for when to end a line of poetry. As you'll see in the following sections, a certain meter may dictate line length, or end rhyme may be involved. Whatever your reasons, though, you should *intentionally* break your lines at an appropriate place. If your lines seem to stop without any reason (or rhyme), experienced readers will be skeptical of your command of the basics of poetry and may dismiss your poem without giving it a fair reading. Unless there is some compelling reason for doing so, stopping your line on relatively unimportant words such as articles ("a," "an," "the"), prepositions ("of," "on," "with"), or coordinating conjunctions ("but," "for," "so") will make your line breaks seem random and careless.

☐ **Do your line breaks surprise your reader?** When we're in the middle of a good book, we can't wait to turn the page to learn what will happen next. Similarly, effective line breaks create suspense for the reader: they make us want to discover what the next line will be. Enjambment is a useful tool for generating suspense. Of course, while you want to avoid entirely predictable line endings, you don't want to replace them with breaks that are merely baffling. A poem that begins, "I can't/figure/out why/I'm breaking my lines here," will disrupt the reader's sense of rhythm before it can ever be established.

☐ **Do you vary your line breaks?** Although plenty of wonderful pre-twentieth-century poems end each line on a mark of punctuation, contemporary poems with nothing but end-stopped lines often feel predictable. Different poets have different aesthetics, but most poets favor a combination of end-stopped and enjambed lines.

☐ **Are you effectively using the white space on the page?** Remember that the more white space you allow on the page, the more focus each word, line, and stanza receives. If you have only a few words per line, do those words merit all the space they are given? If, in contrast, your lines are long and crowded with ideas and images, do you leave your reader feeling overwhelmed? If you have frequent stanza breaks, do the pauses forced on the reader add to or detract from the method and message of your poem? No matter how your poem takes shape, try to take full advantage of the "silence" offered by the white space to increase the impact of your words.

☐ **If your lines are grouped into stanzas, do the groupings make sense?** Readers of poetry expect the poet to have given serious thought to stanza formation. A couplet requires a different sort of attention than a quatrain or a sestet does. Stanzas tend to end on a mark of punctuation, although that isn't always the case. If you do end a stanza midsentence, make sure there's a rationale for that break: when your sentence continues in the beginning of the next stanza, your reader will expect a reason for the exaggerated pause.

# Meter and rhythm ▶

In this section, we look at how meter and rhythm influence the poetic line. **Meter** is the arrangement of words in a poem based on the relative stress of their syllables. If you have written rhyming poems before, you probably composed in meter, even if you didn't realize it at the time. That da-DUM, da-DUM, da-DUM, da-DUM you were hearing in your head is called iambic tetrameter. Rhythm, which also refers to the recurrent alteration of pronounced and softer elements in a line, is generally a less specific term when applied to poetry. All poems have some kind of rhythm, although that rhythm may be closer to free jazz than to the classical precision that meter suggests. Even in metered poems, however, the rhythm of the line is likely to deviate from the meter the poet is using. In the words of Robert Pinsky, "Rhythm is the sound of an actual line, while meter is the abstract pattern behind the rhythm."

Later in this section, we look more closely at free verse—poetry in which the rhythm is metrically irregular. Although free verse now dominates contemporary poetry, metrical verse has had such a profound influence on poetry written in English that we begin by considering its characteristics. In fact, for centuries, English-speaking poets and readers would have wondered how any writing that did *not* employ metrical regularity could dare to claim the name of poetry. Conscious attention to the stressed and unstressed syllables in a line was simply part of what it meant to be a poet.

In her book *The Body of Poetry*, Annie Finch rhapsodizes on this very subject:

> Meter is the gift that poetry gives me before words, through words, and after words. To hear meter is for me the most intimate part of reading and writing a poem, because it is impossible for it to be translated or told: it can only be experienced as the waving form of words and syllables carrying their own spine of metrical energy, the particular current of the rhythm, and everything that rhythm makes visible, audible, palpable.

That's a pretty amazing claim for the power of meter, but many poets who write metrically would probably agree with Finch that its power is hard to overestimate. For formalist poets, taking control of the rhythms of language by consciously manipulating the stressed and unstressed syllables of a line results in a far greater variety of effects than can be achieved otherwise. Meter allows these poets to help their readers more closely experience the same thoughts and emotions as the poets themselves.

Obviously, being able to name the meter that you're using is a big help. If in the past you have felt that something was off about a rhymed poem you wrote, chances are that the meter was irregular. Although **scansion**—the process of counting the number of stressed and unstressed syllables and analyzing their patterns—is a decidedly inexact science, it nevertheless brings some order and system to the language of poetry. As you begin to scan poems yourself, you will quickly notice that we are concerned with syllables rather than words. Each **foot**—the basic metrical unit in poetry—typically consists of one stressed and one or two unstressed syllables.

The ancient Greek plays were written in verse, and the labels we apply to meter come to us from those early comedies and tragedies. Following are the names of the most common types of poetic feet (the adjectival form is in parentheses). Here, an underscore (_) represents an unstressed syllable, while a slash (/) represents a stressed syllable:

> **iamb** (iambic): _ /
> **trochee** (trochaic): / _
> **anapest** (anapestic): _ _ /
> **dactyl** (dactylic): / _ _
> **spondee** (spondaic): / /
> **pyrrhic** (pyrrhic): _ _

The iamb is the most common foot in English poetry, and poets and critics have come up with various explanations for this phenomenon. Robert Pinsky thinks the iambic foot is "like a time signature" in music, guiding the reader "through the infinite, actual variety" of its sounds. Li-Young Lee believes that "meaning is born as the breath dies":

> As we inhale, our bones and muscles actually get very compacted, harder. When we exhale, on the other hand, our bodies become very soft. Ancient Daoists, so I'm told, believe that upon inhalation our ego-self becomes very inflated, while during exhalation our sense of ego and body diminishes and we become more open to a deeper, bigger presence.

That da-DUM may indeed represent the breathing body of the universe. Or it may echo our beating hearts, or the surging of ocean waves. Or there might be a more mundane explanation: the predominance of iambic feet in poetry written in English may simply be a tradition that has been passed down over the centuries. What's important to remember is that experienced readers of poetry, like your instructor, will be aware of the meter you choose—even if you aren't.

Line lengths are also given specific names. Earlier we mentioned iambic tetrameter (four iambic feet), and you may have heard of iambic pentameter (five iambic feet) while studying Shakespeare or other canonical poets. Line lengths are labeled as follows:

> **monometer**: one foot
> **dimeter**: two feet
> **trimeter**: three feet

**tetrameter**: four feet

**pentameter**: five feet

**hexameter**: six feet

**heptameter**: seven feet

**octameter**: eight feet

With all these options laid out before you, you may want to jump in and try your hand at writing dactylic octameter or pyrrhic dimeter. However, a couple of words of warning are in order. Iambs are the prevailing foot in part because it is generally easier to write an iambic line. Certain feet, such as the pyrrhic and spondaic, are fairly rare in poetic lines because in a line of two or more feet, a pattern of stressed and unstressed syllables will reassert itself. Writing a poem in pyrrhic dimeter would be a remarkable feat indeed.

Moreover, very short lines like monometer can, as its name suggests, become monotonous rather quickly. At the other end of the spectrum, once you begin writing lines with more than six feet, it can be difficult to tell the difference between poetry and prose. Some meters are easier to master than others—for example, writing a poem in dactylic octameter wouldn't be quite as daunting as composing one in pyrrhic dimeter. However, if you tried to write either of these as a new poet, most of your efforts would necessarily go into the technical effort of getting the meter correct. You probably wouldn't have much energy left over for the actual poem.

The line lengths of most poems fall somewhere in the middle of very long and very short lines. The longest line in our three model poems is this one from Ruth Stone's "Winter" (individual feet are separated by a vertical bar):

$$\_ \quad / \quad \_ \, / \quad \_ \quad / \quad / \quad / \quad \_ \quad \_ \quad / \quad \_ \quad \_ \quad / \quad \_ \quad /$$
Your heav | y-lid | ded eyes | slip un | der the seal | of my wid | ow hood.

Let's call this seven-foot line iambic heptameter, even though it has an **irregular meter**—that is, not all the feet are the same. We have marked the fourth foot as a spondee and the fifth and sixth feet as anapests. Nevertheless, the prevailing meter is iambic, so the line itself takes that adjective.

Now let's scan one of the short lines in Rae Armantrout's "Duration":

$$\_ \quad / \quad \_ \quad / \quad \quad \_ \, /$$
be yond | the neigh | bor's tree

The line is perfect iambic trimeter, but only one other instance of this meter occurs in the poem. This isn't particularly surprising since neither Stone nor Armantrout employs a regular metrical pattern. It's important to note, therefore, that although both of these poems are in free verse rather than in a strict meter, individual lines can still be scanned. In fact, you can scan almost any written work, including advertising jingles and prose. Scansion is simply a tool for seeing how the stresses in a line are put together.

All this information about meter may seem like a lot to handle, but it does get easier once you put it into practice. Let's give Gail White's "My Personal Recollections of Not Being Asked to the Prom" a full metrical scan:

$$\smile \, / \mid \smile \, / \mid \smile \, / \mid \smile \, / \mid \smile \, / \mid \smile \, /$$
(1) I nev | er mind | ed my | un pop |u lar | i ty

$$\smile \, / \mid \smile \, / \mid \smile \, / \mid \smile \, / \mid \smile \, /$$
(2) in those | days. Books | were friends | and po | ets (dead)

$$\smile \, / \mid \smile \, / \mid \smile \, / \mid \smile \, / \mid \smile \, / \mid \smile \, /$$
(3) were lov | ers. Brain | y girls | were still | a rar | i ty

$$\smile \, / \mid \smile \, / \mid \smile \, / \mid \smile \, / \mid / \, /$$
(4) and boys | pre ferred | big bos | oms to | well-read

$$\smile \, / \mid \smile \, / \mid \smile \, / \mid \smile \, / \mid \smile \, / \mid \smile$$
(5) and sauc | y wits. | I look | back now | with pit | y

$$\smile \, \smile \mid / \, / \mid \smile \, / \mid \smile \, / \mid \smile \, /$$
(6) on the | young Me | I did | n't pit | y then.

$$\smile \, / \mid \smile \, / \mid \smile \, / \mid \smile \, / \mid \smile \, / \mid \smile$$
(7) I did | n't know | that I | was al | most pret | ty

$$\smile \, / \mid \smile \, / \mid \smile \, / \mid \smile \, / \mid \smile \, /$$
(8) and might | have had | a charm | for old | er men.

$$\smile \, / \mid \smile \, / \mid \smile \, / \mid \smile \, / \mid \smile \, / \mid \smile$$
(9) And my | poor mom, | who nev | er bought | a fluf | fy

$$/ \, / \mid \smile \, / \mid \smile \, / \mid \smile \, / \mid \smile \, /$$
(10) ball gown | or showed | me how | to dress | my hair—

$$\smile \, / \mid \smile \, / \mid \smile \, / \mid \smile \, / \mid \smile \, / \mid \smile$$
(11) she must | have won | dered where | she got | this stuff | y

$$/ \, \smile \mid \smile \, / \mid \smile \, / \mid \smile \, / \mid \smile \, /$$
(12) daugh ter. | She did | n't say | it, but | her stare

$$\smile \, / \mid \smile \, / \mid \smile \, / \mid \smile \, / \mid \smile \, /$$
(13) asked wheth | er genes | or nur | ture were | to blame.

$$\smile \, / \mid \smile \, / \mid \smile \, / \mid \smile \, / \mid \smile \, /$$
(14) (But I | got mar | ried, Moth | er, all | the same.)

By scanning the fourteen lines of this sonnet, you can see how carefully attuned White is to metrical concerns. Because she is writing a sonnet, her lines are in iambic pentameter; the line lengths, within a few syllables' variation, are predetermined. Although there isn't as much metrical variation as in a free verse poem, "My Personal Recollections of Not Being Asked to the Prom" does contain a number of substituted feet. The use of several variations—the spondees at the end of line 4, in the second foot of line 6, and at the beginning of line 10; the trochee at the beginning of line 12; the extra unaccented syllables at the end of lines 5, 7, 9, and 11—keeps the poem from sounding like the ticktock of a metronome. Instead, this poem is livelier; it's closer to the way people speak. This rhythmic variety is fairly common in metered poems. Absolute fidelity to a meter generally makes for wearisome reading, and the great masters of iambic pentameter—Shakespeare and Wordsworth, for instance—often employ variations in their lines.

If you have never scanned a poem before, you may feel overwhelmed by how much is going on. As one of my students once said, "Who would have thought that words had so many syllables?" And all these syllables hovering next to one another can make it difficult to tell which are stressed and which are unstressed. But don't become too "stressed" yourself: scansion allows different ways of hearing a line; it is more like taking an educated guess than reaching a definitive answer. Another reader might scan White's sonnet differently, and that would be perfectly all right.

Maybe because all this business about **prosody**—the study of metrical structure—can sound so complicated, new creative writing students often gravitate toward free verse. Of course, students also write free verse because so many of the poets who attract their attention also write extensively in nonmetered poetry. Allen Ginsberg, Gary Snyder, Jack Kerouac, Sharon Olds, Nikki Giovanni, and Billy Collins all make good use of free verse's flexible rhythms and line lengths.

In the early twentieth century, poets such as T. S. Eliot and William Carlos Williams mounted the first sustained and successful challenge to the primacy of metered poetry in English. Williams argued that we "must *listen* to the language for the discoveries we hope to make." He believed that a slavish adherence to a predetermined rhythmic pattern not only made for boring verse but also was in some sense downright *un-American*. (Williams preferred the flexibility of what he called the "variable foot," a concept that traditionalists found maddeningly paradoxical.)

Charles Olson, a slightly younger contemporary of Williams, uses the following formulation to describe the process a free verse poet goes through as his work moves from his mind to the page:

the HEAD, by way of the EAR, to the SYLLABLE

the HEART, by way of the BREATH, to the LINE

Like metrical poets referencing the beating of the heart or the breathing of the lungs, Olson's formulation suggests that writing free verse is not only a mental activity but also a physical one. Our heartbeat and breathing normally come with a steadiness and regularity, but they can also be heightened—when we're running or excited, for example—or slowed down—when we're relaxed or asleep. This open attitude toward line length, which could result in two feet in one line and eight in the next, is one of the chief ways of differentiating free verse from formal verse.

"Free verse is like . . . " Once you complete that sentence, your analogy will probably tell you something about your attitude toward poetry itself. In the past, my students have compared free verse to everything from skydiving, to dancing at Bonnaroo, to cooking without a recipe. Literary critics frequently compare free verse to jazz, which wasn't always considered high art the way it is now. Originally jazz was a daring urban and African American alternative to classical music. When asked to defend "jazz poems," Langston Hughes praised them because their rhythm pulsed with "the tom-tom of revolt against weariness in a white world, a world of subway trains, and work, work, work; the tom-tom of joy and laughter, and pain swallowed in a smile." Of course, if jazz was at one time a revolutionary musical form that inspired poets to break tradition, now it is largely considered boring by young people, who rarely listen to it. (Ironically, hip-hop, today's equivalent of jazz, is much closer to the older forms of strictly metered poetry.)

Mary Kinzie tells us that "the tradition of free verse has permitted two kinds of lineation: lines composed of broken phrases . . . as well as free verse lines organized in syntactically complete units, all the phrases set off and complete." The lines in Rae Armantrout's "Duration" are so brief that they inevitably take the form of "broken phrases," short bursts of energy that propel us from thought to thought and image to image down the page. "Duration" varies in the number of syllables per line, from two in the shortest line to six in the longest. Poets writing in free verse value this elasticity of language, and Armantrout uses it to excellent effect.

If your past efforts as a poet have been in free verse, then you are already aware of its virtues. However, if you're used to writing poems in meter and rhyme, it's helpful to remember that a poem composed in rhyming quatrains may be stronger if it's "translated" into free verse. When you are writing in meter and you realize your poem isn't what you had hoped it would be, allow yourself the freedom to explore other options. John Haines argues that although a poet may begin by working in a prescribed form with a set meter, "when the spirit of things changes, and the inner substance of thought undergoes a transformation, it may turn out that the form is no longer adequate; it ceases to act for us in a vital way and becomes mere formality." A poet true to his or her poem must honor this transformation and alter the form to mirror the new idea:

> The true form thereafter would be one realized in the act of creation—the form in process, to be discovered in the language we speak, in which we express our thought and passion. This speech, carrying with it whatever elements of traditional form we might still feel to be useful and satisfying, would more nearly express for us the truth of our life and time.

Some poetry critics might call the "poems" that I created in the previous section "broken prose." W. H. Auden compared free verse poets to Robinson Crusoe on his desert island: "He must do all the cooking, laundry and darning for himself. In a few exceptional cases, this manly independence produces something original and impressive, but more often the result is squalor—dirty sheets on the unmade bed and empty bottles on the unswept floor." For poets like Auden and Robert Frost, meter provided the spine on which the body of their poems was created. Frost famously said that writing free verse is like "playing tennis with the net down," and one of the perils of writing in free verse is that your lines can become verbose and slack.

Of course, playing tennis without a net may not be the worst thing in the world if you're still having trouble getting your racket to make contact with the ball. Beginning poets who are trying to juggle the demands of meter and rhyme as well as all the other elements of poetry (imagery, figurative language, tone, style, and so on) may simply be overtaxed. Every rule has its exceptions, but my experience over the years is that most students enrolled in an introductory creative writing class find it easier to write a good free verse poem than a good rhyming poem. Although T. S. Eliot's dictum may be true that no verse is free for the person who wants to do a good job, free verse generally provides a wider door for students who are still finding their way into the many-roomed house of Poetry.

## CHECKLIST Meter and rhythm

☐ **If your poem is written in meter, have you scanned the meter to make sure it's doing what you want it to do?** Even if some student readers of your poem aren't aware of the presence or absence of meter, your instructor *will* recognize clumsy handling of regular metrical patterns. If you decide to write in a specific meter, take the time to do it right. Know the name of the meter you're using. Scan your lines repeatedly to determine when, where, and why you are deviating from the pattern you have chosen. Read model poems such as Gail White's to get a sense of how expert poets handle the challenges of meter. Rhyme normally emphasizes meter, so be particularly attentive to the placement of accented syllables if your poem rhymes.

☐ **If you're not writing in meter, does your poem still have a discernible rhythm?** The longer you write poetry, the easier it becomes to hear a poem's rhythm in your head, whether or not that rhythm is based on traditional meter. However, new creative writers sometimes feel that without the aid of meter, their poems' rhythms are too subtle to discern or may be altogether lacking. If you would like more regularity in your lines but you don't want to use traditional meter, try creating lines with the same syllable count. Ten syllables doesn't always equal iambic pentameter, but it comes close. If all the lines of your poem contain basically the same number of syllables, a distinct rhythm will often begin to emerge.

# The music of poetry ▶

Denise Levertov says that "writing poetry is a process of discovery, revealing inherent music, the music of correspondences, the music of inscape." If you have never thought of written or spoken language as musical before, this statement initially may seem a bit baffling. What is the music of "correspondences" and "inscape"? And how can words make music if they aren't being sung?

First, it's helpful to remember that music is the art of ordering sounds into combinations, and words, spoken aloud, do make sounds. We have also looked at the ways that poems use rhythm, another of the elements that poetry shares with music. Greek poetry was originally accompanied by the guitarlike lyre, from which we get the term *lyric poetry*. English ballads like "Lord Randal" and "The Demon Lover" were passed from singer to singer long before they made their way to paper. More recently, Langston Hughes appropriated the blues form for his poetry, and one of the reasons many students sign up for a creative writing course is that they love listening to, analyzing, and writing song lyrics.

In short, making a direct connection between music and poetry isn't as far-fetched as it might seem. Ideally, in a poem, phrases of words are like phrases of music; poets reading from their work are like musicians interpreting the notes on a page. In order to achieve this music in their poetry, poets use a range of devices. This section covers several of the most common tricks of the trade, beginning with the musical aspect of poetry you are probably most familiar with: **rhyme**, a correspondence of sound in two or more words.

Let's take another look at the one rhyming poem among our three models, "My Personal Recollections of Not Being Asked to the Prom":

I never minded my unpopularity
in those days. Books were friends and poets (dead)
were lovers. Brainy girls were still a rarity
and boys preferred big bosoms to well-read
and saucy wits. I look back now with pity
on the young Me I didn't pity then.
I didn't know that I was almost pretty
and might have had a charm for older men.
And my poor mom, who never bought a fluffy
ball gown or showed me how to dress my hair—
she must have wondered where she got this stuffy
daughter. She didn't say it, but her stare
asked whether genes or nurture were to blame.
(But I got married, Mother, all the same.)

As you read the poem, you can see that it has a rhyme scheme—a purposeful arrangement of rhyming words at the end of each line. A shorthand format has evolved over the years to aid us in discussing rhyme schemes. In this format, we give each rhyming word a letter and then put those letters in sequence. Each time a new rhyme occurs in a poem, it receives a new letter. White's sonnet rhymes as follows: *ababcdcd efefgg.* A rhyme scheme is important because it not only brings a sense of order to your work but also signals to your readers that you know what you're doing, that your rhyming is to some larger purpose. A rhyme scheme gives you authority.

White's sonnet employs the most common form of rhyme: **end rhyme**, which Mary Kinzie defines as "the agreement of two metrically accented syllables and their terminal consonants." Kinzie's precise definition tells us what end rhyme is, but it can't, of course, capture all of rhyme's **connotations**—the meanings a word *suggests* rather than specifically names or describes. Among the earliest rhymes we hear are nursery rhymes, which seem to evoke some deeply rooted human pleasure in similar sounds. Many of us take delight in the rhyme of song lyrics, and for poets who work mostly in rhyme, there is no question of its fundamental importance. Rhyme links words not only by sound but also, inevitably, by sense. Consequently, poets use rhyme to underscore the similarities between two words (and ideas) as well as to highlight their differences.

Of course, there is more than one way to rhyme. Consider the rhymes in the first four lines of White's poem: "unpopularity" and "rarity" in the first and third lines, and "dead" and "read" in the second and fourth lines. The no-nonsense single stressed syllables of "dead" and "read" used to be called "masculine rhymes." Not surprisingly, this terminology is now generally considered sexist, and we refer to a masculine rhyme as a single rhyme.

Rhymes such as those that end the first and third lines of the sonnet, "unpopularity" and "rarity," in which the rhyme is a stressed syllable followed by one or more unstressed syllables, used to be called "feminine rhymes" because they were considered "weak." Today, the preferred terminology is **falling rhyme**. "Rarity" and "unpopularity" are actually **triple rhymes**, since both contain the "ar-i-ty" sounds. Drawn-out **polysyllabic rhymes** (rhymes of more than one syllable) like these have long been considered a comic or satirical device in written poetry, and they are basically used for that purpose in White's poem. This particular rhyme, for instance, seems to accentuate the speaker's own awkwardness in social situations. The connection between "fluffy" and "stuffy," the **double rhyme** (with two rhyming syllables) in lines 9 and 11, is ironic, of course, since the stuffy teenager the speaker once was is anything but fluffy. Despite this long association with **light verse**—poetry, usually rhymed, that treats its subject in a comic or good-natured manner—polysyllabic rhymes may be more familiar to your ear from hip-hop, which frequently employs them. However, in rap, double, triple, and even quadruple rhymes are used as often for serious as for comic effect.

"Fluffy" and "stuffy," like "dead" and "read," are **perfect rhymes**: the correspondence between the two rhyme sounds is exact. The effect of perfect rhyme is a closure similar to Yeats's famous statement that "a poem comes right with a click like a closing box." Critic Julie Kane similarly believes that White's lines "snap shut like steel traps each time a rhyme is completed, imparting a sense of completeness to the preceding thought."

A perfect rhyme can indeed be sonorous, lifting readers into the realm of music. However, new poets are likely to overvalue perfect rhyme and ignore other musical effects. One of these variations is called the slant, imperfect, near, or off rhyme. In **slant rhymes**, the vowel sounds may be either similar or significantly dissimilar, and the rhymed consonants may be similar rather than identical. Rae Armantrout makes use of slant rhymes in "Duration," as in the connection between "heav<u>en</u>" and "repet<u>ition</u>'s" in lines 8 and 9.

Eye or **sight rhymes** are words that *look* as if they should rhyme, even though they don't when we say them aloud. Often these words did rhyme in the past, but as the language has evolved, the pronunciation of one of the formerly rhyming words has also changed. "Laughter" and "slaughter" are good examples of eye rhymes, as are "move" and "dove," "laid" and "said," "crow" and "brow," and so on.

**Internal rhyme** occurs within a single line of poetry: "I can't <u>wait</u> to be <u>late</u> for my <u>date</u>." Internal rhyme is used extensively in hip-hop, so much so that many writers of literary poetry have lately begun to shy away from it. Nevertheless, powerful contemporary poets, from Gwendolyn Brooks to Seamus Heaney, have made strong use of internal rhyme, and it can be an effective way to increase musicality in your poem.

Rhyming focuses on the ends of words, but that's not the only way to make connections between similar sounds. **Alliteration** normally refers to the repetition of initial consonant sounds. Gail White uses alliteration in lines 4 and 5 of her sonnet with "<u>b</u>oys," "<u>b</u>ig <u>b</u>osoms," and "<u>b</u>ack." Ruth Stone uses it in lines 19 and 20 of "Winter" with "<u>m</u>inds," "<u>m</u>ounds," and "<u>m</u>otors." And we can find alliteration in Armantrout's "Duration"; lines 5, 9, and 11 are linked by the *w* sound of "<u>w</u>inks," "<u>w</u>here," and "<u>wh</u>istles."

The term alliteration can also be used as an umbrella to cover consonance and assonance. **Consonance**, as its name suggests, is the recurrence of consonant sounds, especially at the end of stressed syllables, but without the similar-sounding vowels. Armantrout employs consonance when she links the *l* sounds of "need<u>le</u>" and "sti<u>ll</u>" in lines 13 and 15. Again, as is the case with rhyme, we can see how linking similar sounds is tied to the linking of similar ideas. The "needle" of the blackbirds' song is "still" on the air throughout the "daylong day." **Assonance** is the repetition of vowel sounds without the repetition of similar end consonants. Assonance is a form of slant or near rhyme, and the terms are often used interchangeably.

Despite its flat statements and "to be" verbs, Ruth Stone's "Winter," which might at first seem rather prosaic, in fact makes extensive use of musical devices. Consider the long *o* assonance in the opening lines of "Winter":

> The ten o-clock train to New York,
> coaches like loaves of bread powdered with snow.

(We can also appreciate the eye rhyme of "powdered" and "snow.") The next line contains both the assonance of the long *e* sound as well as the alliteration from closely repeated *w* sounds:

> Steam wheezes between the couplings.

As we look at the many musical devices our three model poets employ, we begin to realize that the question of whether a poem should or should not rhyme is something of a false one. Gail White may be the only one of these poets writing in consistent end rhyme, but even without this device, good poets can make use of the music of language. To some extent, every poet who attempts to group similar-sounding words into a poem is a "rhyming" poet.

## CHECKLIST The music of poetry

☐ **Does your rhyming poem need to rhyme?** Ask yourself whether the rhyme adds to or detracts from the poem's overall quality. Would the poem be more succinct and specific if it were in free verse rather than rhyme? Your main goal should be to write well, and a well-written poem doesn't have to rhyme.

☐ **If you're committed to keeping a rhyming poem in rhyme, are your rhyming words fresh and intelligent? Have you eliminated all "padding" rhymes?** Again, you should rhyme for a reason: to achieve a certain effect, emphasize the sounds of certain words, or because, in your opinion, your subject demands the special qualities of rhyme. In his satiric poem "A Fit of Rhyme against Rhyme," Ben Jonson warns that rhymes can be guilty of "wresting words from their true calling." That is, rhyme can force us to select an end word simply for its *sound*, when another word would make better overall *sense*. The result can be lines that are garbled and jumbled, with the poet going to elaborate lengths simply to make one word rhyme with another.

☐ **Would slant, internal, or eye rhyme give you more flexibility to say what you really have in mind?** Perfect end rhyme too often leads to cliché because most of the perfect rhymes in English have been used so frequently that it's difficult to do anything original with them. Slant rhymes, in contrast, offer more options and are more likely to allow you to "make it new."

☐ **Do you hear the "music" in your poetry?** Your response to this question may be based on subjective factors; nevertheless, your poem should "sing" to you. (Otherwise, why not just write in prose?) Listen carefully to how you have put your sounds together, and see if you can regroup them in ways that accent meaning. Remember that alliteration, including assonance and consonance, can add musicality to your poem, whether or not it rhymes.

# Images, symbols, and figurative language ▶

*how, don't tell.* Whether your creative writing class is being taught in Maine or Montana or Missouri, you will hear this piece of advice repeatedly from your instructor. The reason is that in nearly every culture, and for as long as we have had poetry, poets and their audiences have decided that imagery must play an integral part in the poetic experience.

C. Day Lewis called the image "a picture made out of words," although "**imagery**" may also refer to the other four senses: taste, touch, smell, and sound. That's a fairly straightforward description, but poets can become quasi-mystical when describing the power of imagery. Ezra Pound called an image "an intellectual and emotional complex in an instant of time." That's a trickier definition but also a more provocative one. Pound seems to be suggesting that one of the key aspects of imagery is that it freezes time, a feat that our rational self tells us is impossible. Yet an image does make us linger. It "thingifies" the world long enough for us to consider it more carefully. Larry Levis focuses on the image's ability to temporarily halt the passage of time when he says, "The images we write hold still, and their stillness is curious because it reminds us that, someday, up ahead, at the end of the story, completion is inevitable but incomprehensible. Freud called it the 'riddle of death,' but a riddle is also an image, a stillness."

One of the most difficult things for new poets to do is to incorporate imagery into their poetry. Students often believe that if they use generalities rather than specific concrete examples, more readers will be able to "relate" to the poem. That argument makes sense from a distance, but it is rarely valid when applied to the actual experience of reading a poem.

For instance, you might think that simply saying, "She's beautiful," will automatically evoke for your readers a mental picture of someone they know who is beautiful. While that may happen occasionally, more often than not, your readers will simply pass over those two words and not "see" the subject of your poem at all. Think back on the way you remember the important events in your own life. Do you think of those events in abstract terms? Or do you retain mental pictures of what happened? Humans tend to process stories in terms of pictures their minds create, and if you don't provide those pictures, your readers will probably tune you out. Images force readers to slow down and see, hear, taste, touch, and smell the world created in the poem.

Because we live in a world that is always rushing toward something else, a poem in which the only description is "She's beautiful" will call forth nothing but a blur. Contrast that statement with, "Her hair was the orange of maple leaves in autumn, her eyes were as blue as the night sky in a painting by van Gogh." That second description requires some mental energy on the part of both the writer and the reader, but it pays off. We may not yet be able to see the face of the beautiful woman, but we are much closer to knowing the color of her hair and eyes. Ultimately, of course, words are too inexact a medium to convey precisely what anyone looks like, but the very fact of language's imprecision means that you owe it to your readers to make at least a gesture toward specificity.

Let's look at another example of how imagery works. One type of poem most often missing concrete imagery is love poetry. This is ironic, of course, given that we almost always claim to love someone because of his or her specific qualities. Yet creative writing teachers frequently receive poems like this one:

My love, you fill my heart with bliss.
　　You give me so much peace,
And bring me joy at the end of each long day.
　　Don't ever go away.

Your eyes are as blue as the sky.
　　Your beauty cannot fade.
Your hair is soft as silk.
　　With you, I'm never afraid.

You never leave my heart alone.
　　You always show you care.
Your smile shines like the sun.
　　You touched my soul forever.

I fell in love at first sight of you,
　　Don't ask me why.
But something about you tells me that
　　I'll love you till I die.

If you received a poem like this from someone you cared about, you would probably be delighted. The poet—let's say it's a young man addressing a young woman—really seems to care about the person he is addressing. He remembers the color of her eyes (always a good sign), and he has even taken the trouble to rhyme! A love poem to a beloved doesn't have to be good; it just has to be sincere.

However, if you were reading this poem in a class, you might have a bit of a queasy feeling. Two abstractions you especially want to avoid are "heart" (shorthand for "romantic love") and "soul" (having to do with all things spiritual). Single words rarely become clichés, but "heart" and "soul" are exceptions. Scan your poems for these words. If you see them, look for ways to eliminate them and replace them with specific, concrete details.

Even though there *are* images in the poem, things we can touch and see, they are all clichés—trite expressions like "blue as the sky," "soft as silk," and "shines like the sun." Clichés persist for a reason: they have an essential truth to them. On clear days, a wide blue sky can make a big impression. Fine silk is indeed very soft. And nothing—in our solar system, at least—shines quite like the sun. But all these images have been used so often and for so long that they no longer make the same impact they once did. Most readers will glide right over them, barely pausing to imagine what they are meant to convey.

Contrast "blue as the sky" with "blue as a painting by van Gogh" or "blue as a bolt of lightning" or "blue as the feathers on a peacock's breast"—or simply "turquoise" or "ultramarine" or "robin's-egg blue." Not only do these revisions bring fresher language into the poem, but they also begin to give us a clearer sense of the individuality of the poet's beloved. Maybe she is brooding and mysterious like van Gogh, or as fiery and explosive as lightning, or as proud as a peacock. The poet doesn't need to explicitly state, "She's mysterious" or "passionate" or "proud"; he can *suggest* those qualities by the images he uses.

Let's take it a step further. Look at the first stanza again:

My love, you fill my heart with bliss.
    You give me so much peace,
And bring me joy at the end of each long day.
    Don't ever go away.

These lines do little to distinguish this love affair from millions of others going on around the planet at this very moment. However, if we look for specifics, we see that there is potential for developing an image centered on the beloved bringing the speaker "joy at the end of each long day." How might that joy be brought? Perhaps the beloved gives the speaker a back rub, or always has a lilac-scented candle lit in the evenings when he comes home from work. And what is the nature of the speaker's "long day"? Does he work construction in Tucson in the summertime? Or is he a mortgage broker in a Boston skyscraper?

The poem seems burdened by its rhymes, so let's see what happens if we drop them:

After a long day hammering nails
in the Arizona sun, I can't wait
to get home to a back rub and a bowl
of gazpacho, spicy and cold.

It's not great, but it's better. The *abcc* end rhyme has been replaced by the assonance of "nails" and "wait" and the slant rhyme of "bowl" and "cold." More important, we get a sense of who the speaker is and what his life is like when he returns to the person he loves. The image of gazpacho, a soup made from chopped raw vegetables, adds an unexpected twist. We tend to think of a love affair as spicy and hot, but maybe "after a long day hammering nails / in the Arizona sun," something cold would be all the more welcome.

All three of our model poems make use of imagery, but Ruth Stone's "Winter" clearly is the most imagistic. Here is the poem again, with each instance of an appeal to one or more of the five senses underscored:

> The <u>ten o-clock train</u> to New York,
> <u>coaches</u> like <u>loaves of bread powdered</u> with <u>snow</u>.
> <u>Steam wheezes between the couplings</u>.
> <u>Stripped to plywood, the station's cement standing room</u>
> imitates a Russian novel. It is now that I remember you.
> Your <u>profile becomes the carved handle of a letter knife</u>.
> Your <u>heavy-lidded eyes slip under the seal of my widowhood</u>.
> It is another <u>raw winter</u>. <u>Stray cats are suffering</u>.
> <u>Starlings crowd the edges of chimneys</u>.
> It is a drab misery that urges me to remember you.
> I think about the subjugation of <u>women and horses</u>;
> brutal exposure; <u>weather that forces, that strips</u>.
> In our time we met in <u>ornate stations</u>
> <u>arching up</u> with nineteenth-century optimism.
> <u>I remember you running beside the train waving good-bye</u>.
> I can produce a facsimile of <u>you standing</u>
> <u>behind a column of polished oak to surprise me</u>.
> Am I going toward you or away from you on this <u>train</u>?
> <u>Discarded junk of other minds is strewn beside the tracks</u>:
> <u>mounds of rusting wire, grotesque pop art of dead motors</u>,
> <u>senile warehouses. The train passes a station</u>;
> <u>fresh people standing on the platform</u>,
> <u>their faces expecting something</u>.
> I feel their entire histories ravish me.

Reading this poem is like watching a short film: with so much imagery, it's difficult *not* to feel as if you have just taken a ride on a train *and* been inside the speaker's mind as she relives selected memories. Even the final line—"I feel their entire histories ravish me"—though primarily composed of abstractions, nevertheless contains, in the word *ravish,* a reference to the physical world. Although today *ravish* has the positive connotations of "to overcome with joy and delight," in earlier centuries it meant "to overcome by violence," and this etymological sucker punch brings home the full power of the poem. Stone leads us to the point where we can begin to feel some of her grief ourselves through her expert use of imagery.

J. A. Cuddon reminds us that "it is often the case that an image is not exclusively one thing or another; they overlap and intermingle and thus combine." Mentioning a freshly baked batch of chocolate chip cookies just being pulled from an oven appeals to our sense of taste, smell, and sight—maybe even touch, if we imagine how hot and gooey they are. Some readers will go on to make associations with the sight and taste of a tall glass of cold milk. "Chocolate chip cookies" may evoke fond memories of childhood, of certain family members, of the look and smell of a kitchen, and so on. In short, the image is a powerful triggering device, even though you can never dictate to your readers exactly what they will experience.

As you consider images for particular moments in your poem, it's important to realize that the more specific the image, the more likely it is to be remembered. Moreover, an image that is unusual yet appropriate is even more likely to make an impression on your readers. Look at how Stone approaches one particular image toward the end of her poem. She first mentions "discarded junk," a rather generic phrase. But she is not content to leave it at that. Instead, we get specific instances of that junk as it is "strewn beside the tracks: / mounds of rusting wire, grotesque pop art of dead motors, / senile warehouses." We see not just wire but "mounds of rusting wire," not just dead motors but "grotesque pop art of dead motors." Even the warehouses are "senile." Like a painter going beyond her original sketch, Stone fills in the details, and she does so with just a few additional words.

Images have their own weight and power, but they have even more impact when they take on the resonance of symbols. Consider the image of the rose as an example. Typically the rose stands for the fleeting nature of love and beauty. There is nothing quite as beautiful as a rose in full bloom, but that bloom doesn't last long, and the rose soon fades, its petals growing brown and discolored and dropping off one by one. Unfortunately, if you put a rose in your poem, this once-terrific symbol will be sapped by its use in countless other poems. There might still be wonderful poems about roses yet to be written, but the poets who compose those poems will need to be exceptionally skillful in avoiding the many clichés now associated with this particular symbol.

If some symbols shout out their meanings, other symbols are so private that only the poet is likely to understand them. Say that you associate telephone poles not with communication or height or a disruption of the natural world—associations that make sense because of the object's function—but with the first thing you saw when you heard the news that your grandfather had passed away. If you place a telephone pole in your poem, alone and without any explanation—"My heart broke when I saw the telephone pole"—your readers will have no idea what associations that extremely personal symbol is supposed to evoke.

To help students avoid both of these pitfalls, authors of creative writing books generally warn against consciously using symbols. Symbols, they say, will emerge from your writing. There's some truth to that. Too much symbolism can ruin a piece of writing. As Umberto Eco says, "Where everything has a second sense, everything is irredeemably flat and dull." Nevertheless, as you grow more confident in your writing, you will often have the feeling that an image works both literally *and* symbolically. That certainly appears to be the case with Armantrout's blackbirds, which might be said to represent the persistence of small things in the face of endless time. (The blackbirds may also allude to Wallace Stevens's famous poem "Thirteen Ways of Looking at a Blackbird"—an **allusion** is a reference to all or part of a previous work of literature.) Similarly, Stone's rusting wire, dead motors, "senile warehouses"—discarded junk—are not only objects one would be likely to see through a train window but also symbols of decay and ruin, images of a world that seems to have passed its prime.

One of the primary ways of bringing imagery and symbols into poetry is through the use of figurative language. In the words of M. H. Abrams, "**Figurative language** is a deviation from what speakers of a language apprehend as the ordinary, or standard, significance of words, in order to achieve some special meaning or effect." Much of the strangeness of poetry, as opposed to everyday conversation and writing, results from the dense use of figures of speech. There are far more of these rhetorical devices than we can cover in this book, so we'll look at only the most common examples.

**Style** in poetry usually refers to the author's selection and placement of words in a line, lines in a stanza, and stanzas in a poem. Aristotle said that the greatest element of style any writer could possess was "a command of metaphor." We'll include similes here also, as Aristotle said that the difference between the two "is but slight." A **metaphor** is a figure of speech in which a word or phrase that ordinarily denotes one thing is applied to something else in order to suggest an analogy or a likeness between the two things: "Your smile is a bouquet of daffodils." A **simile** is a figure of speech that states a likeness between two unlike things: "Your smile is *like* a bouquet of daffodils." I. A. Richards coined the terms **tenor** for the subject to which a metaphor is applied and **vehicle** for the metaphoric term itself. If we say, to borrow an example from Aristotle's *Rhetoric*, that a warrior was a lion in battle, the tenor of the metaphor is the warrior; the vehicle is the lion.

As Ted Kooser says, "If you think of a metaphor as being a bridge between two things, it's not the things that are of the most importance, but the grace and lift of the bridge between them, flying high over the surface." That bridge between the tenor and the vehicle is most fitting when the connection between the thing being described and what it is being compared to is both unexpected *and* somehow fitting. Consider the disappointing figurative language—"blue as the sky," "soft as silk," and "shines like the sun"—from "My Love," our awkward poem of clichés. Overuse has robbed these similes of all their power. In contrast, Ruth Stone's "coaches like loaves of bread powdered with snow" from "Winter" makes inventive use of simile.

Two common variations on metaphor are metonymy and synecdoche. In **metonymy**, the name of something is substituted with the name of something else closely associated with it. When reporters refer to "the White House," for instance, they mean the president of the United States. Similarly, when the president refers to "the press," he is talking about the news media, particularly print journalists. **Synecdoche** is sometimes considered a kind of metonymy, although the term is more often used when a part is used to describe the whole. When the captain of a ship cries out, "All *hands* on deck!" for instance, he wants more than just the hands of his crew members helping out: he wants the sailors themselves. Because metonymy and synecdoche rely heavily on long associations between two things, they are a species of cliché, and you should be wary of using either of them in your poetry.

Another figure of speech is **personification**, the awarding of human attributes to an abstraction or nonhuman thing. In Shakespeare's *Othello,* Iago uses personification when he refers to jealousy as "the green-ey'd monster which doth mock / The meat it feeds on." In his poem "To Autumn," John Keats personifies that season as a woman "sitting careless on a granary floor," her "hair soft-lifted by the winnowing wind." Personification can liven up a poem, but it can also quickly become ridiculous and is probably best used in moderation.

Similar advice goes for the use of the **pun**, a play on the multiple meanings of a word or its relation to other words that sound like it. (In the words of a famous pun, "A pun is its own reword.") There's a delayed pun in Rae Armantrout's "Duration," when she writes, "We're still / on the air," as though she were a radio or TV announcer; the joke is that she has just been discussing blackbirds, who, when they take flight, are also "on the air." Finding puns is especially easy to do when reading Shakespeare, who was enamored of them. Shortly before Mercutio's death in *Romeo and Juliet,* the playwright has Mercutio say, "Ask for me tomorrow and you shall find me a *grave* man." Mercutio is suggesting not only that he will be in a somber frame of mind but also that he will very likely be dead. In a "Hymn to God the Father," John Donne writes, "at my death Thy *Son* / Shall shine as he shines now." Clearly, the pun here implies that Jesus in his glory is as bright as the sun. As the last two quotes indicate, punning has a long history in literature. Still, the value of puns is disputed. Some readers love the wit involved; others find punning a rather low form of comedy. Nevertheless, certain poets who make extensive and skillful use of puns—James Merrill and Stephen Yenser come to mind—focus our attention on the roots of words we have come to take for granted, as well as the interconnectedness of all language.

Finally, we should mention one of the most frequent types of figurative language used in poetry: **irony**, the incongruity between the way things appear and the way they actually are. *Irony* comes from a Greek word meaning "affectation of ignorance," and it's a powerful rhetorical device. **Verbal irony** results when someone says one thing but means another. For instance, when Gail White remarks that "poets (dead) / were lovers," we know she's not a necrophiliac; she is simply saying that the only "lovers" she had were the poets whose work she read in books. And of course Rae Armantrout is being ironic when she writes that "repetition's / not boring" in heaven, when heaven is, by definition, paradise—the opposite of boring.

Gail White's "My Personal Recollections of Not Being Asked to the Prom" is also an example of **situational irony**, in which the results of a situation are distinctly different from what one might reasonably expect. The central character in the poem, the speaker as a teenager, *should* be living a life full of parties and dances; in fact, she prefers books to boys and doesn't even attend her own prom. And Ruth Stone's "Winter" similarly relies on the situational irony that a train ride on a snowy day—which ought to be pleasant, if not downright romantic—evokes such a painful series of memories.

## CHECKLIST Images, symbols, and figurative language

☐ **Do your poems have plenty of concrete, specific, and detailed images? Or are you relying on clichés and bland generalizations?** If the latter is the case, revise your work, looking for places where you can replace an abstraction with something that your reader can see, hear, smell, touch, or taste. According to Ezra Pound, "It is better to present one Image in a lifetime than to produce voluminous works." Pound was given to exaggerated pronouncements, but most beginning writers can benefit from his advice that poets should "go in fear of abstractions." Unless you have good reason to do otherwise, choose the image over the generalization every time.

☐ **Will the symbols in your poetry have resonance for both you *and* your readers?** Symbols that are too public and too obvious won't have much impact. If you use a cross to represent Christianity, for example, or a skeleton to represent death, or a fox to represent cunning, you might as well put up a neon sign announcing the meaning of your poem. But you don't want your symbols to be so private and obscure that no one else will be able to understand them. Find a balance between the two extremes.

☐ **Are you making effective use of metaphors and similes?** Ted Kooser advises poets to consider "writing a poem around a metaphor" because it gives the poet "a head start toward poetry that has integral order and transcends the mere sum of its accumulated words." Try to write a poem built around a central, productive metaphor or simile. Or go back to a poem you have already written and see if you can replace flat and uninspiring language with metaphors and similes that bring your subject to life.

☐ **Is the irony in your poem intentional or unintentional?** Given the prevalence of irony in poetry, it will be difficult for you to write a poem that doesn't make some use of it. The key is for *you*, the poet, to be in control. Look at your poems carefully. Are you aware of potential absurdities in phrasing or situations? Are you handling your language and subject with assurance? Or can your poems be easily misread or misinterpreted? If so, your readers will quickly lose confidence in your poetic voice and authority.

# Diction, syntax, and the language of poetry ▶

Words. They are our greatest delights as poets, but they also present us with our most difficult challenges. Learning how to say something with just the right words is one of the most rewarding achievements you can take away from a creative writing class. When the right words come, we feel as though we are channeling the universe; when we're blocked, those same words may seem incredibly elusive. However, especially in the revision process, you can increase your chances of writing a good poem by selecting the strongest, most suitable words and placing them in the most satisfying and effective order.

Writers using appropriate diction select words that are effective for their purposes. Mary Kinzie tells us that on one end of the spectrum is "plain style," which "employs concrete words, refers to things, objects and feelings, and tends to be monosyllabic." On the other end of the spectrum is "high style," which "employs elevated diction to suggest a refined mode of argument and description and a leisurely, sometimes involuted mode of thought."

Both Rae Armantrout and Ruth Stone use a fairly plain style in their poems. Granted, the absence of transitions from one image and idea to the next lends a certain mystery to "Duration," but we have no trouble understanding the individual sentences of the poem. Stone is more straightforward. "It is another raw winter," she writes. "Stray cats are suffering." Later, she asks the memory of her husband, "Am I going toward you or away from you on this train?" The fact that she uses a relatively matter-of-fact way of speaking in most of the poem highlights the elevated diction of the final line: "I feel their entire histories ravish me." The word *ravish* is not one we use in ordinary conversation, and its use here changes the **tone**—the style and manner of expression—of the poem.

Syntax refers to the way that words are put together to form phrases in a sentence. The task of organizing a sentence for maximum effectiveness is made more complex by the fact that most poets consider the line the basic unit of a poem. When you are ordering the words of your poem, you need to be aware of both how they fit together as a sentence *and* how they appear as a line of poetry. Let's look once more at the first stanza of Gail White's sonnet:

> I never minded my unpopularity
> in those days. Books were friends and poets (dead)
> were lovers. Brainy girls were still a rarity
> and boys preferred big bosoms to well-read
> and saucy wits. I look back now with pity
> on the young Me I didn't pity then.
> I didn't know that I was almost pretty
> and might have had a charm for older men.

White must organize her sentences so that the last word in each line rhymes with the last word in another line. Obviously, there is a real risk of writing sentences with syntax that is badly convoluted simply to ensure that the rhyming words appear at the correct places. Yet White manages to accomplish this difficult task without distorting her syntax. Here's the stanza as a paragraph of prose:

> I never minded my unpopularity in those days. Books were friends and poets (dead) were lovers. Brainy girls were still a rarity and boys preferred big bosoms to well-read and saucy wits. I look back now with pity on the young Me I didn't pity then. I didn't know that I was almost pretty and might have had a charm for older men.

We can still hear the rhymes, but the poet appears to be entirely in control of the syntax she uses.

This double awareness of line and syntax adds an exciting element to poetry. As readers, we are conscious of both when a line ends *and* when a sentence ends. When the endings of both lines and sentences correspond, there is an added emphasis on the closure of that thought. However, when the sentence ends in the middle of a line or a line breaks in the middle of a sentence, we're left hanging. That "unfinished" sense keeps us moving forward, or, as Robert Pinsky says, "The syntax is trying to speed up the line, and the line is trying to slow down the syntax."

Our three model poems—and, indeed, almost all the other poems in this book—are closer to a plain style than to a truly high style that you might associate with someone like Shakespeare. We selected plain-style poems for a good reason: unless you're an experienced and accomplished poet, any attempt to write in a high style might misfire. Why is that? Let's take a look at one of Shakespeare's sonnets to see what high style requires.

In Sonnet XIX, Shakespeare claims that his beloved, even after death, will always remain alive in his verse:

> Devouring Time, blunt thou the lion's paws,
> And make the earth devour her own sweet brood;
> Pluck the keen teeth from the fierce tiger's jaws,
> And burn the long-liv'd phoenix, in her blood;
> Make glad and sorry seasons as thou fleet'st,
> And do whate'er thou wilt, swift-footed Time,
> To the wide world and all her fading sweets;
> But I forbid thee one most heinous crime:
> O! carve not with thy hours my love's fair brow,
> Nor draw no lines there with thine antique pen;
> Him in thy course untainted do allow
> For beauty's pattern to succeeding men.
> Yet, do thy worst old Time: despite thy wrong,
> My love shall in my verse ever live young.

Shakespeare's syntax in this sonnet is extremely complex. The first twelve lines constitute a single sentence containing seven commas, four semicolons, a colon, and an exclamation point: quite an impressive feat! Let's face it: the intricate phrasing of a sentence like this one would be extremely difficult for new creative writers to pull off. Moreover, words such as "thou," "thee," and "thine" and exclamations such as "O!" clearly call forth the diction of an older era. If you're tempted to dip into this **archaic language**—that is, language that evokes an earlier time—remember that a poem making heavy use of deliberately old-fashioned words is more likely to sound like a bad King Arthur movie than a dazzling work of literature. Not surprisingly, most creative writing instructors advise students to start by writing in plain style rather than high style.

Particularly in the revision process, it's important to be aware of diction and syntax, but when you're in the middle of writing a poem, you will probably be more concerned with expressing the emotion or idea that inspired your poem in the first place. That's fine. Getting a rough approximation of what you want to say on the page is a necessary part of the process. But a good poem doesn't stop with the first draft. You must also revise your work, honing your choice of words. Richard Hugo called revision "probably the hardest thing about writing poems. . . . Somehow you must switch your allegiance from the triggering subject to the words." At first glance, this may not sound like an especially tricky task. After all, how else *are* you going to express yourself other than through the use of words? However, as Hugo goes on to remark, there is often a wide gap between the ideas or images that get a poem started and the way they are actually expressed.

And there, as Hamlet said, is the rub. Most poets take years to find their voice, so you probably won't be able to develop your own unique language of poetry in just one semester. What you can do is to *begin* to get a sense of how poetry differs from everyday language and how you might infuse it with your own personality and habits of thinking. One of the best ways of doing this is to steer clear of some of the bad habits that many new poets develop.

First, remember that writing a poem doesn't mean you can throw all the rules of grammar out the window. Poetry allows you to write fragments, play around with punctuation, experiment with unusual phrasing, or scatter your words and lines across the page. However, to quote Ezra Pound again, "Poetry must be at least as well written as prose." One way to test this is to eliminate the line breaks from your poem (as we just did with White's sonnet) and read it aloud. Does it sound awkward and forced, or eloquent and compelling? Even if you are experimenting with form and content, poetry doesn't give you the freedom to stop thinking clearly. Nor should you ignore the basic duty of every writer: carefully proofreading your work.

Avoid clichés—the old creative writing joke goes—like the plague. Clichés are a form of laziness: something comes into your head, and by virtue of its being there, you commit it to paper. The problem is that the phrase is in your head because you have heard it a thousand times before. That's not poetry;

it's "received language." You can avoid most clichés by never settling for less than the most precise word or phrase. As Hugo says, look for "those words you can own and ways of putting them in phrases and lines that are yours by right of obsessive musical deed."

That's an interesting phrase: "obsessive musical deed." It hints at the way your own idiosyncratic ways of encountering the world can be a great strength as a poet. "A poet is materially estranging her language, all the time," Heather McHugh tells us. "Her own language must become strange to her." One of the great pleasures of poetry happens when you know that you're writing both inside and outside yourself, when you hear voices you didn't know were in your head.

It's useful to take the advice of McHugh and other creative writing instructors: *Compose toward clarity. Revise toward strangeness.* If in your early drafts you try to get your poem as close as possible to the way that you want it, in your later drafts you will feel more comfortable about eliminating the verbiage and clichés and introducing elements that keep the poem from being merely average. Those later drafts are crucial: again it's the rare poem that can't benefit from careful revision.

Remember, finally, that philosophy and poetry are different enterprises, especially for new poets. Some outstanding poetic works do in fact deal with complicated metaphysical issues, but these poems are nearly always written by highly experienced poets. You should master the fundamentals of poetry before you attempt to tackle questions about the meaning of the universe. "Great is the enemy of good," the writing theorist Donald Murray often said. Don't worry about earth shaking profundity until you have written a decent poem.

## CHECKLIST Diction, syntax, and the language of poetry

- ☐ **Do your diction and syntax reflect the goals of your poem?** As you reread your work, make sure you have selected the most accurate and powerful words and arranged them in the most powerful order. Of course, you can be flexible with your diction and syntax, but be wary of choosing highfalutin words like "morphophonemics" or "disestablishmentarianism" unless you have good reason to use them. And don't wrench your sentences around simply to sound different or to catch a rhyme: inverted syntax poetic is not.

- ☐ **Are you using archaic, antiquated language?** Stephen Minot reminds us in *Three Genres* that poetry written this year ought to sound as if it was written this year: "Every age has its own linguistic flavor, and like it or not, you're writing for the twenty-first century." That does not mean that all poets will have the same voice—far from it. But your poem should not sound as though it was composed using a quill pen in some long-ago world of dragons and damsels in distress.

☐ **Have you eliminated all the clichés from your poems?** As you reread your poetry, consider whether a phrase you're using is one you have heard many times before. If so, change it. Say something unexpected. Use an image or a metaphor or a simile that no one has ever tried before. When you start writing poetry, especially if you haven't read a lot in the past, you run the risk of repeating language previous writers have used. Finding a careful yet sympathetic reader for your early drafts is always helpful.

☐ **Are you seriously considering the revision advice of your instructor and peers?** Even if you have been writing for some time, you will never grow as a writer if you're not willing to seriously consider and learn from the advice of more experienced writers. Not all advice is good advice, but if you hear the same critique repeatedly, there may be some merit in your readers' recommendations.

# Poetic forms ▶

Inspiration doesn't always arrive when you need it, and coming up with ideas for a new poem can be difficult. Fortunately, over the centuries, poets have developed hundreds of specific poetic forms. The Academy of American Poets lists some of these patterns on its Poetic Forms and Techniques Web page (poets .org). Lewis Turco's *Book of Forms*, now in its fourth edition, is another wonderful resource, as is *Patterns of Poetry* by Miller Williams. The great number and variety of forms *can* be a bit overwhelming, so for our purposes, a few of the most common forms should suffice.

## Sonnet

Many stanza patterns are organized around rhymes, with the sonnet being perhaps the best-known example. A **sonnet** is fourteen lines of rhymed iambic pentameter, with varying rhyme schemes. Phillis Levin claims that the sonnet—"a meeting place of image and voice, passion and reason"—"has resulted in some of the greatest lyric poetry" by "almost every notable poet writing in a Western language."

When you write a sonnet, you become part of a long tradition, but the form continues to welcome newcomers. In part, that's because its rules help poets move from point to point, as though they were following road signs on a highway. Yet those guideposts allow a remarkable amount of freedom. Let's look at another sonnet by Shakespeare, the well-known Sonnet XVIII, as an example:

Shall I compare thee to a summer's day?
Thou art more lovely and more temperate:
Rough winds do shake the darling buds of May,
And summer's lease hath all too short a date:

Sometime too hot the eye of heaven shines,
And often is his gold complexion dimmed,
And every fair from fair sometime declines,
By chance, or nature's changing course untrimmed:
But thy eternal summer shall not fade,
Nor lose possession of that fair thou ow'st,
Nor shall death brag thou wander'st in his shade,
When in eternal lines to time thou grow'st.
So long as men can breathe, or eyes can see,
So long lives this, and this gives life to thee.

Sonnet XVIII is called an English sonnet, or more commonly, a **Shake-spearean sonnet**, which means that its three rhyming quatrains—*abab cdcd efef*—are followed by a final couplet that rhymes *gg*. Note that Gail White's sonnet also employs the rhyming couplet characteristic of a Shakespearean sonnet, but she breaks her poem into two stanzas—an opening **octave** of eight lines and a closing sestet of six. The octave and sestet give "My Personal Recollections of Not Being Asked to the Prom" elements of the Italian or **Petrarchan son-net**, although that form traditionally rhymes *abbaabba cdecde*. This mixing and matching among the different sonnet rhyme schemes (there are many more we could name) is common and increases your flexibility as you scout out appropriate rhymes.

One feature common to both Shakespeare's and White's sonnets is the *volta* (Italian for "turn"). You will notice that after the eighth line, the poems change the direction of their "arguments": in Sonnet XVIII, Shakespeare begins to make the case that, unlike the short-lived pleasures of a summer day, his beloved will not grow old because he or she is being memorialized in poetry; White shifts to the disappointment her mother suffered over her daughter's lack of dating skills. Shakespeare uses a colon to signal this change, and White begins a new stanza altogether. Not all sonnets make this swerve after the eighth line, but every real sonnet does take a turn toward some unexpected place before it is finished.

# Villanelle

Another popular form, this one with French origins, is the **villanelle**. A vil-lanelle consists of five tercets and a final quatrain. Strictly speaking, all these lines should be in iambic pentameter, although that rule is often broken. The first and third lines of the first stanza alternately repeat as the third line in the subsequent tercets. (A repeating line or phrase is called a **refrain**.) In the qua-train, the first line of the first stanza is the next-to-last line, and the third line of the first stanza is the final line of the poem. The villanelle has only two rhymes. The first and third lines of every tercet rhyme with each other, and the second lines of every stanza have the same rhyme.

This sounds more complicated than it actually is. If we were to sketch out the rhyme scheme line by line, it would look like this, with the rhyming words in parentheses:

1. Refrain 1 (a)
2. (b)
3. Refrain 2 (a)

4. (a)
5. (b)
6. Refrain 1 (a)

7. (a)
8. (b)
9. Refrain 2 (a)

10. (a)
11. (b)
12. Refrain 1 (a)

13. (a)
14. (b)
15. Refrain 2 (a)

16. (a)
17. (b)
18. Refrain 1 (a)
19. Refrain 2 (b)

Initially, writing a villanelle might seem like a rather daunting task, but once you come up with a first and third line that are both powerful and flexible enough to be used in several different contexts, much of your work is already finished: you have written eight of the nineteen lines of your poem.

Two examples of villanelles follow. Both take a few liberties with the repeating lines. In "A Way of Healing," Perie Longo's poem about the grieving process, the refrain changes from "Only look to the outpouring of spring" to "Of looking to the outpouring of spring" in the final stanza. Chryss Yost's refrain mutates even more significantly. In her poem—which implies that leaving Los Angeles is as difficult as trying to escape from the Disneyland ride called Autopia—the line "I, Miss Highway, I couldn't drive off track," becomes "You have to stay. I couldn't drive off track," then, "And anyway, I couldn't drive off track," and finally, "and be okay. I couldn't drive off track." Nevertheless, the basic idea and pattern remain, and fudging the refrain is not uncommon among contemporary American poets.

Here is Perie Longo's poem, "A Way of Healing":

Only look to the outpouring of spring

To know how sitting in wait may open the heart,
How storm and bluster release a hidden thing

That first in stark silence set us reeling.
But as we listen, words like blossoms spark—
Only look to the outpouring of spring.

What seemed dead rises, begins the healing.
Little by little old thought comes apart.
How storm and bluster release a hidden thing.

Time is essential to grow wholeness of being.
Then weed what intrudes, tender caring remark,
Only look to the outpouring of spring,

The rush of river over rock to help us sing
And dance, beat the drum, decipher the dark.
How storm and bluster release a hidden thing.

Should those who seek soul's comfort cling
To what anchors change, offer the art
Of looking to the outpouring of spring.
See how storm and bluster release a hidden thing.

And now Chryss Yost's poem, "Escaping from Autopia":

but even leaving, longing to be back,
to do again what I did yesterday—
I, Miss Highway, I couldn't drive off track

or crash. I joined the candy-coated pack
to follow yellow lines and concrete, gray
but even. Leaving. Longing to be back

beyond those lines, in other lines. Like smack
these flashback rides, E-ticket crack: You pay
you have to stay. I couldn't drive off track,

or spin to face my enemies' attack.
The road signs told me "NOW LEAVING L.A."
but even leaving, longing to be back

to go again. I knew I had a knack
for getting there and going. Child's play,
And anyway, I couldn't drive off track,

once safety-strapped onto that strip of black.
I couldn't lose or get lost on the way,
but even leaving, longing to be back
and be okay. I couldn't drive off track.

# Rondeau

Another French form heavily reliant on repetition is the **rondeau**, which has fifteen lines in three stanzas: a quintet, a quatrain, and a sestet. Two rhyme sounds repeat themselves throughout the poem. The opening words of the first line reappear as a refrain at the end of the second and third stanzas. The pattern of the lines is as follows, with the rhyming words in parentheses:

1. (a)
2. (a)
3. (b)
4. (b)
5. (a)

6. (a)
7. (a)
8. (b)
9. Refrain

10. (a)
11. (a)
12. (b)
13. (b)
14. (a)
15. Refrain

Our two examples of a rondeau follow the pattern carefully. Each of these famous poems tackles an extremely serious subject: Paul Laurence Dunbar's "We Wear the Mask" is about racism experienced by African Americans; John McCrae's "In Flanders Fields" memorializes the dead killed in a World War I battle. First, Dunbar's "We Wear the Mask":

> We wear the mask that grins and lies,
> It hides our cheeks and shades our eyes,—
> This debt we pay to human guile;
> With torn and bleeding hearts we smile,
> And mouth with myriad subtleties.
>
> Why should the world be overwise,
> In counting all our tears and sighs?
> Nay, let them only see us, while
>     We wear the mask.
>
> We smile, but, O great Christ, our cries
> To thee from tortured souls arise.
> We sing, but oh the clay is vile
> Beneath our feet, and long the mile;

But let the world dream otherwise,
We wear the mask!

Now McCrae's "In Flanders Fields":

In Flanders fields the poppies blow
Between the crosses, row on row,
That mark our place; and in the sky,
The larks, still bravely singing, fly,
Scarce heard amid the guns below.

We are the dead; short days ago
We lived, felt dawn, saw sunset glow,
Loved and were loved, and now we lie
In Flanders fields.

Take up our quarrel with the foe:
To you from failing hands we throw
The torch; be yours to hold it high.
If ye break faith with us who die
We shall not sleep, though poppies grow
In Flanders fields.

# Rondelet

As its name suggests, the **rondelet** is a shorter version of the rondel and a cousin of the rondeau. It consists of a single stanza of seven lines. The first line, which has four syllables, serves as a refrain that is repeated in the third and final lines. The remaining lines have eight syllables and rhyme with one another. The pattern of the lines is as follows, with the rhyming words in parentheses and the syllable count listed afterward:

1. (A) Four syllables
2. (b) Eight syllables
3. (A) Repeat line 1
4. (a) Eight syllables
5. (b) Eight syllables
6. (b) Eight syllables
7. (A) Repeat line 1

Two examples follow by May Probyn, both entitled "Rondelet." In the first, she carries on a conversation with someone who wants to know where her lover has gone. In the second, the speaker demonstrates an iron will about not changing her mind. In both poems, the speaker's preoccupation (not to say obsession) with an intense situation makes her repetition of the refrain seem natural. She can't get something out of her head; therefore, it's appropriate that she says it again and again.

"Which way he went?"
I know not—how should I go spy
Which way he went?
I only know him gone. "Relent?"
He never will unless I die!
And then what will it signify
Which way he went?

———

Say what you please,
But I know I shall not change my mind!
Say what you please,
Even, if you wish it, on your knees—
And, when next you hear me defined
As something lighter than the wind,
Say what you please!

And here are two outstanding contemporary examples by Caroline Parker. The first is "Snake Eyes":

Not every dream
about Vegas is a nightmare;
not every dream
creeps right up to its flame-thin edge,
but this one does. I am lucid
enough to leave Nevada, but
not every dream.

The second poem, *"Rondolet d'automne,"* puns cleverly on its sensual refrain:

Bare naked limbs
without their luminous chaos
bare naked limbs
I consider trimming myself,
but let it slide a bit longer;
better to get Hector with his
bare naked limbs.

## Triolet

Like the rondelet, the **triolet** is a very short French form that employs repetition and two rhymes to create its effect. It is an eight-line poem in iambic tetrameter, with two refrains—*A* and *B*—and a rhyme scheme as follows:

1. (A)
2. (B)
3. (a)
4. (A) Repeat line 1

5. (a)
6. (b)
7. (A) Repeat line 1
8. (B) Repeat line 2

Again, as in all other poetic forms relying on one or two recurring phrases, much of the important work is done generating the repeating lines. As you draft, try to come up with lines that are open to multiple interpretations and that end on a word that has many rhymes. In Thomas Hardy's "How Great My Grief," for instance, there are hundreds of rhymes for words with a long *u* and long *e* sound. Although he needs only two (*a*) rhymes and one (*b*) rhyme, Hardy has provided himself with a great many options. Here is his poem:

> How great my grief, my joys how few,
> Since first it was my fate to know thee!
> -Have the slow years not brought to view
> How great my grief, my joys how few,
> Nor memory shaped old times anew,
>     Nor loving-kindness helped to show thee
> How great my grief, my joys how few,
>     Since first it was my fate to know thee?

Because the first and second lines are repeated as a couplet at the end of the poem, in the intervening six lines something must happen to alter their original tone or meaning. We see that subtle transition in each of Adrienne Bond's "Triolets for a Three-Time Loser." In "Whee!" the woman initially appears bold when confronting the man, who tells her not to walk on the grass; however, the final line sounds a note of frustration, possibly even resignation. In contrast, the narrator of "Aha!" works herself up in the middle of the poem and seems angrier at her partner at the end than at the beginning. And in "Sigh!" the loss alluded to in the opening line feels more substantial by the poem's conclusion because the speaker has given us concrete examples of what she has lost.

### Whee!

"Do not walk on the grass," said he.
She asked, "What would you have me do?
Lay down sidewalks as I go?"
"Do not walk on the grass," said he.
"Let's leap like squirrels from tree to tree,"
she cried. "Let's raise a hullabaloo!"
"Do not walk on the grass," said he.
She asked, "What would you have me do?"

### Aha!

You think I don't know where you've been
or would forgive you if I knew

you'd been cavorting on the green.
You think I don't know where you've been?
I'm sharp-eyed as a peregrine;
you're as obvious as a horny gnu.
You think I don't know where you've been
or would forgive you if I knew.

Sigh!

We only save the things we've lost;
the rest can change beyond belief.
Kept bread becomes a moldy crust.
We only save the things we've lost;
Lost lovers keep our youthful trust;
the one we've wed disturbs our peace.
We only save the things we've lost;
the rest can change beyond belief.

## Sestina

The **sestina** was originally an Italian form. It consists of six sestets in iambic pentameter followed by a tercet or, as it is commonly called, a triplet, which constitutes the envoi, the concluding remarks of the poem. The final words in each line (indicated by capital letters) repeat themselves as follows, with the envoi including all six words in its three lines:

Stanza 1: ABCDEF

Stanza 2: FAEBDC

Stanza 3: CFDABE

Stanza 4: ECBFAD

Stanza 5: DEACFB

Stanza 6: BDFECA

Envoi: Variable

The reason for the end words' arrangement is shrouded in mystery (although some critics believe it has to do with numerology), but, again, the pattern is not *quite* as complex as it looks at first. As you can see, each new stanza repeats the final words of the previous stanza in the order 6–1–5–2–4–3; the only exception is the envoi.

"Sestina," a nineteenth-century poem by Edmund Gosse, imagines the medieval French troubadour Arnault Daniel's first attempts at writing in the form:

In fair Provence, the land of lute and rose,
Arnaut, great master of the lore of love,
First wrought sestines to win his lady's heart,

For she was deaf when simpler staves he sang,
And for her sake he broke the bonds of rhyme,
And in this subtler measure hid his woe.

'Harsh be my lines,' cried Arnaut, 'harsh the woe
My lady, that enthorn'd and cruel rose,
Inflicts on him that made her live in rhyme!'
But through the metre spake the voice of Love,
And like a wild-wood nightingale he sang
Who thought in crabbed lays to ease his heart.

It is not told if her untoward heart
Was melted by her poet's lyric woe,
Or if in vain so amorously he sang;
Perchance through cloud of dark conceits he rose
To nobler heights of philosophic song,
And crowned his later years with sterner rhyme.

This thing alone we know: the triple rhyme
Of him who bared his vast and passionate heart
To all the crossing flames of hate and love,
Wears in the midst of all its storm of woe,—
As some loud morn of March may bear a rose,—
The impress of a song that Arnaut sang.

'Smith of his mother-tongue,' the Frenchman sang
Of Lancelot and of Galahad, the rhyme
That beat so bloodlike at its core of rose,
It stirred the sweet Francesca's gentle heart
To take that kiss that brought her so much woe
And sealed in fire her martyrdom of love.

And Dante, full of her immortal love,
Stayed his drear song, and softly, fondly sang
As though his voice broke with that weight of woe;
And to this day we think of Arnaut's rhyme
Whenever pity at the labouring heart
On fair Francesca's memory drops the rose.

Ah! sovereign Love, forgive this weaker rhyme!
The men of old who sang were great at heart,
Yet have we too known woe, and worn thy rose.

"You've got two basic tactics with those repeated end-word," Lewis Turco says. "You can try to hide them or you can use them as hammers." If Gosse's poem tends toward the former tactic, Barry Spacks's contemporary take on the form, "Sestina on Sestinas," leans toward the latter approach. The repeating words are "sestinas" and clever variations on the words "blur," "rush," "enter," "inside," and "build." Spacks mostly employs iambic pentameter, but many contemporary poets find that varying the meter, as well as modifying the repeating words, results in a stronger poem. Spacks's sestina has a decidedly humorous edge to it, which is often a characteristic of "these Seuss-y structures sadist poets build." (You can read dozens of examples of excellent contemporary sestinas on the Web site of *McSweeney's* literary magazine at mcsweeneys.net.) Here is Spacks's "Sestina on Sestinas":

> Hard labor, pals, to push through most sestinas.
> They'll natter on, repeating in a blur
> like unremembered dreams, a madding rush
> where meanings seldom dare to break and enter.
> What battering-ram could sneak a thought inside
> these Seuss-y structures sadist poets build?
>
> Myself, I'd rather garden plants than build
> such tottering, tumbling towers of words. Sestinas
> we're liable to survive, once locked inside,
> are those where proper warnings are not blurred:
> "Abandon hope, all ye who choose to enter
> here!" But some tout punchlines so we'll rush
>
> toward absent consequence, a tourist crush
> of scanning through the rooms of cunning buildings
> where every stanza we expect to enter-
> tain us looks the same! Yet rare sestinas
> *sing.* God bless the mark! I'd write a blurb
> for any of that ilk: "One finds inside
>
> this stream of sound, dear Reader, an Insider-
> Spirit who will lift you from the rushes,
> (saved like Moses) clarify your blurry
> Senses. . . ." Ha! We all know why the builders
> place no exit doors in their sestinas:
> so they can drive us bonkers once we enter
>
> the long internment's torture. Fellow Enter-
> tainers, Stand-Ups, Poets, deep inside
> we should be wise enough to skip sestinas,
> yet we endure them—hey, we even rush
> to try our hands at tools intent to build
> such insubstantial substance, one long blurt
>
> of deadend clauses, high barbaric blurbles
> over rooftops sense can't dent, er-
> roneously passing as a sort of *Bild-*
> *ungsroman* that plush lives are boxed in. Side
> by side our gross sestinas pant like Russian
> dancers kicking boots, boots, boots! Sestinas

claim we'll even live through most sestinas, blurs
of rushing time spring every trap we enter
insideout, such tricksy lives we build!

## Cinquain

One final French form, the **cinquain** (from the French word *cinq,* meaning
"five"), is much easier to write. In the broadest sense, a cinquain is simply a five-
line stanza. However, the cinquain as it is now usually written has the following
syllable count per line:

1. two syllables
2. four syllables
3. six syllables
4. eight syllables
5. two syllables

The American poet Adelaide Crapsey established this use of syllabic lines in
cinquains. Here are three examples of the form by Glenna Luschei:

> Writing
> poems of five lines
> is beautiful but hard.
> Hail to pioneer Adelaide
> Crapsey!
> ("Cinquain")

> I pray
> professors sign
> my dissertation, leave me
> free for my true work, writing
> cinquains.
> ("Dissertation")

> I buy
> an amber watch
> spider ensnared thirty
> million years, a great way to spend
> spare time.
> ("Amber")

## Haiku

The Japanese **haiku** is a very short and highly imagistic poem, often evoking the
natural world during a particular season. Robert Hass tells us that "insistence on
time and place was crucial" for early writers of haiku—poets like Bashō, Buson,
and Issa. In fact, Hass points out, the "practice was sufficiently codified . . . there

was even a rule that the seasonal reference should always appear either in the first or third unit of the three phrase poem."

In its American form, the haiku often contains three lines of five, seven, and five syllables, although this is by no means an unbreakable rule. Many poets use one or two lines, or three lines with a looser syllable count. "What distinguishes a haiku," says Cor van den Heuvel, "is concision, perception and awareness—not a set number of syllables." Van den Heuvel believes haiku is "about having an openness to the existence around us—a kind of openness that involves seeing, hearing, smelling, tasting, and touching."

Moreover, while the natural world remains a touchstone for many haiku, American poets have expanded the form's subject matter considerably. Urban scenes, family life, even war have found vivid poetic expression in haiku. Jack Kerouac, who wrote haiku on a variety of topics, believed they "must be very simple and free of all poetic trickery and make a little picture and yet be as airy and graceful as a Vivaldi Pastorella." Ultimately, according to Bruce Ross, the best haiku "should convey a moment of insight experienced by a poet in real time through real beings and objects, a moment the reader may enter and share."

Writing haiku can be addictive. In the last year and a half of his life, the great American novelist Richard Wright abandoned prose altogether and wrote nothing but haiku, more than 4,000 of them. He wrote about everything that came into his view, from stray cats to spiderwebs to a little girl spanking her doll, demonstrating what all practitioners of the form know: the great variety of the world can be parsed down to just a few well-chosen words.

Seven haiku follow on a variety of subjects by another contemporary master of the form, Alexis Rotella. Rotella does not employ a set syllable count, but she does follow the haiku practice of announcing her subject in the first line (or phrase), then requiring us to approach that subject in a novel way through imaginative use of additional sensory detail.

Summer afternoon:
the smell
of inner tubes.

——

Yachts all docked—
the tinkle
of ice.

——

She's running for office—
for the first time
my neighbor waves.

——

A butterfly lands on Park Place.

_____

After an affair
sweeping
all the rooms.

_____

Snow on the graves—
the sound
of a distant plane.

_____

Christmas cookies—
nibbling
stars.

## Pantoum

The **pantoum**, which originated in Malaysia, has become another staple of American poetry. It consists of any number of quatrains that rhyme *abab*, with the second and fourth lines of one quatrain repeating as the first and third lines of the following quatrain. Like the villanelle, the pantoum requires strong repeating lines with flexible meanings and in return provides the poet with a clear structure. Because of the repeating lines, half of each new stanza is already written for you. New poets also appreciate the fact that the pantoum's end words, unlike the villanelle, do not have to rhyme.

In her pantoum "Braids," which *does* rhyme, Lois Klein uses the repeating lines to emphasize the poignancy and loneliness of childhood, a time and place "both charmed and cruel":

The way Mother gripped my hair to wind in braids
her blue-veined hands cool and deft
as if remembering a shadow time:
her fault the man had left.

Her blue-veined hands cool and deft
against my forehead when I lay ill.
Her fault the man had left,
her old mistakes regretted still.

Against my forehead when I lay ill
striped sunlight through venetian blinds.
her old mistakes regretted still,
no defense could ease the pain.

Striped sunlight through venetian blinds
like prison bars enclosed my world.
No defense could ease the pain.
Braided hair bound tight my curls.

Prison bars enclosed my world.
Mother's hands that twirled and gripped
my hair tight against my head.
No strand escaped or ever slipped.

Mother's hands that gripped and twirled,
hands that seemed both charmed and cruel.
My hair tight against my head
yet she would place a ribbon there.

Her hands that seemed both charmed and cruel
as if remembering a shadow time,
yet she would place a ribbon there
despite the way she gripped my hair.

## Ghazal

Another popular non-Western poem is the **ghazal**, derived from Persian and Urdu sources. Ghazals traditionally (1) consist of five to twelve loosely related but self-contained couplets of approximately the same length; (2) have a melancholy subject, often the hopelessness of an unsatisfied romantic attachment; and (3) repeat the final word or words of the second line at the end of all the second lines. Ghazals written in English often break at least one rule of this form.

The ghazal became popular in the 1960s and 1970s when poets such as Jim Harrison began writing and publishing them. Many purists, then and now, derided these American versions of the form as watered down or off the mark altogether, but ghazals are now a familiar form in many creative writing classes.

In his ghazal "After the Holidays," John Ridland effectively evokes a mood of doomed love. However, unlike the poet of the traditional ghazal, who laments the absence of a lover, Ridland mourns the impending departure of children and grandchildren:

*—For Jenny and Sasha leaving after Christmas*

They are sorting and packing, picking up
Loose ends, toys, ribbons, bits and pieces of the heart.

I am father and grandfather, sitting by,
Letting the sorrow of parting wash into my heart.

Nonna is out doing errands, picking up more
Bits for attention, devotion, pumped along by her heart.

Each year this happens: together for a fortnight we build
A delicately balanced construction, learn it by heart,

Then dismantle it, leaving the floor of the mind flat
While the veins return their used blood to the heart.

Not sorrow, no: *fondness.* Fondness is all.
We all remember what absence does to the heart.

## Prose poem

One final form to consider is poetry written in prose. Just about any reader of literature will acknowledge that there has been "poetic prose"—that is, prose that is rhythmic, imagistic, and condensed—for as long as there has been literature. Yet the term **prose poem** is relatively recent, dating to the work of nineteenth-century French poets such as Charles Baudelaire, Arthur Rimbaud, and Stéphane Mallarmé. As we suggested in the introduction to this chapter, the very term *prose poem* is considered an oxymoron by some poets. How, they ask, can poetry be prose?

For our purposes, a prose poem is any short, compact, "musical" piece of writing that does not have line breaks but which its author sees as a poem rather than a paragraph or paragraphs of fiction or nonfiction prose. Because this type of poem has no line breaks, prose poets pay attention to the sentence rather than the line, and the careful crafting of those sentences is essential to the form's success. Among the other elements necessary for a well-written prose poem, anthologist Michael Benedikt lists "skill at managing metaphor"; "a keen ear for unusual, unconventional . . . sounds & music"; and "an especially keen ear for rhythm, and for the rhythms of natural speech in particular."

Prose poems are hybrids not only in form but also in content. They can be both lighthearted (one anthology of prose poems is called *The Party Train*) and ambitious (another anthology is called *Models of the Universe*). They are often surrealistic and experimental (see the work of Charles Simic, Russell Edson, and James Tate for American examples of this strain of the prose poem). The prose poem also has a freedom that allows what Brooks Horvath calls "fugitive content: a place where one may give voice to the otherwise no longer sayable, as well as to the yet-unsaid." David Soucy calls the prose poem "a flying trapeze act without a net," and it is this element of risk taking and exploration that draws many poets to the form.

The following five prose poems from Gertrude Stein's book *Tender Buttons* give a sense of the playfulness and resistance to easy interpretation characteristic of the experimental prose poem. Although the titles of the poems promise something straightforward, the sentences themselves at first seem to have only a tangential relation to their supposed subjects. Yet the longer one tries to match the title with the poem, the more possibilities open up, and it quickly becomes apparent that striving toward meaning, despite all the obstacles Gertrude Stein places in our way, is part of what these prose poems force us to do:

> A charm a single charm is doubtful. If the red is rose and there is a gate surrounding it, if inside is let in and there places change then certainly something is upright. It is earnest.
>
> ("Nothing Elegant")

> If lilies are lily white if they exhaust noise and distance and even dust, if they dusty will dirt a surface that has no extreme grace, if they do this and it is not necessary it is not at all necessary if they do this they need a catalogue.
>
> ("A Red Stamp")

> A blue coat is guided guided away, guided and guided away, that is the particular color that is used for that length and not any width not even more than a shadow.
>
> ("A Blue Coat")

> A purse was not green, it was not straw color, it was hardly seen and it had a use a long use and the chain, the chain was never missing, it was not misplaced, it showed that it was open, that is all that it showed.
>
> ("A Purse")

> A feather is trimmed, it is trimmed by the light and the bug and the post, it is trimmed by little leaning and by all sorts of mounted reserves and loud volumes. It is surely cohesive.
>
> ("A Feather")

Like Stein's pieces, "Hideous Towns" by David Case has a sense of humor. Yet Case's prose poem is both darker and closer to the world we know. It is an admission that we are all connected, no matter how much we might wish that wasn't the case:

> Turns out there's a song called "Hideous Towns" by The Sundays. I haven't heard it, I don't need to—I drove through Selma, Alabama, I've seen Needles, California. In hideous towns, there are real months of Sundays, the feeling at each sunset of crushing things to come, a doubtful tingling of the fingers as all unreliably mapped space starts moving in: possums in the yard trailing naked tails through ill-clipped shrubs. Even the Dairy Queen shut down, the tiny Free Will churches packed—satellite dishes crying for remote possibilities.
>
> They are, those in the hideous towns, cousins once removed, twice removed, a defeated people who open filling stations in Peach Springs, Arizona, with office door signs reading: Sorry, We're Open.

Jim Peterson's "The Empty Bowl," about the refusal of an old dog to eat its meals, is similar to Case's poem in that it discovers an element of strangeness, even dread, in our everyday life:

A man's dog was very old and crippled. Each morning she sniffed her food, giving it a few licks. Then she would drag herself over to an empty red bowl that had belonged to a previous dog. She would lick the empty bowl and shove it along the boards of the porch with her nose. The man would pick her up, crooning softly, "You must eat, Old Lady," and place her next to her own bowl of food. She would stand there and smack her lips a few times, then drag herself over to the empty bowl. The man tried different food, but that never worked. He tried putting the food in the red bowl, but she only reversed the process, sniffing the meaty morsels, then dragging herself resignedly to her own empty bowl. He tried removing one of the bowls, but then the old dog would haul herself around the porch, down the steps falling on her face at the bottom, then out into the yard and under every tree and bush looking for the empty bowl. So the man would put both bowls back on the porch to keep her happy. Every morning it was the same. The scruffy white hair of her muzzle, the raw floppy ears pestered by gnats and flies, that half-seeing gaze through cataracts. He couldn't understand how she survived without food. She looked so bad it embarrassed him for the neighbors to see her. "Maybe I should put her to sleep. That would be the merciful thing to do." All the way to the vet's office she lay on the front seat beside him with her head in his lap. If he took his hand away from her head, she would stare at him until he put it back. In the car there were no gnats or flies to nag her ears. No space demanding she drag herself here or there. When he arrived and lifted her from the seat, she was limp in his arms, pink tongue dangling lazily from her mouth.

## CHECKLIST Poetic forms

☐ **Do you understand all the rules of the form in which you are working?** Some forms are fairly self-explanatory, but others have rather complex requirements. Breaking these rules can be part of the fun, but you should at least be aware of the rules you're ignoring. Get a feel for the form before trying to write in it. It's helpful to reread the form's description; then try to match it up against several examples by other poets.

☐ **Does the form enhance your content rather than limit it?** When a form is working for your poem, it seems to propel what you have to say forward, sparking unexpected language and ideas. When the form is working against you, you will feel it dragging down your writing. Different forms fit different poems, so don't hesitate to try your idea in a pantoum rather than a sonnet, or a villanelle rather than a sestina. And an unsuccessful formal poem often opens up when it is recast in free verse.

# Getting started writing poetry ▶

As Wendy Bishop tells us, "There is no single, best . . . invention technique that will get all writers drafting productively." Nor is there a "preferable sequencing system," with one type of exercise building on another. Instead, Bishop believes that "invention activities should provide students with exploratory moments and drafting options that develop flexibility and fluidity in a writer."

In short, not everything works for everyone, and you won't know what works for you until you try it. Moreover, you may find that a technique that inspires a poem one day won't yield much the next day, while an invention activity that seems useless this week will work for you next month. The brain remains a mysterious organ, and, as we have noted, poetic inspiration is unpredictable. Most poets will tell you that the more you experiment, try and fail, and try again, the more likely you are to ultimately come up with a group of poems you will be proud to have written. So write, write, *write*!

Over the years, my students have found the following kick-starts quite useful. At least one of them should result in a poem you are proud to include in your final portfolio.

## ▶ KICK-STARTS Beginning your poems

▶ **1.** Keep a journal in which you write down *everything* that might become material for a poem: ideas, observations, images, words, phrases, lines, and stanzas. If in the process you feel a poem igniting, start writing it, but don't worry if you end up with fragments and false starts. The more material you collect, the more likely some of it will begin to cohere into a fully formed poem.

▶ **2.** Find a book full of interesting words. It could be this one, or an anthology of literature, an encyclopedia, or a dictionary. Open up the book at random, and skim the page until a word catches your eye. It might be an unusual word like *kleptomaniac*, or it might be a common or evocative word such as *bruise* or *salt*. Write it down quickly and move on. Try to avoid abstractions and instead seek out words that are concrete and specific. Put real *things* into your poem (peach preserves and wedding rings, dishwater and cobwebs) and look for strong, clear verbs ("slash," "punch," "stroke," "sneeze"). Go easy on the adverbs and adjectives. Once you have jotted down ten to fifteen good words, use as many of them as you can in a short poem. Try to keep your poem fairly serious (it's tempting to transform this word salad into a comic jumble) and see if you can finish it in fifteen to twenty minutes. You'll often be amazed at the results.

▶ **3.** Read published poems (in this book, in an anthology, or online) and respond to them with poems of your own. It doesn't matter whether you respond to the subject of the other person's poem or just a single line or image. Generally it's most effective to find the moment of maximum energy or tension in the published poem. Identify what excites you about the poem; then make the same thing happen in your own work.

4. A variation on exercise 3 is to write a poem beginning and/or ending with one or more lines by another poet. Choose a line that you find particularly marvelous, and write from or toward it. Many poets ultimately transform or eliminate the model poet's line from their own poem. (If you choose not to, be sure to give the other poet credit for his or her work.)

5. Respond to poems written by poets you know personally, such as fellow students or friends who write poetry. Exchange your poems by hand or through e-mail. If you know someone is waiting to read your poetry, you are much more likely to write it.

6. Write a poem inspired by one of the other arts. For example, does a painting you love seem to want you to tell its story in words? If you haven't found that painting yet, the art section of your library will have plenty of books with full-color illustrations, or you can go online to a virtual gallery such as the WebMuseum (ibiblio.org/wm). Do more than simply describe the scene in front of you: set your imagination free, and consider using what you see as a springboard for something more personal. You can also use music as an inspiration. For instance, write a poem that evokes a Chopin étude or a punk song by Extreme Noise Terror. Excellent poems have also been written about dance, theater, and even architecture.

7. Everyone who has ever composed a poem for a special occasion such as a birthday or an anniversary knows this desire to connect with someone else. We want to please that person by showing that we have thought longer than we normally would about the event at hand. Write a poem that celebrates some special occasion, whether it be an **epithalamium** for a marriage; an **elegy** for someone who has passed away; or an **ode,** which can commemorate everything from a military victory to the painting on a Grecian urn to the song of a nightingale.

8. Write a poem in a form not discussed in this chapter. (You can find descriptions in Lewis Turco's *Book of Forms,* Miller Williams's *Patterns of Poetry,* on the Academy of American Poets' Web site, or simply by Googling "poetic forms and techniques.") Write a **ballad** (a narrative poem in quatrains rhyming *abcb,* with alternating four- and three-beat lines) or a poem in **terza rima** (a poem in three-line stanzas, in which the end words of the first and third lines rhyme, and the end word of the second line becomes the rhyming word in the following stanza). You can spend your lifetime as a writer working in the hundreds of patterns that previous poets have devised. If you are drawn to the challenge and boundaries of forms, experiment with as many of them as possible.

9. Begin writing a poem. When you reach what feels like a natural pause—a period, a comma, or just a lull in the sentence—break the line and begin a

new stanza. Count the lines in your first stanza, and then make sure all subsequent stanzas have the same number of lines as the first. Whether you're writing in couplets, tercets, quatrains, quintets, or an even longer group of lines, the regularity of your stanzas will oblige you to make interesting choices about diction and enjambment and where and how to conclude your poem.

**10.** Write a poem that describes and focuses on an unusual object that is right in front of you. Students have written poems about everything from stuffed animals to old pocket watches to Christmas ornaments to bottle openers. In the best of these poems, careful depiction of the object merges with storytelling and the creation or re-creation of vivid memories.

**11.** Write the poem behind a news story that captures your attention. Your poem may stick to the facts as much as possible, or it may begin from a charged moment in the story and quickly become a pure creation of your imagination. Consider writing the poem from an unusual point of view. A poem about a kidnapping, for instance, might be told from the perspective of the kidnapper or the person who has been kidnapped, but it also might be seen from the vantage point of the kidnapper's neighbor or the kidnapped person's childhood friend. Text-based sources—that is, newspapers and newsmagazines (in print or online)—tend to work better than television stories because the facts remain in front of you for easy perusal.

**12.** Write a poem in the form of a letter. Richard Hugo's book *31 Letters and 13 Dreams* is a great source for these types of poems. Hugo addresses poems to close old friends and to newer friends he doesn't yet know well. He brings these people detailed news of his own life and asks for information about their world. However, because the letter is in the form of a poem, Hugo condenses what he has to say and presents the material as eloquently—and as imagistically—as possible.

**13.** Write a poem in the persona of someone other than yourself. In this type of poem, also called a **dramatic monologue**, you become a character from history or of your own invention. Usually set during a moment of crisis in the speaker's life, the dramatic monologue is addressed to an audience of one or more silent listeners and gives the inside story from the perspective of someone who, on the exterior, may not be an especially sympathetic character. The friction between how we are likely to see the speaker and how he or she sees himself or herself has resulted in some outstanding work. Among the master poets who have worked extensively from behind the mask of personae are the British Victorian poets Robert Browning and Alfred Tennyson and the contemporary American poets C. K. Williams, Richard Howard, Robert Hayden, and Ai.

# An Anthology
# of Poems

## Kim Addonizio

## For You

For you I undress down to the sheaths of my nerves.
I remove my jewelry and set it on the nightstand,
I unhook my ribs, spread my lungs flat on a chair.
I dissolve like a remedy in water, in wine.
I spill without staining, and leave without stirring the air.
I do it for love. For love, I disappear. ◀

## Elizabeth Alexander

## House Party Sonnet: '66

Small, still. Fit through the bannister slit.
*Where did our love go? Where did our love go?*
Scattered high heels and the carpet rolled back.
*Where did our love go? Where did our love go?*
My brother and I, tipping down from upstairs
Under the cover of "Where did our love go?"
Cat-eyed Supremes wearing siren-green gowns.
Pink curls of laughter and hips when they shake
Shake a tambourine *where did our love go?*
*Where did our love go? Where did our love go?*
Stale chips next morning, shoes under the couch,
Smoke-smelling draperies, water-paled Scotch.
Matches, stray earrings to find and to keep—
Hum of invisible dancers asleep. ◀

# Sherman Alexie

## Basketball

After a few beers here, every Indian is a hero of "unbroken horses." Someone always remembers I was the Reservation point guard with the Crazy Horse jump shot. Someone always wants to go one-on-one in the alley while Lester FallsApart balances on a garbage can, his arms forming the hoop. Someone always bets his ribbon shirt against mine, and we play, and I win. Someone always finishes the night bareback, like it should be, while I go home, hang another shirt in my closet, another Crazy Horse dream without a skeleton or skin. ◄

# Agha Shahid Ali

## Postcard from Kashmir

Kashmir shrinks into my mailbox,
my home a neat four by six inches.

I always loved neatness. Now I hold
the half-inch Himalayas in my hand.

This is home. And this the closest
I'll ever be to home. When I return,
the colours won't be so brilliant,
the Jhelum's waters so clean,
so ultramarine. My love
so overexposed.

And my memory will be a little
out of focus, in it
a giant negative, black
and white, still undeveloped.

for Pavan Sahgal ◄

## Todd Boss

# The World Is in Pencil

—not pen. It's got
that same silken
dust about it, doesn't it,
that same sense of
having been roughed
onto paper even
as it was planned.
It had to be a labor
of love. It must've
taken its author some
time, some shove.
I'll bet it felt good
in the hand—the *o*
of the ocean, and
the *and* and the *and*
of the land.  ◀

## Ciaran Carson

# Campaign

They had questioned him for hours. Who exactly was he? And when
He told them, they questioned him again. When they accepted who
        he was, as
Someone not involved, they pulled out his fingernails. Then
They took him to a waste-ground somewhere near the Horseshoe
        Bend, and told him
What he was. They shot him nine times.

A dark umbilicus of smoke was rising from a heap of burning tyres.
The bad smell he smelt was the smell of himself. Broken glass and
        knotted Durex.
The knuckles of a face in a nylon stocking. I used to see him in the
        Gladstone Bar,
Drawing pints for strangers, his almost perfect fingers flecked with
        scum.  ◀

# Lorna Dee Cervantes

## Poem for the Young White Man Who Asked Me How I, an Intelligent, Well-Read Person, Could Believe in the War between Races

In my land there are no distinctions.
The barbed wire politics of oppression
have been torn down long ago. The only reminder
of past battles, lost or won, is a slight
rutting in the fertile fields.

In my land
people write poems about love,
full of nothing but contented childlike syllables.
Everyone reads Russian short stories and weeps.
There are no boundaries.
There is no hunger, no
complicated famine or greed.

I am not a revolutionary.
I don't even like political poems.
Do you think I can believe in a war between races?
I can deny it. I can forget about it
when I'm safe,
living on my own continent of harmony
and home, but I am not
there.

I believe in revolution
because everywhere the crosses are burning,
sharp-shooting goose-steppers round every corner,
there are snipers in the schools . . .
(I know you don't believe this.
You think this is nothing
but faddish exaggeration. But they
are not shooting at you.)

I'm marked by the color of my skin.
The bullets are discrete and designed to kill slowly.

They are aiming at my children.
These are facts.
Let me show you my wounds: my stumbling mind, my
"excuse me" tongue, and this
nagging preoccupation
with the feeling of not being good enough.

These bullets bury deeper than logic.
Racism is not intellectual.
I can not reason these scars away.

Outside my door
there is a real enemy
who hates me.

I am a poet
who yearns to dance on rooftops,
to whisper delicate lines about joy
and the blessings of human understanding.

I try. I go to my land, my tower of words and
bolt the door, but the typewriter doesn't fade out
the sounds of blasting and muffled outrage.
My own days bring me slaps on the face.
Every day I am deluged with reminders
that this is not
my land
and this is my land.

I do not believe in the war between races.

but in this country
there is war. ◀

# Marilyn Chin

# Repulse Bay

*Hong Kong, Summer 1980*

1

Washed ashore
At Repulse Bay

Creatures that outgrew their shells—
I saw a mussel hang
On a shell's hinge: the sun
Turned its left side brown
What remained carried
Around the lips
Like a human tongue
Unfit for speech

Suddenly, the sea
Sweeps it up, with
A stub-necked bottle, bits of feces and the news
Printed in red and black
Bilingual editions for the Colonialists
And two-bit Japanese tourists
Seeking thrills

2

Back to Kowloon, in Granny's
One room apartment, her laundry waves
On her sun-filled balcony—
I recognize some of mine: blue jeans, bright T's
A black lace bra on a hook . . .
Two stories below, an old hawker
Selling abalone on a stick, chicken asses
Pig ears, tripe of all species burnt pink—
Looks up, shakes his fist

3
The rain over Hong Kong falls
Over all of us, Li Ching, though
This postcard will tell you nothing
About the country I have lost

Overhead, a building blinks
Of Rolex, Omega and yet
Another brand that ticks

4

Last night, drunk out of my mind
I promised everybody visas and a good time
(should they make it to America)

Autumn is here now, though
There are no rustling New England leaves
Or Oregon grapes tugging the vines

5

How the sun shines through the monsoon brightly
On the small men selling viscera
On the dead and swimming creatures of the sea  ◀

# Billy Collins

## Nostalgia

Remember the 1340s? We were doing a dance called the Catapult.
You always wore brown, the color craze of the decade,
and I was draped in one of those capes that were popular,
the ones with unicorns and pomegranates in needlework.
Everyone would pause for beer and onions in the afternoon,
and at night we would play a game called "Find the Cow."
Everything was hand-lettered then, not like today.

Where has the summer of 1572 gone? Brocade and sonnet
marathons were the rage. We used to dress up in the flags
of rival baronies and conquer one another in cold rooms of stone.
Out on the dance floor we were all doing the Struggle
while your sister practiced the Daphne all alone in her room.
We borrowed the jargon of farriers for our slang.
These days language seems transparent, a badly broken code.

The 1790s will never come again. Childhood was big.
People would take walks to the very tops of hills
and write down what they saw in their journals without speaking.
Our collars were high and our hats were extremely soft.
We would surprise each other with alphabets made of twigs.
It was a wonderful time to be alive, or even dead.

I am very fond of the period between 1815 and 1821.
Europe trembled while we sat still for our portraits.
And I would love to return to 1901 if only for a moment,
time enough to wind up a music box and do a few dance steps,

or shoot me back to 1922 or 1941, or at least let me
recapture the serenity of last month when we picked
berries and glided through afternoons in a canoe.

Even this morning would be an improvement over the present.
I was in the garden then, surrounded by the hum of bees
and the Latin names of flowers, watching the early light
flash off the slanted windows of the greenhouse
and silver the limbs on the rows of dark hemlocks.

As usual, I was thinking about the moments of the past,
letting my memory rush over them like water
rushing over the stones on the bottom of a stream.
I was even thinking a little about the future, that place
where people are doing a dance we cannot imagine,
a dance whose name we can only guess.  ◀

## Vona Groarke

# Why I Am Not a Nature Poet

has to do with Max and Nemo
scarcely out of a plastic bag three weeks ago
and into our new fishbowl
when Nemo started swelling up,
spiking pineapple fins and lying sideways
like a drunk in a gutter
lipping some foul-mouthed shanty to the moon.
"Dropsy," Ed in the Pet Centre said, who,
three weeks ago, swore they could live fifteen years.
"Put him in the freezer. Kill him quick.
Don't leave him in the bowl to rot
or the other one will eat him and die too."
I buy drops instead that cost
what three new goldfish would.
Eve makes a *Get Well Nemo* card
and talks to him when she passes,
calling him "little guy" and "goldilocks,"
playing "Für Nemo" on her keyboard.
I don't know. Max, I think, fine-tunes

his hunger and has a bloodless, sly look
to him now. He knows I'm on to him.
I tap the glass, shoo him away
whenever I see him closing in
on Nemo's wide-eyed slump
but I can't stand sentinel all night.
I'm in the kitchen when I hear the shout,
"Come up, see what's going on."
I take the stairs two at a time,
ordering the right words in my head:
*Choice . . . Fault . . . Nature . . . Destiny.*
Eve's face is level with the fish
and behind the bowl so it's magnified,
amazed, like an open moon.
"Max is nudging Nemo," she says.
"He's helping him turn round." ◀

## Kimiko Hahn

# Yellow Jackets—

protect through venom and candor.

While timing their own dinners
to mother's tray, father's tongs,

or baby's saucer-sized cheeks,

they can sting any intruder repeatedly
unlike the honeybee's suicidal sortie.

I like that. I like X
who calls people out at brunch

through simple narration:
*your mouth never stops moving.*

Or, *you eat off other plates as if they're your own.*

Or, *you check your BlackBerry when nobody is talking about you.*
Or, *you laugh whenever you insult someone.*

A starling attribute I wish I could emulate
if only my spine possessed such integrity. ◀

# Joy Harjo

## Santa Fe

The wind blows lilacs out of the east. And it isn't lilac season. And I am walking the street in front of St. Francis Cathedral in Santa Fe. Oh, and it's a few years earlier and more. That's how you tell real time. It is here, it is there. The lilacs have taken over everything: the sky, the narrow streets, my shoulders, my lips. I talk lilac. And there is nothing else until a woman the size of a fox breaks through the bushes, breaks the purple web. She is tall and black and gorgeous. She is the size of a fox on the arm of a white man who looks and tastes like cocaine. She lies for cocaine, dangles on the arm of cocaine. And lies to me now from a room in the DeVargas Hotel, where she has eaten her lover, white powder on her lips. That is true now; it is not true anymore. Eventually space curves, walks over and taps me on the shoulder. On the sidewalk I stand near St. Francis; he has been bronzed, a perpetual tan, with birds on his hand, his shoulder, deer at his feet. I am Indian and in this town I will never be a saint. I am seventeen and shy and wild. I have been up until three at a party, but there is no woman in the DeVargas Hotel for that story hasn't yet been invented. A man whose face I will never remember, and never did, drives up on a Harley Davidson. There are lilacs on his arm, they spill out from the spokes of his wheels. He wants me on his arm, on the back of his lilac bike touring the flower kingdom of San Francisco. And for a piece of time the size of a nickel, I think, maybe. But maybe is vapor, has no anchor here in the sun beneath St. Francis Cathedral. And space is as solid as the bronze statue of St. Francis, the fox breaking through the lilacs, my invention of this story, the wind blowing. ◀

# Geoffrey Hill

## September Song

*born 19.6.32–deported 24.9.42*

Undesirable you may have been, untouchable
you were not. Not forgotten
or passed over at the proper time.

As estimated, you died. Things marched,
sufficient, to that end.

Just so much Zyklon and leather, patented
terror, so many routine cries.

(I have made
an elegy for myself it
is true)

September fattens on vines. Roses
flake from the wall. The smoke
of harmless fires drifts to my eyes.

This is plenty. This is more than enough.  ◀

# Brenda Hillman

## Shadows in Snow

When shadows are unhinged from bodies,
     they make chords with clouds
          impossible to hear.

In the end, there will be nothing wrong.
Tonight red ring surrounds the moon
like a hurt boy
following a married woman;

you hurry along, tired of your travels,

& the dense beauty from whose demands
     you never recover
stays beside you
as the orchid keeps the black stripe
of its personal winter—  ◀

# Major Jackson

## The Giant Swing Ending in a Split

Why was I ashamed to be seen on the waterfront
with her? We both felt the past slip
from our shoulders, rose lipped and listening to

jet engines Doppler across the night.
Wasn't I also me when I lay with her?
Maybe frighteningly more. My sleepsmile
and low whispers hers, too. O
delicious agony, I'm divided right
to my body's historic wharf. I only trust the sweat
salting down my back her fingernail tracks. ◄

# June Jordan

## Ghazal at Full Moon

I try to describe how this aching begins or how it began
with an obsolete coin and the obsolete head of an obsolete Indian.

Holding a nickel I beheld a buffalo I beheld the silver face
of a man who might be your father: A dead man: An Indian.

I thought, "Indians pray. Indians dance. But, mostly, Indians do
      not live
In the U.S.A.," we said, "the only good Indian is a dead Indian."

Dumb like Christopher Columbus I could not factor out the obvious
denominator: Guatemala/Wisconsin/Jamaica/Colorado: Indian.

Nicaragua and Brazil, Arizona, Illinois, North Dakota, and New
      Mexico:
The Indigenous: The shining and the shadow of the eye is Indian.

One billion-fifty-six, five-hundred-and-thirty-seven-thousand people
breathing in India, Pakistan, Bangladesh: All of them Indian.

Ocho Rios Oklahoma Las Vegas Pearl Lagoon Chicago
Bombay Panjim Liverpool Lahore Comalapa Glasgow: Indian.

From a London pub among the lager louts to Machu Picchu
I am following an irresistible a tenuous and livid profile: Indian.

I find a surging latticework inside the merciless detritus of diaspora.
We go from death to death who see any difference here from Indian.

The voice desiring your tongue transmits from the light of the clouds
      as it can.
Indian Indian Indian       Indian Indian Indian Indian. ◄

## Allison Joseph

# On Being Told I Don't Speak like a Black Person

*Emphasize the "h," you hignorant ass,*
was what my mother was told
when colonial-minded teachers
slapped her open palm with a ruler
in that Jamaican schoolroom.
Trained in England, they tried
to force their pupils to speak
like Eliza Doolittle after
her transformation, fancying themselves
British as Henry Higgins,
despite dark, sun-ripened skin.
Mother never lost her accent,
though, the music of her voice
charming everyone, an infectious lilt
I can imitate, not duplicate.
No one in the States told her
to eliminate the accent,
my high school friends adoring
the way her voice would lift
when she called me to the phone—
*A-ll-i-son, it's friend Cathy.*
*Why don't you sound like her,*
they'd ask. I didn't sound
like anyone or anything,
no grating New Yorker nasality,
no fastidious British mannerisms
like the ones my father affected
when he wanted to sell someone
something. And I didn't sound
like a Black American,
college acquaintances observed,
sure they knew what a black person
was supposed to sound like.

Was I supposed to sound lazy,
dropping syllables here and there
not finishing words but
slurring their final letters
so each sentence joined
the next, sliding past the listener?
Were certain words off limits,
too erudite for someone whose skin
came with a natural tan?
I asked them what they meant
and they stuttered, blushed,
said *you know, Black English,*
applying a term from that
semester's text. *Does everyone
in your family speak alike,*
I'd ask, and they'd say *don't
take this the wrong way,
nothing personal.*

Now I realize there's nothing
more personal than speech,
that I don't have to defend
how I speak, how any person,
black, white, chooses to speak.
Let us speak. Let us talk
with the sound of our mothers
and fathers still reverberating
in our minds, wherever our mothers
or fathers come from:
Arkansas, Belize, Alabama,
Brazil, Aruba, Arizona.
Let us simply speak
to one another,
listen and prize the inflections,
never assuming how any person will sound
until his mouth opens, until her
mouth opens, greetings welcome
in any language. ◄

## Donald Justice

# Variations for Two Pianos

*For Thomas Higgins, pianist*

There is no music now in all Arkansas.
Higgins is gone, taking both his pianos.

Movers dismantled the instruments, away
Sped the vans. The first detour untuned the strings.

There is no music now in all Arkansas.

Up Main Street, past the cold shopfronts of Conway,
The brash, self-important brick of the college,

Higgins is gone, taking both his pianos.

Warm evenings, the windows open, he would play
Something of Mozart's for his pupils, the birds.

There is no music now in all Arkansas.

How shall the mockingbird mend her trill, the jay
His eccentric attack, lacking a teacher?

Higgins is gone, taking both his pianos.
There is no music now in all Arkansas. ◀

## Jane Kenyon

# The Blue Bowl

Like primitives we buried the cat
with his bowl. Bare-handed
we scraped sand and gravel
back into the hole.
                    They fell with a hiss
and thud on his side,
on his long red fur, the white feathers
between his toes, and his
long, not to say aquiline, nose.

We stood and brushed each other off.
There are sorrows keener than these.

Silent the rest of the day, we worked,
ate, stared, and slept. It stormed
all night; now it clears, and a robin
burbles from a dripping bush
like the neighbor who means well
but always says the wrong thing. ◀

# Galway Kinnell

## That Silent Evening

I will go back to that silent evening
when we lay together and talked in low, silent voices,
while outside slow lumps of soft snow
fell, hushing as they got near the ground,
with a fire in the room, in which centuries
of tree went up in continuous ghost-giving-up,
without a crackle, into morning light.
Not until what hastens went slower did we sleep.
When we got home we turned and looked back
at our tracks twining out of the woods,
where the branches we brushed against let fall
puffs of sparkling snow, quickly, in silence,
like stolen kisses, and where the *scritch scritch scritch*
among the trees, which is the sound that dies
inside the sparks from the wedge when the sledge
hits it off center telling everything inside
it is fire, jumped to a black branch, puffed up
but without arms and so to our eyes lonesome,
and yet also — how could we know *this?—happy!*
in shape of chickadee. Lying still in snow,
not iron-willed, like railroad tracks, willing
not to meet until heaven, but here and there
making slubby kissing stops in the field,
our tracks wobble across the snow their long scratch.
Everything that happens here is really little more,
if even that, than a scratch, too. Words, in our mouths,

are almost ready, already, to bandage the one
whom the *scritch scritch scritch*, meaning *if how when*
we might lose each other, scratches scratches scratches
from this moment to that. Then I will go back
to that silent evening, when the past just managed
to overlap the future, if only by a trace,
and the light doubles and shines
through the dark the sparkling that heavens the earth. ◀

## Yusef Komunyakaa

# A Voice on
# an Answering Machine

I can't erase her voice. If I opened the door to the cage & tossed the magpie into
the air, a part of me would fly away, leaving only the memory of a plucked string
trembling in the night. The voice unwinds breath, soldered wires, chance, loss,
& digitalized impulse. She's telling me how light pushed darkness till her father
stood at the bedroom door dressed in a white tunic. Sometimes we all wish we
could put words back into our mouths.

I have a plant of hers that has died many times, only to be revived with less
water & more light, always reminding me of the voice caught inside the little
black machine. She lives between the Vale of Kashmir & nirvana, beneath a bipo-
lar sky. The voice speaks of an atlas & a mask, a map of Punjab, an ugly scar from
college days on her abdomen, the unsaid credo, but I still can't make the voice
say, Look, I'm sorry. I've been dead for a long time. ◀

## Ted Kooser

# Mourners

After the funeral, the mourners gather
under the rustling churchyard maples
and talk softly, like clusters of leaves.
White shirt cuffs and collars flash in the shade:
highlights on deep green water.

They came this afternoon to say goodbye,
but now they keep saying hello and hello,
peering into each other's faces,
slow to let go of each other's hands. ◀

# Ben Lerner

## We Have Assembled

WE HAVE ASSEMBLED for the athletic contest in tiered seats. Once, we assembled in a central core with mobile spiral arms. Or, lying on our backs, we formed a radiating cluster, imposing animal figures and names upon the stars. Now we watch heavily armored professionals assume formations on a grid of artificial grass. Wishbone. Shotgun. Power I. ◀

# D. Nurske

## Left Field

Told I threw *like a girl*
I waited out in the shadows

while the infielders made spectacular leaps
—by luck or memory of the future?

Some threw like older girls,
some hurled streaks of evening,

all grew equally remote
as night fell and the voices
singing *no batter, no pitcher*
faded under crickets.

I pounded my glove,
spat, dug my cleats
savagely in the sod
and growled *swing.*

Secretly, I was proudest of my skill
at standing alone in darkness. ◀

## Naomi Shihab Nye

# I Feel Sorry for Jesus

People won't leave Him alone.
I know He said, *wherever two or more
are gathered in my name* . . .
but I'll bet some days He regrets it.

Cozily they tell you what He wants
and doesn't want
as if they just got an e-mail.
Remember "Telephone," that pass-it-on game

where the message changed dramatically
by the time it rounded the circle?
Well.
People blame terrible pieties on Jesus.

They want to be his special pet.
Jesus deserves better.
I think He's been exhausted
for a very long time.

He went *into the desert*, friends.
He didn't go into the pomp.
He didn't go into
the golden chandeliers

and say, *the truth tastes better here*.
See? I'm talking like I know.
It's dangerous talking for Jesus.
You get carried away almost immediately.

I stood in the spot where He was born.
I closed my eyes where He died and didn't die.
Every twist of the Via Dolorosa
was written on my skin.

And that makes me feel like being silent
for Him, you know? A secret pouch
of listening. You won't hear me
mention this again. ◄

# Mary Oliver

## Crossing the Swamp

Here is the endless
    wet thick
        cosmos, the center
            of everything—the nugget
of dense sap, branching
    vines, the dark burred
        faintly belching
            bogs. Here
is *swamp*, here
    is struggle,
        closure—
            pathless, seamless,
peerless mud. My bones
    knock together at the pale
        joints, trying
            for foothold, fingerhold,
mindhold over
    such slick crossings, deep
        hipholes, hummocks
            that sink silently
into the black, slack
    earthsoup. I feel
        not wet so much as
            painted and glittered
with the fat grassy
    mires, the rich
        and succulent marrows
            of earth—a poor
dry stick given
    one more chance by the whims
        of swamp water—a bough
            that still, after all these years,
could take root,
    sprout, branch out, bud—
        make of its life a breathing
            palace of leaves. ◀

# David O'Meara

## The Game

The trees skitter past, a rush of verticals
at the roadside, I'm fifteen
in the rear-view, off to play
the softball tournament at Golden Lake.

There's Tommy, Trevor, and me.
And Trevor's older brother, Kevin,
who shit-grins behind the steering wheel,
getting us there for the 10 a.m. pitch.

Somewhere down these back routes,
just for kicks, he guns the rusted chassis
at rising humps in the road,
full speed, trying to jimmy us

loose from gravity, and slip
a fat envelope of air
between our wheels and the earth.
Each time we land, our tailbones jab

the vinyl seats, and the stitched gloves
jostle in our laps, their punched palms
a darker tan than last summer.
Kevin's loving the morning breeze

forced through the rolled-down windows,
but especially the looks of panic
on his passengers' faces,
as if we were clean, plush cushions

he'd been itching to knock
the stuffing from. "Watch
this," he says, pushing the gas pedal
to the dusty mat, then charges

the wrong side of the next blind hill.
Our heads are numb; our stomachs roll
and clutch, I catch my own eye
in the side mirror, giddy with the look
of death, every bit as close as it might appear. ◀

# Deborah Parédez

## Bustillo Drive Grocery

On the corner of Bustillo Drive
in the years before the campaign
to widen the street so cars veered off
Roosevelt Avenue right into mailboxes
right into stray dogs and second cousins,
in the years before we found the cockroach
floating inside a bottle of R.C. Cola
and swore off sodas forever
our righteous boycotts lasting
only halfway through Lent,
in the years before the thieves
tore through the screen doors and cracked
open the cash registers and *Abuelito's*[1] head
with the butts of their guns, in the years
before I turned sour as *chamoy*[2]
coarse and tough as stale *chicharón*,[3]
I was in charge of *los dulces*.[4]
In those years, *Abuelita*[5] harnessed
me with my first job, setting me on a stool
behind the counter, setting me
like chocolate poured—quick—into the
candy mold before it hardens.
In the afternoons I fulfilled my duties
with a reverence for the expansive variations,
the countless shapes of sweetness:
aligning cylinders of Life Savers by flavor,
the Milky Ways near the Three Musketeers,
the dainty swirled straws of pixie sticks near
the prized plastic heads of Pez dispensers,
the packets of pop rocks in grape, cherry and orange.

---

1. **Abuelito:** Grandpa
2. **chamoy:** savory sauce made from pickled fruit
3. **chicharón:** a dish made from fried pork rinds
4. **los dulces:** the sweets or candies
5. **Abuelita:** Granny

I sat tall in my stool, a big girl, I was in charge
of *los dulces*. In the shelves above my reach
jars of Spanish olives, bottles of Bayer aspirin,
rolls of Charmin stood at attention,
awaiting their orders, but I could not be bothered
by the weight of such practical inventory.
I cared only for saccharine indulgence
so when on Friday nights the regular crowd
of relatives arrived for the gossip and the gambling,
I descended from my *dulce* throne
leaned coyly against the domino table
until Uncle Louis finished off his Falstaff
slapped his last domino down and with the same
triumphant hand, grabbed hold of me, swooped me up,
the fringes of my crocheted *poncho*[6] fanning out in radiant plume.
He would lower me into the cavernous
depths of the oldtime soda water cooler
that ran the length of the front wall, the length of a coffin
and twice as deep, my body plunged head first
into the cool humming darkness, arms outstretched,
hands grabbing hold of a slender bottleneck
and just then—catch complete—my plumed body
in pelican dive—I went soaring again—
Uncle Louis pulling me out from the depths,
*poncho* fringes fluttering, giggles spouting
from my mouth, syrupy bubbles erupting
from the opened bottle of my shaken Orange Crush.
In those years, my unwavering devotion to *los dulces*,
my faith in the choreography of return spurred
every harrowing descent, brought me back
every time—flushed and dizzy and eager for more. ◄

## Bradley Paul

# Short Ends

I thought my dog would die for a while.
Her kidneys were gone for a while.

---

6. **poncho:** a blanket-like outer garment

I paid to get them back for a while.
For a while my dog won't die.

They were shooting a movie at the state beach for a while.
The sea grapes popped underfoot for a while.
My dog insisted she swim for a while.
For a while I was next to the sea.

In the cooler it was cool for a while.
The flesh of the pear was cold for a while.
The Coke was not flat for a while.
For a while there was something to eat.

But where is my brother? He was here for a while.
Where is my mother? She was here for a while.
They were healthy as my dog for a while.
For a while we made quite a scene. ◀

# Molly Peacock

## Instead of Her Own

Instead of her own, my grandmother washed my hair.
The porcelain was cold at the back of my neck,
my fragile neck. Altogether it was cold there.

She did it so my hair would smell sweet.
What else is like the moist mouse straw
of a girl's head? Why, the feeling of complete

peace the smell brings to a room whose window
off oily Lake Erie is rimmed with snow.
Knuckles rasping at young temples know,

in the involuntary way a body knows,
that as old is, so young grows. Completion
drives us: substitution is our mission.

Thin little head below thin little head grown old.
Water almost warm in a room almost cold. ◀

## Patricia Smith

# Listening at the Door

Beneath the door, I could practically see
the wretched slither of tobacco and English Leather.
Hiding on the other side, I heard Mama giggle
through clenched teeth, which meant potential
husband sitting spitshined on our corduroy couch.
The needle hit that first groove and I wondered
why my mama had chosen the blues,
wrong, Friday-angled, when it was hope
she needed. I pressed my ear against the door,
heard dual damp panting, the Murphy bed squeal,
the occasional directive,
the sexless clink of jelly jar glasses.

What drove me to listen on those nights
when my mother let that fragrant man in,
banished me to the back of the apartment,
pretended she could shine above hurting?
I'd rest my ear against the cool wood all night
as she flipped through the 45s—
looking for Ray Charles, Stevie Wonder,
somebody blind this time,
somebody crawling on his knees toward love. ◀

## Gary Snyder

# I Went into the Maverick Bar

I went into the Maverick Bar
In Farmington, New Mexico.
And drank double shots of bourbon
                    backed with beer.
My long hair was tucked up under a cap
I'd left the earring in the car.

Two cowboys did horseplay
　　　　　　by the pool tables,
A waitress asked us
　　　　　　where are you from?
a country-and-western band began to play
"We don't smoke Marijuana in Muskokie"
And with the next song,
　　　　　　a couple began to dance.

They held each other like in High School dances
　　　　　　in the fifties;
I recalled when I worked in the woods
　　　　　　and the bars of Madras, Oregon.
That short-haired joy and roughness—
　　　　　　America—your stupidity.
I could almost love you again.

We left—onto the freeway shoulders—
　　　　　　under the tough old stars—
In the shadow of bluffs
　　　　　　I came back to myself,
To the real work, to
　　　　　　"What is to be done." ◄

## Gary Soto

# What Is Your Major?

One spring I thought that maybe archeology
Was better than mortuary studies,
That a person scanned the wreck of a pagan temple
And by intuition commanded, "This is where we dig."
I knew people died like minutes,
And that someone had to tie shoelaces one last time
And fiddle with the collars before the coffins,
Soft as pin cushions, were closed.
I knew they were similar, the ancient dead
Washed by the rise and fall of the Nile,
And the recent dead, like Mrs. White's husband,

Poor man whose head fit through the rollers
Of industrial machinery. I knew
Mr. White would go nowhere, even if his coffin rotted
And rain washed over his face,
Now narrow as a hatchet.
He wouldn't get up and scare me,
And the temples wouldn't litter
My back with goose bumps.
I had outgrown ghost stories,
And at night I was not in the least scared
Of petting my own flesh,
Eventual fodder for the carnivorous earth.
I was nineteen, in junior college,
Piling up units so that I could help the dead.
I wanted to use my hands,
Either by shoveling for pharaohs by the Nile,
Or, in the college basement under a twenty-watt bulb,
Patting rouge on a poor fellow,
Cooing, "Come on, friend, let's make a good show." ◄

## James Tate

# Teaching the Ape to Write Poems

They didn't have much trouble
teaching the ape to write poems:
first they strapped him into the chair,
then tied the pencil around his hand
(the paper had already been nailed down).
Then Dr. Bluespire leaned over his shoulder
and whispered into his ear:
"You look like a god sitting there.
Why don't you try writing something?" ◄

# Gloria Vando

## new shoes and an old flame

```
        shopping today i see a pair of kinky
       yves st. laurent
     shoes and
    think of you
  now why do you
  suppose my mind
  not unlike bubble
   gum pushed to its
    very limits springs
      back upon your image
        sticking to the thought
          of you wondering how
            you'd feel about those
              skinny call-girl heels cause
            i'm still    coming on to you
            you see        even though i
            tell my-          self you're gone
            now one            of those people we
            speak               of with reverence or
            a hint                of smile suggesting something
            deeper                 than we ever let on  your name
            still                    makes me smile and think of
            high-                      heel shoes—the higher, the better ◀
```

## David Wojahn

# The Assassination of John Lennon as Depicted by the Madame Tussaud Wax Museum, Niagara Falls, Ontario, 1987

Smuggled human hair from Mexico
Falls radiant upon the waxy O

Of her scream. Shades on, leather coat and pants, Yoko
On her knees—like the famous Kent State photo

Where the girl can't shriek her boyfriend alive, her arms
Wind-milling Ohio sky.
                              A pump in John's chest heaves

To mimic death-throes. The blood is made of latex.
His glasses: broken on the plastic sidewalk.

A scowling David Chapman, his arms outstretched,
His pistol barrel spiraling fake smoke

In a siren's red wash, completes the composition,
And somewhere background music plays "Imagine"

Before the tableau darkens. We push a button
To renew the scream.
                              The chest starts up again.  ◀

## Matthew Zapruder

# Automated Regret Machine

My friend and I were watching television
and laughing. Then we saw
white letters begin to crawl along
the bottom of the screen.
People were floating on doors and holding
large pieces of cardboard
with telephone numbers scrawled

in black fear up to the helicopters.
The storm had very suddenly
come and now it was gone.
I saw one aluminum rooftop flash
in sunlight, it would have burned
the feet of anyone trying to wait there.
My friend by then had managed
to will her face into that familiar living
detachment mask. I thought
of the very large yellow house
of the second half of my childhood, how through
my bedroom window I could reach my hand
out and upward and touch
the branch of an elm. At night
in the summer I heard the rasp
of a few errant cicadas whose timing
devices had for them tragically drifted.
And the hoarse glassy call
of the black American crow.
Though I am at least halfway through
my life, part of my spirit
still lives there, thinking very soon
I will go down to the room where my father
carefully places his fingers on the strings of the guitar
he bought a few years before I was born.
Picking his head up he smiles
and motions vaguely with his hand, communicating
many contradictory things.  ◀

# 2

# Writing the Short Story

## ▶ A few things you should know about the short story

What is **fiction**? In the largest sense, it is something that's made up. Of course, a story can be entirely fabricated, or just *not quite* true, although as literary critics have often said, it's hard to tell the truth even when we want to. The word "fiction" comes from a Latin root meaning "to shape or fashion," and whenever we recount some past event, even if it's only what we did yesterday, we inevitably include certain details and leave others out. We shape what we have to say to make a point or produce a desired effect. Through this process, raw material becomes fictionalized.

And fictions are everywhere, from the implied stories in magazine advertisements ("using this product will make you more attractive to other people"), to politicians' speeches, to the extended stories, or **narratives**, found in films. Indeed, any form of communication that relies extensively on imagination might be labeled fiction, which brings us into potentially dangerous territory: a definition isn't worth much if it is all-inclusive.

Of course, even if we limit our discussion of fiction to creative writing, **poetry**—the other genre in this book—also falls into that category. Fortunately, we can distinguish what we generally call fiction from poetry because fiction is written in **prose**, the ordinary language of speaking and writing. Poetry—highly charged and rhythmic language—may be notoriously difficult to define, but it is relatively easy to identify on the page: prose moves in a straight line from the left to the right margin, while the right-hand margins of a poem are ragged, with each line ending where it does for added emphasis (the **prose poem** notwithstanding).

The difference between fiction (and poetry) and **creative nonfiction**—literary writing that claims to be true—is more striking. Writers of creative nonfiction are always accountable to the evidence. James Frey, for instance, found himself in hot water when it was revealed in 2006 that his Oprah Winfrey-endorsed, best-selling book *A Million Little Pieces*, which he called a memoir, actually included a number of incidents that either were exaggerated or hadn't occurred at all. Had the book been labeled a novel, no one would have blinked an eye: novelists, after all, are *supposed* to make things up.

We have a further sense of how liberating the word "fiction" can be when we look at what is called historical fiction, in which the author's perspective on the facts inevitably affects how these particulars are presented. Even though more fact finding may be involved in this enterprise than with other types of fiction writing, we still read a historical novel rather than a nonfiction book of history because we want to be caught up in the *story*. E. L. Doctorow, for example, carefully researched General William Tecumseh Sherman's advance through the South for his novel *The March* and adheres to the broad outlines of what really happened. However, his book is admired not primarily for its documentation of the Civil War but because readers enjoy being inside the minds and hearts of the characters he has created.

*The March*, written by a great American author, is clearly a literary novel, while a novel such as John Jakes's *North and South,* about the same time period, is likely to be labeled "genre fiction." What's the difference? Genre fiction, which includes romance, spy/thriller, horror, fantasy, science fiction, and the like, requires the writer to adhere to certain conventions, such as good triumphing over evil. In a romance novel, for instance, we know that early on, a man and a woman will fall in love but will be prevented from coming together by a series of obstacles. Yet no matter how many plot complications ensue, just at the point when those barriers seem insurmountable, the conventions of a romance require that the two lovers ultimately unite. Fans of the genre know the basic story line by heart—indeed, they *demand* that the writer stick to it—and they receive pleasure from watching the author work variations on time-honored themes.

In contrast, writers of literary fiction go in fear of adhering too closely to a standard set of expectations. Knowing that there are only a handful of basic plots on which to draw, literary writers look to evoke the specific, the individual, the original. They value character over plot, and they spend a great deal of time on the nuances of authorial voice and style. John Jakes may provide us with a great page-turner, but E. L. Doctorow makes us want to slow down and savor each sentence of his prose, each moment of his narrative.

Literary fiction values ambiguity. Although they rarely occur in real life, happy endings are something we love, and writers of genre fiction cater to that desire. Many recreational readers savor a pleasant diversion that doesn't require much investment of mental energy, and they prefer all the questions and complications in a story to be resolved by the end. But writers and readers of literary fiction value uncertainty; they enjoy the possibility that a character or situation can be interpreted in more than a single way. Life is complex, their thinking goes; fiction should be, too.

# The elements of fiction ▶

Depending on the number of students enrolled in your class and duration of your academic term, your instructor may choose to focus on either short-shorts or stories that are more fully developed. Fortunately, the similarities between the short and longer forms are more pronounced than are the differences. The one-page short-short, the ten-page short story, and, for that matter, the thousand-page novel all make use of the same basic elements of fiction. The focus of this chapter is on those fundamentals that are most pertinent to the short fiction you will be writing. Each of these elements will be discussed in more detail later in this section; for now, let's get acquainted with the terms.

▶ **Structure and Design**   Obviously novelists need a plan to carry them through their projects. But writers of short stories must also consider structure and design, perhaps more so because they have relatively little room to maneuver. In a strong work of short fiction, every piece of the story must interact effectively with the others.

▶ **Character**   The **characters**—the people in your story—should be recognizable as human beings, showing both their good and bad sides, and should be *capable* of changing, even if they don't ultimately rise to the challenges that face them.

▶ **Dialogue**   The **dialogue** is what characters say to one another. The best dialogue not only reveals who the characters are but also moves the story along. Some stories have no dialogue at all, but most have at least some conversation, and learning how to write significant and selective dialogue is an essential skill.

▶ **Setting**   The **setting** is where and when the story takes place. Like good dialogue, deft use of detail and description both illuminates character and propels a scene forward.

▶ **Point of View, Tone, and Style**   These allow us into, or keep us out of, the characters' minds; they dictate how much we learn of their internal, unspoken thinking. According to I. A. Richards, tone is a literary speaker's "attitude toward his listener." And **style** is how writers say what they have to say. Point of view, tone, and style are covered together because, especially in the short story, *who* is telling the story and *how* it's told are closely intertwined.

# The short story: Three models ▶

We have said that fiction is imaginative writing in prose. It encompasses the novel, the novella, the short story, and the short-short story. How long *is* a short-short story? Different writers and critics give different answers, but most would agree that the short-short is at least 100 but probably no more than 1,000 or 1,500 words. In a semester-length two-genre creative writing class, students often have time to write longer stories of up to four or five thousand words. This turns out to be a fairly broad range, from less than one double-spaced page to twenty pages. Still, this is a relatively small canvas, and readers expect that every moment of a story will engage their interest.

Perhaps the most important thing to remember about the short story is that it is *not* a fragment. It is a complete work, with a beginning, a middle, and an end. Granted, parts of the short-short may be drastically condensed, and the art of fiction is, in part, the art of learning which things to include and which to omit. However, even in a fifteen-page story, everything that doesn't deepen our understanding of the characters and contribute to the forward momentum of the narrative will be eliminated.

Even if your instructor has not yet given you your fiction writing assignment, the moment you feel the urge to begin stringing words together into a story, *go for it*. Creative impulses don't necessarily arrive on a schedule, and whether you begin your story now, or after reading every word in this chapter, any time that you feel like writing is a good time.

Assuming, however, that the Muse hasn't struck you while reading the last few pages, you'll probably want to become familiar with a few examples of short stories before you start writing your own. For our model stories, we have two short-shorts of fewer than 1,000 words, and a longer story of about 2,500 words. These three stories, all quite different from one another, give you a range of models. Isaac Babel's dark and descriptive "Crossing the River Zbrucz" (108) shows war at its grimmest. In sharp contrast, Donald Barthelme's "The Baby" (110) takes a potentially grim situation and turns it into comedy. Finally, Stephanie Vaughn's "We're on TV in the Universe" (112) is a humorous yet ultimately poignant look at a young woman's car accident in an ice storm.

Taken together, these three stories provide material for a discussion of the elements of fiction. We will make frequent reference to the three stories, so it's worth reading each one at least twice. If you're still not ready to write after reading about the basics of fiction, turn to the "kick-starts" writing prompts in "Getting Started Writing the Short Story." And because reading is so often a trigger for writing, the mini-anthology of short stories that concludes this chapter is another potential source of inspiration.

"The human being is a storytelling animal," Salman Rushdie says, "or actually, *the* storytelling animal, the only creature on earth that tells itself stories in order to understand what sort of creature it is." As you write your own story, you may, like Rushdie, find yourself coming to know just what sort of creature you are.

## Isaac Babel

# Crossing the River Zbrucz

The Russian writer Isaac Babel (1894–1940) is considered to be one of the greatest writers of short fiction of the twentieth century. Francine Prose praises the way Babel typically introduces "some element of unease" so that his paragraphs "make us catch our breath in the final sentence." And Tom Teicholz writes: "He stands in the footsteps of the reader, alternately awed, impressed and horrified by [his] characters and their world."

Babel was a war correspondent for his country during World War I, so he had firsthand knowledge of the conflict between Russia and Poland described in this story, which was first published in his 1926 collection, *The Red Cavalry Stories*. It is important to remember, however, that even though "Crossing the River Zbrucz" is written in the voice of a callous Russian army officer, Babel himself was Jewish, and his real sympathies are clearly with the Jewish family whose home has been invaded. Although Babel enjoyed considerable success while he was alive and he is generally considered one of the masters of the short story, his life was cut tragically short. Never one to mute his condemnation when he saw injustice, Babel ran afoul of the Soviet authorities and was arrested by the secret police and "disappeared" in 1939. It was later learned that not long after the arrest, he was executed and his body was thrown into a communal grave.

The commander of the Sixth Division reported that Novograd-Volynsk[1] was taken at dawn today. The staff is now withdrawing from Krapivno[2], and our cavalry transport stretches in a noisy rear guard along the high road that goes from Brest to Warsaw, a high road built on the bones of muzhiks[3] by Czar Nicholas I.

Fields of purple poppies are blossoming around us, a noon breeze is frolicking in the yellowing rye, virginal buckwheat is standing on the horizon like the wall of a faraway monastery. Silent Volhynia[4] is turning away, Volhynia is leaving,

---

1. **Novograd-Volynsk:** A city in the border region between Russia and Poland
2. **Krapivno:** A town in that same region
3. **muzhiks:** Peasants
4. **Volhynia:** The name of the area in which the story is set

heading into the pearly white fog of the birch groves, creeping through the flowery hillocks, and with weakened arms entangling itself in the underbrush of hops. The orange sun is rolling across the sky like a severed head, gentle light glimmers in the ravines among the clouds, the banners of the sunset are fluttering above our heads. The stench of yesterday's blood and slaughtered horses drips into the evening chill. The blackened Zbrucz roars and twists the foaming knots of its rapids. The bridges are destroyed, and we wade across the river. The majestic moon lies on the waves. The water comes up to the horses' backs, purling streams trickle between hundreds of horses' legs. Someone sinks, and loudly curses the Mother of God. The river is littered with the black squares of the carts and filled with humming, whistling, and singing that thunders above the glistening hollows and the snaking moon.

Late at night we arrive in Novograd. In the quarter to which I am assigned I find a pregnant woman and two red-haired Jews with thin necks, and a third Jew who is sleeping with his face to the wall and a blanket pulled over his head. In my room I find ransacked closets, torn pieces of women's fur coats on the floor, human excrement, and fragments of the holy Seder plate that the Jews use once a year for Passover.

"Clean up this mess!" I tell the woman. "How can you live like this?"

The two Jews get up from their chairs. They hop around on their felt soles and pick up the broken pieces of porcelain from the floor. They hop around in silence, like monkeys, like Japanese acrobats in a circus, their necks welling and twisting. They spread a ripped eiderdown[5] on the floor for me, and I lie down by the wall, next to the third, sleeping Jew. Timorous poverty descends over my bed.

Everything has been killed by the silence, and only the moon, clasping its round, shining, carefree head in its blue hands, loiters beneath my window.

I rub my numb feet, lie back on the ripped eiderdown, and fall asleep. I dream about the commander of the Sixth Division. He is chasing the brigade commander on his heavy stallion, and shoots two bullets into his eyes. The bullets pierce the brigade commander's head, and his eyes fall to the ground. "Why did you turn back the brigade?" Savitsky, the commander of the Sixth Division, shouts at the wounded man, and I wake up because the pregnant woman is tapping me on the face.

"Sir," she says to me, "you are shouting in your sleep, and tossing and turning. I'll put your bed in another corner, because you are kicking my papa."

She raises her thin legs and round belly from the floor and pulls the blanket off the sleeping man. An old man is lying there on his back, dead. His gullet has been ripped out, his face hacked in two, and dark blood is clinging to his beard like a clump of lead.

---

5. **eiderdown:** A comforter filled with the soft feathers of eider ducks

"Sir," the Jewess says, shaking out the eiderdown, "the Poles were hacking him to death and he kept begging them, 'Kill me in the backyard so my daughter won't see me die!' But they wouldn't inconvenience themselves. He died in this room, thinking of me. . . . And now I want you to tell me," the woman suddenly said with terrible force, "I want you to tell me where one could find another father like my father in all the world!" ◄

# Donald Barthelme

# The Baby

Donald Barthelme (1931–1989) was a founding member of the prestigious creative writing program at the University of Houston and one of the most widely respected writers of fiction in the twentieth century. Many of his stories appeared in the *New Yorker*, and Barthelme was partly responsible for bringing "postmodern" fiction into the mainstream. He is also a master of the short-short, as evidenced in collections such as *Sixty Stories* (1981) and *Flying to America* (2007).

Barthelme often wrote about family themes, though in wild and unlikely permutations, as in "The Baby," originally published as "The First Thing the Baby Did Wrong" in *Overnight to Many Distant Cities* (1983) and later reprinted with its current title in *Forty Stories* (1987). Playful and experimental in his writing, Barthelme can veer from philosophy to parody in an instant. Above all, he is a writer with a pronounced sense of humor and irony. He locates the comic in the absurd and in the horrifying—as in this story about parents who take childhood discipline to ridiculous lengths. A consummate craftsperson, Barthelme is particularly well suited to the short-short story, in which every sentence must be well made and every word matters.

The first thing the baby did wrong was to tear pages out of her books. So we made a rule that each time she tore a page out of a book she had to stay alone in her room for four hours, behind the closed door. She was tearing out about a page a day, in the beginning, and the rule worked fairly well, although the crying and screaming from behind the closed door were unnerving. We reasoned that that was the price you had to pay, or part of the price you had to pay. But then as her grip improved she got to tearing out two pages at a time, which meant eight hours alone in her room, behind the closed door, which just doubled the annoyance for everybody. But she wouldn't quit doing it. And then as time went on we began getting days when she tore out three or four pages, which put her alone in her room for as much as sixteen hours at a stretch, interfering with normal feeding and worrying my wife. But I felt that if you made a rule you had to stick to it, had to be consistent, otherwise they get the wrong idea. She was about fourteen months old or fifteen months old at that point. Often, of course, she'd go to sleep, after an hour or so of yelling, that was a mercy. Her room was very nice, with a nice wooden rocking horse and practically a hundred dolls and stuffed animals. Lots of things to do in that room if you used your time wisely, puzzles and things. Unfortunately sometimes when we opened the door we'd find that she'd torn more pages out of more books while she was inside, and these pages had to be added to the total, in fairness.

The baby's name was Born Dancin'. We gave the baby some of our wine, red, whites and blue, and spoke seriously to her. But it didn't do any good.

I must say she got real clever. You'd come up to her where she was playing on the floor, in those rare times when she was out of her room, and there'd be a book there, open beside her, and you'd inspect it and it would look perfectly all right. And then you'd look closely and you'd find a page that had one little corner torn, could easily pass for ordinary wear-and-tear but I knew what she'd done, she'd torn off this little corner and swallowed it. So that had to count and it did. They will go to any lengths to thwart you. My wife said that maybe we were being too rigid and that the baby was losing weight. But I pointed out to her that the baby had a long life to live and had to live in a world with others, had to live in a world where there were many, many rules, and if you couldn't learn to play by the rules you were going to be left out in the cold with no character, shunned and ostracized by everyone. The longest we ever kept her in her room consecutive was eighty-eight hours, and that ended when my wife took the door off its hinges with a crowbar even though the baby still owed us twelve hours because she was working off twenty-five pages. I put the door back on its hinges and added a big lock, one that opened only if you put a magnetic card in a slot, and I kept the card.

But things didn't improve. The baby would come out of her room like a bat out of hell and rush to the nearest book, *Goodnight Moon* or whatever, and begin tearing pages out of it hand over fist. I mean there'd be thirty-four pages of *Goodnight Moon* on the floor in ten seconds. Plus the covers. I began to get a little worried. When I added up her indebtedness, in terms of hours, I could see that she wasn't going to get out of her room until 1992, if then. Also, she was looking pretty wan. She hadn't been to the park in weeks. We had more or less of an ethical crisis on our hands.

I solved it by declaring that it was all right to tear pages out of books, and moreover, that it was *all right* to have torn pages out of books in the past. That is one of the satisfying things about being a parent—you've got a lot of moves, each one good as gold. The baby and I sit happily on the floor, side by side, tearing pages out of books, and sometimes, just for fun, we go out on the street and smash a windshield together.  ◀

# Stephanie Vaughn

# We're on TV in the Universe

Stephanie Vaughn was born in a military family and raised in Ohio, New York, Texas, Oklahoma, the Philippines, and Italy. A professor of English at Cornell University, Vaughn is a two-time recipient of a National Endowment for the Arts Individual Artist Fellowship. Her stories have appeared in the *New Yorker* and in numerous anthologies, including *American Short Stories since 1945* and *The Vintage Book of Contemporary American Short Stories*. Her collection *Sweet Talk*, which contains "We're on TV in the Universe," was originally published in 1990 and was republished in 2012.

"Hers is a wise, touching, extraordinary voice," Joshua Henkin said in a review of *Sweet Talk*, and critics have been nearly unanimous in their praise of the book. The *Washington Post* suggested that "Vaughn's world is full of imaginative metaphors, including microcosmic worlds, suggesting hidden possibilities and longings." While the two previous model stories are freighted with direct conflict, the "trouble" in "We're on TV in the Universe" is more muted and internal. Obviously, longer stories have more room for nuance, for "hidden possibilities and longings," but notice, too, that the narrator faces immediate and numerous obstacles to reaching her journey's goal. No great tragedies occur in "We're on TV in the Universe," but the narrative pace is brisk, and there is an understated tension throughout the story.

My theory of the universe is that it's not moving outward from a Big Bang nor collapsing backward into the center. It's moving back and forth, breathing in and out, just like lungs. Sometimes, when the universe is running uphill, it breathes faster, and the stars from our vantage point in the Milky Way whip left and right like windshield wipers. The universe, when it is in deep sleep at five o'clock in the morning, has a heartbeat of 124 beats per minute, the same heartbeat that an unhatched chicken has just before it begins to crash its head against the shell.

Last winter I wrecked my car during an ice storm on Interstate 17. I had a chicken in a cage on the front seat beside me. I had the cage strapped in with the passenger seat belt, and a towel draped over the cage, so that the chicken wouldn't have to look at the weather. I was on my way to a party, and I was wearing my only party outfit, a black satin dress with a giant belt that was actually a music box in disguise—when you pressed the buckle, it played "Stars and Stripes Forever." The chicken was actually a young rooster who hadn't yet learned his own music. When he tried to crow a cock-a-doodle-do, he made a horrible scraping metal sound that came out "er-err-errr." It was early evening, black and snowy, the roadbed hissing beneath my tires, the chicken going "er-err-errr" every so often beneath the towel.

"So you don't want to go to a party?" I said to the chicken. I knew by then that I was driving on a chancy road, and I was trying to keep myself going with the chicken talk. "So you don't want to go to a party?" I said. "You want to go back home and become drumsticks and Hot Buffalo Wings?"

"Er-err-errr," the chicken said.

"Just kidding," I said. The chicken was going to be a present for a man who lived in the country and owned ducks, geese, and a swan. One thing I knew about this man was that he liked his birds the way some people like dogs and cats, and he probably wouldn't eat them. I was trying to picture the chicken in his new home when I crossed a bridge over the Susquehanna and encountered the silence of black ice. The tires lost their hiss, the chicken shut up, and about fifty yards after I hit the ice, I hit a Tioga County Sheriff's Department car. The car was parked on the road berm just beyond the bridge, and inside the car a sheriff was radioing for a tow truck, as if he knew I was coming and that when I got there, our two cars were going to need help.

My car did a kind of simple dance step down the highway on its way to meet the sheriff's car. It threw its hips to the left, it threw its hips to the right, left, right, left, right, then turned and slid, as if it were making a rock-and-roll move toward the arms of a partner.

Before the impact, when my car was still grace on ice, when my car was no longer in touch with the planet but now sliding above a thin layer of air and water, four thousand pounds of chrome and steel, bronze metallic paint, power steering, power brakes, AC, AM/FM, good tires, fine upholstery, all the things you like to see in an ad when you're looking for a big, used American car, when it was gliding through that galaxy of flashing lights, on its way through Andromeda, Sirius, and the Crab Nebula, it crossed my mind that surely it was against the laws of physics to hit a patrol car. If you were sliding above ice, you might hit a regular car, or a pole, or a fence, or an asteroid, but you could not hit the car of a man with a badge, a gun, bulletproof windows, citations forms in his pocket, handcuffs, the power to arrest you, a man working hard on a bad night.

Just about all of those things did really fly through my head and, recognizing the impossibility of the event, as my car slid sideways toward the side of the other car, I felt weightless and invisible. I felt harmless and happy.

Even for a sheriff, Officer Mike Cook was very tall. Officer Cook was linebacker tall, he was Jack-and-the-Beanstalk tall, he was as tall as my desire to be back home. Looking up at him, at the black silhouette of his hat, at the crazed lights on the top of his car slinging snowfish around his head, I lost contact with my native language. He put his hands on his hips and waited. When he perceived that words for me were as ephemeral as snowflakes, he said in his deep patrolman's voice, his made-for-TV-voice, "We're not having a very good evening, are we?"

*We*, he said. Officer Cook had embraced me with his pronoun.

It was then that I knew I loved Officer Cook, the blackness of his huge wet boots, the tenderness of his large hands as he lighted the flares and placed them along the roadside. People died that night on Interstate 17, and we were alive. We were alive! I loved Officer Cook for having survived the double whump of my car smashing into his car, nose to tail, and tail to nose, and then having thought of something to say about it afterward. We hit him twice, the chicken and I, before we spun out again heading back down the road in the direction we had been going before the accident. It took me a moment to realize that we were still moving and that the wheels had caught their traction again and needed an application of the brakes.

"Is it over?" I said to the chicken. When I lifted the towel, he was walking in small circles around the cage, looking for an escape perhaps. Poor creature, who in the early A.M. that day had been a resident of Old MacDonald's Pet Shop eating yellow corn and practicing his ridiculous crow in front of cooing children.

The reason Office Cook had been radioing for a tow truck was that another car had already hit the ice slick and had departed from the road. It had slid down a steep bank and been caught by drifts. The owner was standing now on the safe side of the guardrail waiting for the truck. He was a juggler, a college kid who had just driven four hundred miles on his way home from a Springsteen concert.

"I'm only twenty miles from home," he said.

"Me, too," I said. "Twenty miles from home and ten miles from a big party."

He had three snowballs and was tossing them in the air as we talked. He tossed them so high that they disappeared into the feathered darkness before they met his lightning hands again.

"You want a ride home?" he said. "Your car's done for the night." In fact, my car was going to need three thousand dollars in body work plus the four-hundred-dollar transmission job I had been postponing, and therefore it was done forever. I looked down at his red Mustang held by snow.

"How do you know *your* car's not done for the night?"

"My car didn't hit a police car," he said.

I don't know why the TV crew didn't put the juggler in the picture, maybe because they believed that the real story lay in the irony of a patrolman's needing help. The crew arrived breathlessly, a van from a station in Binghamton. One of them had a video camera, and the other did the talking. Officer Cook, who was back in his car talking on the radio, got out in order to say, "We don't want any more vehicles on this roadside. Move along now."

Traffic was moving very slowly past us in the far lane, cars, an eighteen-wheel rig, their drivers invisible behind black glass, straining to see us, I imagined, our little tableau, a cautionary tale.

"How many cars involved here?" the TV man said.

"Three," Officer Cook said, turning to get in his car.

"Anybody hurt? Anybody injured?"

"I don't think so," Officer Cook said. "Get off the road," he said, and slammed his door.

Just then I leaned against the car so that I could prop my elbows on the roof, and my belt buckle broke into "Stars and Stripes Forever." The TV man turned and took me in for the first time and then noticed the juggler, who by then was throwing five snowballs into the air and was all concentration.

"Did you hit the cop, or did he hit you?"

"I hit him," I said. I could see the TV man thinking about it—here were a juggler in the snow, a cop with a wrecked car, and a woman who sounded like brass band, maybe there was a story here—and then he shook his head no.

"Let's get out of here," he said to his cameraman.

They jogged to the van, and before they got in I heard the TV man say, "I know there's a better wreck somewhere down the road."

I looked at the juggler, who dropped his hands and let the balls fall past him like tiny comets. "You fail the wreck test," he said. "They're looking for an A-plus wreck. They're looking for something with bodies."

The belt had arrived at the piccolo section of the march, the silvery shooting-star solo of the brave little instrument soaring above the heavy brass ones. The juggler and I paused to listen to it. We tapped our feet in the slush and kept time with our bodies. When the march was over, the juggler said, "Nice belt."

The happiest person I met that night was the tow-truck driver. She was making lots of money in the bad weather and knew how to handle the roads. "My policy is people first and then their wrecks," she told us. "You might have some aches and pains, or your feet might be froze." So we got in the cab, the juggler, the chicken, and I, and rode one mile to the exit and a gas station, where we waited for the tow truck to bring in our cars. Officer Cook had to stay behind and wait for a policeman to come and fill out an accident report. That was the last I saw of him until the eleven o'clock news.

At the station, there were already three other drivers waiting for their cars. We all still had that adrenaline high you get from a close call, and we kept taking turns describing our accidents. We kept embellishing as we went, so that the accidents got more frightening as we added the sounds of breaking glass (my taillights) and the screech of metal (the juggler's bumper scraping the end of the guardrail), things you hear but don't listen to when the car is still moving. Someone wanted to know if I was a veterinarian. In the spirit of the moment,

I said, "Not exactly," and they all looked skeptical—We're all truth-tellers here, they seemed to say. "Actually, this is a birthday present for a veterinarian who lives in the country," I said. That was true enough to make sense of where I was and how I happened to arrive there with a live chicken. I played John Philip Sousa for them. The juggler juggled some soda cans. We asked him what the hardest things were to juggle and he said, "Live lobsters." A famous juggler in New York City had tried live lobsters once on a dare from someone in the audience, but the lobsters kept snapping at him. The chicken drank some water from a paper cup and, feeling more himself again, began to speak his peculiar chicken language.

In the end, I didn't accept a ride home with the juggler, because I had decided he was probably doing a little speed. Instead, I took a room at Koch's Universe Motel, which had a giant neon sign depicting stars and spaceships. I gave the chicken to the tow-truck driver. She had three children who wanted a pet, and she was the only one at the gas station who promised she wouldn't eat it. At eleven o'clock I got a glimpse of Officer Cook on TV. The camera panned over his car, pausing at the crushed front fender and the popped hood. Then it cut to him just long enough for him to say, "We don't want any more vehicles on this roadside," and then the report hurried on to the "better wrecks." Just before Officer Cook got to the word "roadside," I got a hazy look at myself in the background, separated from Officer Cook by the hood of his car and streaks of falling snow. There we were, together again. There we were, the two of us locked forever in the frame of a TV screen, bouncing off of satellites and caroming over the planet. We were still going places. We were leading off the transmission from earth in front of sports and weather, the late-night talk shows, and old movies. We were going to be up there with everybody who had ever been on TV. Truman and Eisenhower, JFK and LBJ. You name it. Pete Rose and Gloria Steinem. We were moving fast, already on our way to the moon. Pretty soon we'd be passing through the orbit of Mars, then Jupiter, Saturn, Uranus, Neptune, and Pluto. We'd be going to Andromeda and who knows where else. What a vacation.

A confession now. What was I doing on the road with a live chicken and a musical belt? I was going to a party where I imagine that I would be noticed as an interesting person. The Poultry Woman. The Marching Band Woman. A woman you would like to discover at a party. There were going to be famous people at that party, Watkins Glen race drivers, glass sculptors from Corning, writers from New York City, maybe even athletes and actors. I was between jobs again and living alone. When I set out in bad weather I had a feeling. Something was going to change for me that night, something was going to relocate me in the universe. Watching television in the motel, I thought about it. I was right. Something happened. ◀

# Structure and design ▶

A **story**, according to E. M. Forster in his book *Aspects of the Novel*, is "a narrative of events arranged in their time-sequence. . . . The king died and then the queen died." A **plot** is also a narrative of events but with the emphasis on causality: "The king died, and then the queen died of grief." Forester tells us, "if it is in a story, we say 'and then?'" If it is in a plot, we ask 'why?'"

Both story (the *what*) and plot (the *why*) have to do with events occurring in time. Dealing with time is one of the most challenging aspects of fiction writing because what is on the page rarely corresponds with the passage of real time. A character may have a memory that lasts for pages, although in life, those pages would have passed in only a second or two. Conversely, fiction writers can make lifetimes disappear with just a wave of their typing fingers. "Centuries passed," we say, and, as far as the story or book is concerned, they have.

A **chronology** is an account of the way time actually moves, from past to present to future. In novels and longer stories, chronology may be all jumbled up. A story may begin just as the **protagonist**—the main character on whom our attention is centered—is about to die. The narrative then might return elsewhere in time via a **flashback**: the sudden intrusion of past events in the middle of a description of current action. The story might then **flash forward**—cutting to the future—after the protagonist has passed away and all his family are gathered at his funeral. We are accustomed to this jumping around in time from watching movies, in which filmmakers often cut to another scene just when something important is about to happen in order to increase **suspense**, that anxiety about the outcome of an event that audiences find so painfully delicious.

However, in your short story you should avoid being seduced by a convoluted plot. Keep flashbacks and flash forwards to a minimum. If you do decide that it is briefly necessary for your narrative to provide information from the past or the future—as Stephanie Vaughn does in "We're on TV in the Universe"—it may help to graph your story as a time line:

——Past Events——|The Story|——Future Events——

If you're conscious of when something occurred in relation to the main story that is "happening" as the reader reads it, you're less likely to get tripped up with chronology. Your protagonist may be bewildered about when something takes place but you shouldn't be.

Even if the information never makes it into the story itself, thinking about what comes before and after what is actually written on the page can be of real value to the writer. Ernest Hemingway's "iceberg theory" is especially relevant for writers of the short story: "If it is any use to know it, I always try to write on the principle of the iceberg. There is seven-eighths of it underwater for every part that shows. Anything you know you can eliminate and it only strengthens your iceberg. . . . If a writer omits something because he does not know it then there is a hole in the story."

Screenwriters are told they must be able to summarize their movies in a **logline**, a one-sentence summary of twenty-five words or less. "A soldier encounters a chilling surprise in the home he occupies overnight." "A baby receives comically disproportionate punishments for tearing out the pages of books." "After hitting a police car on an icy road at night, a young woman reexamines her life." These three loglines don't do justice to our three model stories, but they do demonstrate that the basics of each story can be encapsulated in a few words. Readers of literary fiction normally don't demand a synopsis, but if you can't summarize your story in a few sentences, you may not yet know the story well enough to tell it properly.

Once you have decided on your story, you need to decide where on the time line of events to begin. Too often, students write about that moment in the story that first occurs to them, although the more intriguing conflict actually takes place at another point in the chronology of events. Say, for instance, that you want to write about a couple breaking up. It might seem logical to begin with the last fight between the two lovers, yet their very first fight two years earlier may be the real crux of the story, long before the breakup occurred. Or perhaps the story you really want to tell only briefly references the couple's rift. What interests you is how, after the breakup, your protagonist wandered forlornly into a city park and got into a fight with an old acquaintance.

Just about every fiction writer will tell you to find the moment when your protagonist is close to a disaster of some sort. In the words of Lajos Egri, a story "must open with a crisis which is the sole point of attack—in the life or lives of one or more of the characters. A decision must be imminent and the characters must be ready to take action." The ancient Greeks called this technique of beginning a story in the midst of the main action **in medias res**: "in the middle of things." It was good advice for storytellers then, and it is even more valid now, when we have so little tolerance for entertainment that does not engage us immediately.

A story that begins with three pages of background about how Princess Palonia has spent years battling witches and dragons in her quest for the magic crown of Capel Tywynsoch simply won't hold the attention of most readers. **Exposition** or **backstory**—the history leading up to the present moment in the story—may be provided quickly at the beginning, or a sentence or two at a time over the course of the story, or through the dialogue the characters speak, but it should be extremely condensed in a short-short and only slightly less so in the longer story. Your focus is on *now*, not *then*.

Remember that the burden is always on you, the author, to draw your readers in. If you're worried about whether you're off to a strong start, imagine an intelligent, interested, but not entirely patient reader who will give you about half a page to make your story come to life. If you haven't hooked your reader by then, chances are he or she will probably stop reading. Lights out, game over. Begin again.

Our three model authors are very aware of the need to start strong and economically. Let's look at how skillfully they use their openings to create fictional worlds.

Isaac Babel writes:

> The commander of the Sixth Division reported that Novograd-Volynsk was taken at dawn today. The staff is now withdrawing from Krapivno, and our cavalry transport stretches in a noisy rear guard along the high road that goes from Brest to Warsaw, a high road built on the bones of muzhiks by Czar Nicholas I.

Babel could have begun "Crossing the River Zbrucz" during the morning's heated battle—that certainly would have made for some exciting writing. But the heart of his story is the protagonist's encounter with the Jewish girl and her dead father. All that fighting—the explosions and gunfire, the blood and suffering— ultimately would have been wasted words, so much hot air standing between the reader and the story's moment of crisis. Babel's opening has only two sentences, but they are crammed with information. Even if we know nothing at all about the people and places involved, we do know that a battle has taken place, with one side capturing a city or region, and that portions of the army are now on the move to consolidate that victory. The details of the battle, the cause of the war, who's right and who's wrong: none of this material is essential to the story about to be told, so Babel leaves it out.

Here is Barthelme's opening gambit:

> The first thing the baby did wrong was to tear pages out of her books. So we made a rule that each time she tore a page out of a book she had to stay alone in her room for four hours, behind the closed door. She was tearing out about a page a day, in the beginning, and the rule worked fairly well, although the crying and screaming from behind the closed door were unnerving.

In only three sentences, we are brought immediately into the perverse but ultimately comic universe of the story. Sentence 1 gives us a hint that something may be wrong with the speaker's parenting style: after all, can a baby really do anything "wrong"? Sentence 2 introduces the first of the many ridiculous punishments the parents mete out to their child (*four hours* behind a closed door for tearing out the page of a book?). Now we *know* something is seriously amiss. And sentence 3 further heightens the narrator's skewed, even cruel, perspective: despite his infant's "unnerving" crying and screaming, the father sticks with his draconian punishment. It's a testament to how adroitly Barthelme uses exposition in the form of description and action that after only seventy-six words, we sense that we have entered a seriously dysfunctional home. The fun comes when the author abruptly reverses our expectations and leads us on the humorous romp that follows.

Because her story is longer, Vaughn's opening is a bit more leisurely. While her first paragraph is beautifully crafted, it is also somewhat cryptic. It isn't until later in the story that we come to understand her unusual "theory of the universe" and the significance of an unhatched chicken "just before it begins to crash its head against the shell." We might be wondering at this point just what "We're on TV in the Universe" is about; not surprisingly, in the second paragraph Vaughn transitions directly into a traditional story hook:

> Last winter I wrecked my car during an ice storm on Interstate 17. I had a chicken in a cage on the front seat beside me. I had the cage strapped in with the passenger seat belt, and a towel draped over the cage, so that the chicken wouldn't have to look at the weather. I was on my way to a party, and I was wearing my only party outfit, a black satin dress with a giant belt that was actually a music box in disguise—when you pressed the buckle, it played "Stars and Stripes Forever."

These sentences are intriguing. Not only are we promised the excitement of a car accident, but we are told that it occurred during an ice storm while the narrator drove to a party wearing a novelty belt buckle, with a chicken riding shotgun.

Vaughn could have chosen to start the story at a different point. She could have shown us the narrator receiving the invitation and imagining how she might make a splashy entrance. She might have shown the narrator preparing for the party, slipping on her black dress and gimmicky belt, then heading out to the car and strapping the chicken into the passenger seat. But what would be the point of including this extraneous material in the story? "We're on TV in the Universe" is about what happens when the narrator hits black ice and slams into a patrol car. The accident and its fallout are the story's focus: Vaughn wants to get us there as expeditiously as possible.

Every part of a story is important, but the middle—the longest part—is often the most difficult to sustain. Let's say you have managed to pique your readers' interest in the scene and characters. Now what? Once you have begun, you will want to make the central conflict immediately apparent. "Where's the trouble?" James Gordon Bennett used to say in his fiction workshops. Bennett felt that a story didn't really begin until we knew the crisis afflicting the main characters, and most fiction writers would agree: *conflict* in some form is at the center of every good story.

We may all wish for a calmer, gentler life, but fiction is not the place to seek that tranquility. Your reader will quickly become bored if nothing significant happens to your protagonists. "Do not be nice to your characters," Romelda

Shaffer advises; "slap them with one problem after the other. What is compelling about a nice, smart, handsome, rich man?" The answer in real life is "Quite a lot." But in fiction, nice guys (and gals) often do finish last.

There is nothing especially nice about the characters in "Crossing the River Zbrucz." The narrator is insensitive at best. His hosts are war-shocked and bedraggled. Trouble is everywhere in this battle-scarred landscape, but the real trouble, we learn in the second half of the story, is located in the repercussions of one particularly loathsome act of torture and cruelty. "Crossing the River Zbrucz" is designed so that we move from the very large to the very small, from history to one family's personal tragedy. We can imagine a cinematic equivalent of the story, beginning with a shot of a map of eastern Poland that dissolves into a long shot of the landscape. The camera follows the army across the river; then we focus in on the narrator as he enters the home of the Jewish family. The closer we get to the action, the more our curiosity grows: What is on the other side of this black and foaming river? What is at the end of this troubling road?

In contrast to Babel's concentration on a single day, Donald Barthelme's "The Baby" covers an indeterminate time span, although it seems to be at minimum a duration of several weeks—from the time we first hear of the baby's "misbehavior," through the many punishments that continue right up until the day the father finally gives up on disciplining his child and joins the baby in smashing the windshields of cars. If Babel's strategy is gradually to close in on his subject, Barthelme keeps us involved by very briefly describing key scenes: the baby tearing out first one page at a time, then two, then swallowing them, then tearing a corner when she thinks her father isn't looking, and so forth. Stuart Dybek believes it is possible to "argue that the art of the short story is the art of transition," and Barthelme has mastered this art. He clearly signals the passage of time, the relation of one action to the next: "The first thing the baby did wrong. . . . So we made a rule. . . . She was tearing out about a page a day, in the beginning. . . . But then as her grip improved she got to tearing out two pages at a time. . . . But she wouldn't quit doing it. . . . And then as time went on. . . ." We are inside the story because with each transition, we are *shown* events rather than just being told about them.

Vaughn's strategy for sustaining our interest through the middle of "We're on TV in the Universe" is to keep us wondering about the outcome of the narrator's accident. How bad will her luck be? Surely, she thinks, as her car slides across "the silence of black ice," it is "against the laws of physics to hit a patrol car." That turns out not to be the case. When she first sees Officer Cook, he is "linebacker tall, Jack-and-the Beanstalk tall." Briefly we wonder if she will be arrested and tossed in the back of his car. Fortunately, it turns out the sheriff is a fairly tolerant man. He isn't going to handcuff and cite her, but she must face the dispiriting likelihood that her car is totaled. Shortly afterward, a TV crew arrives to compound her humiliation. And what is she going to do once they leave, stranded in the snow, miles from home, with no transportation? We are intrigued by her situation as one problem follows hard on the next. After the initial accident, none of her difficulties are life threatening, and the narrator manages to face them with surprising good humor. Yet there is an urgency to her situation. It's night; it's cold. She may have been lucky enough, as the juggler puts it, to fail "the A-plus wreck" test, but she's still in trouble.

Fiction writers generally accelerate their characters' agitation as the story draws to its close. This sense of increasing turbulence and distress is similar to what Aristotle called "**rising action**," the escalation and complication of the central conflict. Short-shorts are often too brief to have a true rising action, but even the shortest stories transition from moments of lesser to greater tension.

This increase of conflict and trouble can be represented as an inverted check mark, with the peak of the check signifying the **climax**, the point of maximum dramatic attention, and the turning point in the narrative.

$$\wedge$$

Traditionally what follows the climax is called the **resolution**—the "falling action," or the working out of the remaining complications. This process is also called the **denouement** (French for "untying")—in this case, untying the knot of the plot. Even in a novel, the resolution is normally quite brief. In a short story, the resolution will be even more compressed, and in a short-short, there is likely to be no resolution at all. We reach the climax, and the story is over. Like someone who has been punched in the stomach by a stranger, we're left gasping *What?* or *Why?*

Isaac Babel is especially good at delivering this final blow in his short fiction, and the concluding sentences of "Crossing the River Zbrucz" make for a superlative twist to his story:

> "Sir," the Jewess says, shaking out the eiderdown, "the Poles were hacking him to death and he kept begging them, 'Kill me in the backyard so my daughter won't see me die!' But they wouldn't inconvenience themselves. He died in this room, thinking of me. . . . And now I want you to tell me," the woman suddenly said with terrible force, "I want you to tell me where one could find another father like my father in all the world!"

We don't know the narrator's response to this sudden, awful revelation (although we can imagine that even he is taken aback). Yet there is no need to show his reaction on the page: we readers have essentially become the narrator at this point, so we respond for him. Babel rightly wants the focus to remain on the woman and her story; if we were to see the narrator speechless and aghast or hear whatever inadequate response he might mutter, some of the power of that final moment would be diminished.

Even though Barthelme's denouement is brief, it is nevertheless more extended than Babel's. Following the climax—when the narrator finally admits that he and his wife have "more or less of an ethical crisis on [their] hands"—the story ends with a resolution of the many complications brought on by the baby's page-tearing proclivities:

> I solved it by declaring that it was all right to tear pages out of books, and moreover, that it was *all right* to have torn pages out of books in the past. That is one of the satisfying things about being a parent—you've got a lot of moves, each one good as gold. The baby and I sit happily on the floor, side by side, tearing pages out of books, and sometimes, just for fun, we go out on the street and smash a windshield together.

The sense of gleeful bad judgment that runs throughout the story receives one final hallelujah here. If we were at all worried that this was a real story about a real baby, those worries have been banished.

"We're on TV in the Universe" is the longest of the three model stories, so it's appropriate that its denouement is the most prolonged. After the narrator checks into Koch's Universe Motel, she sees Officer Cook and, briefly, herself on television. Suddenly an evening in which everything had gone wrong seems to make sense. The narrator begins imagining the satellite signal, in these days of pre-cable television, transmitting out into space, so that presidents and baseball players and movie stars, along with noncelebrities like herself—"everybody who had ever been on TV"—are joined together in one cosmic "vacation" in outer space.

This comforting vision leads to the discomfiting final paragraph in which she admits that at the time of the accident she was lonely and without direction, that she'd been going to the party because she wanted to be the sort of "woman you would like to discover at a party." The story of the journey—the hero or heroine overcoming obstacles and attaining a blessing or gift—goes back to the beginnings of literature. Keeping the protagonist from reaching his or her goal is a time-honored variation on that theme. This is the fate of Vaughn's narrator, interrupted in her quest to "be noticed as an interesting person." The story's final line, "Something happened," is sadly ironic. Yes, something happened, but it wasn't what the narrator expected. She'd hoped to be discovered by celebrities. Instead, she has an epiphany: all our fates are "locked forever" together, not just in the "frame of a TV screen," but in the universe itself.

For Russell Banks, the end of the story has an almost mystical significance for the writer. It is "the most exhilarating moment of writing fiction—getting to that point where the stakes are so high that who you are will emerge with those last couple of sentences." Charles Baxter has a somewhat more pragmatic way of deciding whether a story is complete: "If, no matter how many times I have reread it, I can't think of anything else to do to it, it's probably finished." You will need to come up with your own criteria for deciding when your story is over, but in general it is better to stop earlier rather than later.

Of course, when we analyze polished, published stories—as we have just been doing—it might seem as though the authors knew exactly what they were doing from the very start. That, however, may be far from the truth. Jill McCorkle admits, "Most of my stories surprise me." For Tobias Wolff, "Stories tend to grow in the writing of them, and to begin to define themselves as I work on them." You will often learn what you really need to know about your story by writing a first draft. If you realize that the structure you thought was inevitable is in fact a maze from which you cannot seem to emerge, knock down the walls that are blocking your way. Redesign your story. Tell it differently. Just because you initially envisioned things happening one way, don't feel bound to that version of events in subsequent drafts.

Even as vigorous a proponent of story structure as Madison Smartt Bell acknowledges that the "experience of imagining and composing any story is much more fluid than any reverse-engineering analysis could convey." Be mindful of the words you are actually putting on the page; they will usually tell you what is still missing and what needs to be taken out. George Saunders says it well: "Simply pay full attention to the place you are in the text, with real concentration and real openness, then you can't go wrong, because the next moment will respond to the previous one, and so on and so on."

In short, while it often helps to have a plan in mind as you draft, you should be open to the possibility that an unexpected twist or turn will restructure your story, transforming it into something that surprises even you with the ingenuity of its design.

## CHECKLIST Structure and design

☐ **Have you begun your story at the most opportune moment?** In short fiction, there is no room for elaborate preambles. Babel begins his story as the Russian army crosses into Poland. Barthelme drops us directly into the life of his wacky, dysfunctional family. After her first paragraph, Vaughn's narrator is on the road and about to hit black ice. In general, you will want to start your story as *late* in the narrative as possible. The conflict and tension should already be present in the situation: you just need to put your characters down in the midst of it.

☐ **Is the story's conflict immediately clear?** You may think that a story about a man wandering up and down the city streets contemplating the meaning of life will wow your readers with its profundity. Think again. The "navel-gazing narrator" is usually a bore. Too often he or she is simply an excuse to keep you, the author, from delving into more emotionally troubling, but far more interesting, material. Your reader should be able to answer the crucial question, "Where's the trouble?" by the end of the first page—at the very latest. It's possible to write a story in which a character is in conflict only with his or her environment, but it's much easier to bring two people into conflict. Someone wants something, but a second person is in the way. It is the oldest plot formula in the world—which means that it has been working for millennia.

☐ **Does some significant change occur during the course of your story?** Shorter stories operate on truncated principles, so there isn't time for the extended rising action of a novel or a long story. Still, there must be movement in your narrative. Maybe your protagonist, like the young woman in "We're on TV in the Universe," must accommodate herself to a sudden change in her expectations. Perhaps, like the narrator of "The Baby," he significantly modifies his own beliefs. Or maybe, like the narrator of "Crossing the River Zbrucz," he encounters some aspect of the world so chilling that it stuns him into silence. Your characters might succeed, or they might fail, in facing the challenges in front of them, but at the end of the story, they should be different than they were when it began.

☐ **Does your story end at the best possible place?** You may feel that your story requires a bit of tying up, as in the pieces by Barthelme and Vaughn. Or you may follow the example of Babel and stop at the point of maximum impact. You don't want to end before your conflict has played itself out, but don't hang around too long after the climax. Consider deleting the last paragraph or two of your first draft. Leave it to your reader to puzzle out the ultimate meaning of your story.

# Creating characters ▶

The convoluted plots of horror tales, romances, and espionage thrillers generally don't work well in the confines of the short story. But if your story doesn't recreate the twists and turns of your favorite movie or genre novel, what will be its focus? In all likelihood, the answer is your characters.

If we catch glimpses of "real" human beings in your main characters, we are more likely to connect with them, to understand and sympathize with them—even if they are engaged in activities that we do not approve of. From Odysseus to Emma Bovary to Holden Caulfield, readers have always cherished the imperfect yet vividly rendered protagonist, and contemporary short stories tend to succeed or fail based on the believability of their fictional inhabitants. Therefore, one of your chief jobs is to create characters that readers will find authentic. But how?

Experienced readers of fiction will expect your characters to show both their good and bad sides, and characters rarely offer excuses for their shortcomings. In the words of Tana French, "Your character is always right. No real person thinks they're being stupid or misguided or bigoted or evil—so your characters can't, either." Since everyone, alas, is flawed, a character who is perfect is also implausible. An imperfect character is more likely to be **round**, or **three-dimensional**. According to E. M. Forster, such a character is someone whom we can credit with actually being alive. "The test of a round character," Forster says, "is that it is capable of surprising in a convincing way." Not only must the character startle us with a behavior or comment we weren't expecting, but she or he must do so "in a convincing way." Lynne Sharon Schwartz believes writers can find the failings in their characters by looking hard at themselves: "A writer's nerve consists in serving as his own specimen of human nature and looking at the very things he would most like to overlook—not only the standard character flaws, but the secret weaknesses, the perversities of every kind, the meannesses and stupidities, the fear, obsessive mistakes, blindness and deafness, grossness, and the whole residue of infantile cravings."

We noted that fictional characters are generally expected to be at least somewhat different at the end of the story than they were at the beginning. The character's transformation must be prepared early on, and we can see this authorial groundwork in "We're on TV in the Universe." The opening presents us with a narrator who both reflects on the nature of the universe and has conversations in her car with a chicken. When her car begins skidding on the black ice, she seems strangely unafraid of toppling over the bridge into the freezing Susquehanna River. Instead, she compares the car's back-and-forth motion to "a rock-and-roll move" and says that sliding on black ice is like gliding through the galaxy past "Andromeda, Sirius, and the Crab Nebula." Throughout the story, the narrator has a strong desire to make an impression on other people. This is what motivates her to drive to a party in an ice storm with a chicken. She is, like all of us, something of an egotist. However, we see in her response to the accident that she has a fanciful imagination and is capable of accepting bad luck with a sense of humor. Therefore, at the story's conclusion, after all her plans for the evening have fallen through, we aren't entirely surprised by her elaborate vision of how we're all on TV in the universe.

Forster contrasts round characters with **flat**, or **two-dimensional**, characters. Flat characters are caricatures, incapable of surprise or complexity, yet they are often necessary as plot devices that throw the three-dimensional characters into greater relief. Forster says that in "their purest form, they are constructed around a single idea or quality: when there is more than one factor in them, we get the beginning of the curve towards the round." The two red-haired men in "Crossing the River Zbrucz" who help the woman clean up after their home has been ransacked are flat characters. The narrator says that they "hop around in silence, like monkeys, like Japanese acrobats in a circus." Their primary function in the story seems to be to disguise the fact that the third man in the room is dead and to highlight the more three-dimensional daughter, whose passionate denunciation of the men who killed her father is "the beginning of the curve towards the round." Similarly, in "We're on TV in the Universe" the television reporter from Binghamton, with his cursory questions about the accident, does little more than throw the more three-dimensional characters—the narrator, Officer Cook, and the juggler—into sharper relief.

"Fiction is about trouble," says Rick DeMarinis. "Trouble is a direct consequence of desire. Characters are living embodiments of desire. A character without desire is immobilized." Obviously troubled people are more likely to find themselves in trouble, and as you consider which characters will star in your story, you should think first of people whose lives are in turmoil. We may love being in the company of that sunshiny person whose every decision seems blessed and who has a correspondingly optimistic vision of the world. Unfortunately, people like that tend to make poor protagonists for a story. Think instead of individuals you avoid because they make embarrassing comments in restaurants, or have a habit of choosing the wrong partners, or always start fights at family reunions. Memorable characters are often based on people the writer knows who don't always do the right thing, and who suffer the consequences as a result.

Authors often speak of their characters as though they were real human beings rather than just fictional constructs, and in a sense that's understandable. Nearly always, we draw on our own lives or on the lives of people we have met to create characters. In fact, the desire to put ourselves in a story and to render friends, relatives, lovers, acquaintances, and enemies on paper is what compels many writers to write in the first place. Not surprisingly, good fiction writers are usually good people watchers: they remember little tics of speech, characteristic gestures, details of face and dress. If, for instance, you can capture in a story your aunt Consuela's odd scent of rosewater and freshly baked bread and sweat, or your first boyfriend's habit of wetting his little finger before he smoothed down his eyebrows, you are well on your way to creating vividly rendered characters.

One common misperception new writers have is that characters based on real people must be as close to those individuals as the writer can make them. That is not the case, especially if your protagonist resembles yourself. When you create characters, invention is at least as important as including (auto)biographical details. As Grace Paley reminds us, even if your characters are based on real people, once they inhabit your fictional world, "you don't really know them, so you're going to start inventing right away." A piece of dialogue you heard last night will find its way into a character's mouth. A trip you took to the Grand Canyon a year ago suddenly seems just the sort of vacation your character ought to be thinking about at the top of page two. Everything you have ever seen or heard or done is potential material for character development. The well is deeper than you know. Dip into it.

Most convincing fictional creations are composites of ourselves and our friends, family, and acquaintances. When you create an amalgamation of several real people, you can bring in the most interesting aspects of each one. If you combine your mother's need to wash and put away every dish before she goes to bed, your father's love of old issues of *National Geographic*, your own fondness for the Black Keys, and your little sister's habit of beginning every other sentence with, "So anyways . . . ," things start to get interesting.

Not only do composite characters make the people in your story more believable, but they also give you license to go beyond what really happened—to take your characters in more intriguing directions than those normally provided by real life. Moreover, composite characters get you off the hook from the accusation every writer fears hearing from a friend or relative: the person in your story is *exactly* like me!

However your characters come into being, you must be able to see the world through their eyes. "Each character needs to be real to me," says Sue Miller. "I inhabit each of them. I try to give them my sympathy, even the ones I don't like very well: to understand why they are as they are, what they do to make what they do defensible to them." This is crucial: the less appealing a character is, the more she or he requires the *possibility* of redemption. If your protagonist is an unloving stepmother, for example, what about her own life made her that way? You probably won't have time to give a detailed personal history, but you can hint at the origins of a character's defects. Readers of a short story won't be expecting characters as nuanced as David Copperfield or Anna Karenina, but they will be looking for a suggestion of complexity: the well-thumbed black-and-white photo of her own mother that the stepmother carries in her purse; the offhand remark she makes about being struck by her father that time she forgot to bring in the clothes from the clothesline before a storm.

When you begin your story, you may well figure that it's best to get all the characterization out of the way in the first paragraph or two so that you can get down to the story itself. You might, for example, write this:

> Jezebel Johnson was five feet seven inches tall, weighed 130 pounds, and had hair dyed the color of ripe peaches. Smart and lively, she had a lacerating wit but crummy taste in men. Jezebel's parents had divorced when she was eight, and she always blamed that traumatic event on her propensity to be either hopelessly romantic or wildly cynical about love. There was no in between as far as Jezebel was concerned: you were either drowning in a sea of hearts and violins, or looking down on the ocean of love from a very high cliff with a bad taste in your mouth. Jezebel's weakness was handsome slackers who reminded her of her father. She was always falling for them at the worst possible time. Sleepy-eyed, unshaven Harvard Koonin was just the latest in a long line of bad choices.

In addition to being a pile-up of clichés, this description tries to do all the work of characterization much too fast. Rather than *showing* us Jezebel in action—letting us hear who she is through her conversations with Harvard, or providing us with a flashback to her parents' divorce—we are given the CliffsNotes version of characterization.

Developing a convincing character may take the entire length of your story. You know from watching films that we learn about characters by what they do and say, scene by scene, and Stephen Minot reminds us that "in order to maintain the reader's sense of personal discovery, the writer of fiction has to supply a series of little hints, and they have to be slipped in stealthily." The shorter the story, the more important it is to dole out that information bit by bit: If your reader knows everything at the beginning, there won't be any room for surprise at the end.

Somerset Maugham said, "You can never know enough about your characters." For many writers, getting to know their characters begins with naming them. Characters are less likely to be named in very short stories than in longer works of fiction, but whether you call someone "the young man" or Edgar, you should have a sound reason for doing so. As you consider names, don't just use the first one that pops into your head. A name's **connotation**, its associations and related meanings, is important, and you ignore it at your peril. Jezebel Johnson, the creation above, has an awful name. It may be memorable, but what contemporary parents would christen their child after the wicked queen in the Bible who was thrown out of a window and eaten by dogs? Simply giving someone the name Jezebel makes her less believable as a character. (Instead, why not call her Jessie, or Jasmine, or Jules?) Make sure, too, that the names of your main characters aren't easily confused with one another. Generally names in a short story should not begin with the same letter. Joe and John are not as distinguishable from each other as Joe and Ricardo.

Of our three model stories, only "We're on TV in the Universe" has an important named character: Officer Cook. You might wonder why the narrator, the main character, doesn't have a name, but no one she meets in the story knows her, and it would be awkward for her to introduce her name without a reason. In any case, we learn a great deal about her likes and dislikes, her fears and aspirations—we don't really need to know her name. Officer Mike Cook is a figure of authority. He provides a moment of real tension when the narrator is uncertain how he will react to the fact that she has just crashed into his car. Appropriately, he never actually introduces himself in the story; he's too laconic for introductions (presumably the protagonist learns his name because it is on his badge). Vaughn has chosen a good name for a big, blunt man with "a deep patrolman's voice." Mike Cook: two monosyllables concluding with the harsh, no-nonsense sound of a *k*. "Officer Aloysius Shallow" wouldn't be nearly as convincing.

Once you have decided what to call your characters, you will realize that there is still quite a lot about them that you don't know. We have mentioned Hemingway's "iceberg theory of character," which Kim Edwards summarizes as "the idea . . . that what's unstated must nonetheless exist clearly in the author's mind for a character to have sufficient depth." Novelists and writers of extended stories frequently write many pages of notes about their characters. They jot down everything from their characters' heights, weights, birthplaces, and dates of birth to their current addresses and their biggest dreams and fears. The shortest stories may reveal only the tip of the iceberg, but that's all the more reason for you to have a clear sense of who your characters are so that you can convey their personalities in just a few well-chosen words.

The following questions will help you think more thoroughly about your main characters. This is just a start, though. To delve more deeply, you'll want to make up your own questions and answer them in some detail.

- Where were they born?
- How old are they?
- What do they look like (for example, their race and ethnicity, height, weight, eye and hair color, and other physical characteristics)?
- What type of music and movies do they like?
- What jobs do they have?
- How do they get to work?
- What are their biggest dreams? Greatest fears?
- What do they want more than anything else in the world?

Spending fifteen or twenty minutes brainstorming about each of your central characters may save you a great deal of time later. As you decide whether your characters were born in São Paulo, Brazil, or Santa Fe, New Mexico, whether they listen to Bob Marley or Franz Schubert, whether they commute in a Porsche 911 Carrera S Cabriolet or on the city bus, and whether they work as corporate lawyers or salesclerks at The Gap, you begin to make them come alive, to distinguish these *particular* characters from all the other people about whom you might have written.

Although much of this material may never wind up in your story, going through the process helps you gain a clearer sense of who your characters are. As you begin to write, your character profile will serve as a biographical reference point, a summary that will help guide your decisions about a character's appearance, speech, actions, and motivations.

A word of caution: Although it's good to be concrete and detailed when describing your characters, it's also possible to be too specific. Suppose Alberto glances at someone he has never seen before and then describes that person as "six feet two and a half inches and 342 pounds." It's much more likely that the character doing the observing would register something along the lines of "over six feet and nearly 350 pounds." Unless Alberto works for the FBI or guesses heights and weights for a carnival, don't give him greater powers of observation than most of us possess.

In general, though, as Dan Chaon remarks, "The more you have [characters] observe things, the more you get to know them." What characters do or don't notice makes them who they are. In the opening paragraph of "Crossing the River Zbrucz," for instance, the narrator seems to have the cool, detached perspective of a military officer, yet he also takes time to describe the natural beauty of the setting in some detail. This appreciation of the region's beauty makes him seem more likable. However, when he enters the home of his hosts later, he notices only "ransacked closets, torn pieces of women's fur coats on the floor, human excrement, and fragments of the holy Seder plate that the Jews use once a year for Passover." Rather than feeling sympathy for the plight of these people, he becomes furious. "Clean up this mess!" he shouts. "How can you live like this?" Perhaps his anger is a measure of his insensitivity, or maybe he is just masking the guilt he feels at intruding on such a devastated family. Either way, what he doesn't initially register is the corpse on the floor. All he sees is "a third Jew who is sleeping with his face to the wall and a blanket pulled over his head." When that sleeping person is revealed to be a bloody and mutilated body, we understand that the narrator has been psychologically damaged by war: even though he may be able to wax poetic about "flowery hillocks," he is someone who is incapable of seeing something horrible right at his own feet.

If Babel's protagonist is ultimately unsympathetic, he nevertheless seems real to us because his observations show him to be a round character. He may act like a tactless bully, but he is not entirely bad. Even the biggest fictional villains normally have some traits that make them seem human, and your job is to find a moment or moments when you can catch those people in a more sympathetic light. Robin Hemley says of "bad, immoral, selfish, mean, or obnoxious" characters: "You must make us care about them. You must make them capable of change, whether they, in fact, *do* change, or at least you should intimate that they were not always as low-down as they appear now."

Again, that possibility of change is crucial. For many readers, the essence of a short story is a notable transformation in one or more main characters, although that alteration doesn't have to be life changing or even noticeable to a casual observer. Jerome Stern points out that "change usually means psychological change—realization, revelation, revision, epiphany, understanding, decision." In other words, you don't have to shoot your characters to make them realize the error of their ways. In fact, it's usually a bad idea to make something *too* drastic happen to a character in short fiction. Big, dramatic events—explosions and tornadoes and earthquakes—typically require many pages of setup, and you don't have that luxury in a short story. Instead, think small: it's better to have someone slapped on the cheek than blown away by an Uzi.

The change—modest or otherwise—that occurs in the main characters of two of the three model stories is partially a matter of guesswork on our part, since in a short story we don't normally see the extended effects of a character's actions or encounters. We don't know how the narrator of "Crossing the River Zbrucz" responds to the revelation that the old man he had thought was sleeping in a corner is actually dead, or what he thinks of the daughter's pronouncement that "I want you to tell me where one could find another father like my father in all the world!" Yet we can surmise that this information has at least as much of an impact on the narrator as it does on us.

In the final paragraph of "We're on TV in the Universe," the narrator confesses that she was "on the road with a live chicken and a musical belt" because "I was going to a party where I imagined that I would be noticed as an interesting person. The Poultry Woman. The Marching Band Woman. A woman you would like to discover at a party." Yet she is far from confident. Her life is in flux; she is "between jobs again and living alone." She says: "When I set out in bad weather I had a feeling. Something was going to change for me that night, something was going to relocate me in the universe. Watching television in the motel, I thought about it. I was right. Something happened."

What was that something? The narrator is unclear, and readers' interpretations of the cryptic final line will vary. Did the narrator realize all of us are cosmically connected? Or, conversely, that we are all alone, nothing more than beams of light lost forever in the eternities of space? We know that the story took place recently—"last winter"—but we don't have any real evidence that the accident "relocated" the narrator in the universe. Nevertheless, in her authorial voice there is a note of the wisdom that sometimes comes with experience. Perhaps the something that happened was simply that she became more competent at dealing with life's inevitable adversities.

Only the preposterously comic narrator of "The Baby," who decides to smash car windows with his infant daughter rather than punish her, shows an unmistakable change, but the exaggerated nature of his about-face is in keeping with the overall absurdist tone of the story.

Finally, be wary of nonhuman characters, especially nonhuman narrators. The chicken in "We're on TV in the Universe" provides a good bit of comic relief, but we never mistake it for the thinking, feeling equivalent of a human being. You may believe that telling a story from the point of view of a housefly or juniper bush is extremely clever, but chances are your instructor won't agree. Of course, great writers have given us everything from the talking cockroach that recounts the events of Franz Kafka's "The Metamorphosis" to the dog who narrates Paul Auster's *Timbuktu*, but the risk of ending up sounding supremely silly is very real. Stick with people when you write your story: unless you are a horse whisperer or have a very clear memory of your previous life as a snail, human beings are what you know best.

## CHECKLIST Creating characters

- [ ] **Do you know your main characters and their desires well?** You should have a strong sense of who your characters are, where they have been, and where they live. You, and your readers, should be able to quickly identify the driving forces that make them act: what they want and what they're prepared to do to get it.

☐ **Does your story show us only the *essential* aspects of your characters?** While it's important that you know your characters thoroughly, you will be revealing only a tiny sliver of that information on the page. Show your characters being themselves, only more so. Whatever conflict they are involved in should bring out a heightened sense of who they really are.

☐ **Can you eliminate any characters? Or can you combine two or more characters into a single character?** In general, two or three main characters are about all you'll be able to develop well in a story. If you need more people to complete the action of your story, try combining several characters into one. Remember that unless someone is intentionally two-dimensional, characters should be as complex as possible.

☐ **Is your description of each character appropriate to, and necessary for, that character's function in the story?** You, the author, should always have a clear mental picture of your characters. However, each piece of physical description you actually use should be carefully chosen. Is it really important for your reader to know that a character is 165 pounds and five feet nine and a half inches tall, or can you just say "medium weight and height"? And do weight and height, or eye and hair color, matter at all in your story? Unless some physical aspect of your character is essential to her or his personality as it emerges, leave out the description.

☐ **Are the characters' names appropriate?** In a short story, having too many people with similar-sounding names can be confusing. If Stan wishes Steve would just leave him alone and pick on Stewart or Sterling instead, we're likely to forget who is who. It is better to have Luis square off with Terrance, or have Leticia face down Phuong.

☐ **Do your characters need to be named at all?** Of course, one option is to forgo names altogether. Only one character in the three model stories is named, possibly because naming them might distract a reader from the characters' main actions. Whatever you decide to do with your protagonists and **antagonists**—the protagonists' opponents or adversaries—you should avoid naming minor characters in short fiction. For instance, if a busboy at a restaurant comes to clear the table where the two main characters are having a conversation, do we really need to know that his name is Cumbert Wilson-Smith? Especially if Cumbert never makes another appearance in the story, it's better to keep him and other minor characters anonymous so that they don't sidetrack our focus from what is important.

☐ **Are your main characters different at the end of the story than they were in the beginning?** "The idea is to turn flesh and blood into literary characters," says Philip Roth, "and literary characters into flesh and blood." Remember that convincing fictional characters, like real people, are both consistent and surprising. Reread the opening and concluding sections of your story. Do you see a difference in how your protagonist began and how he or she ends?

# Writing dialogue ▶

Dialogue is what the people in your story say to one another. Some stories, like "We're on TV in the Universe," make extensive use of dialogue; others, like "The Baby," contain little or no conversation between characters. Dialogue may not be mandatory, but when it is employed skillfully, it can bring a story to life. Good dialogue contributes to character, introduces backstory, and advances plot. It adds an immediacy to fiction, and crafting it can be a great deal of fun.

Indeed, fiction writers seem to love talking about dialogue almost as much as they love writing it, so there is no shortage of advice on this element of storytelling. "Dialogue should do two things," says Melanie Bishop. "It should sound like people talking minus the *umms* and stumbling, and it should move your story forward." Rick DeMarinis reinforces the idea that even though "dialogue must have all the spontaneity of real-life speech, it is in fact nothing like real-life speech. It is a carefully timed give-and-take: a slow dance, a brisk sparring session, or a merciless pummeling. It is carefully and artfully crafted." In other words, dialogue should be an integral part of your story, not just an opportunity for your characters to open their mouths and yap about the weather.

The great Irish writer Elizabeth Bowen had this to say about dialogue:

**1.** Dialogue should be brief.

**2.** It should add to the reader's knowledge.

**3.** It should eliminate the routine exchanges of ordinary conversation.

**4.** It should convey a sense of spontaneity but eliminate the repetitiveness of real talk.

**5.** It should keep the story moving forward.

**6.** It should be revelatory to the speaker's character, both directly and indirectly.

**7.** It should show the relationships among people.

Of course, like any other advice, we can take this with a grain of salt. Writers like Ernest Hemingway, some of whose stories consist almost entirely of dialogue, would be ill served by Bowen's first rule. Still, Bowen was a master of the short story, and overall her advice is sound, particularly for writers of very short stories, in which everything must be brief. Even when your story is composed mostly of dialogue, if that dialogue is to be effective, it should adhere to most of Bowen's suggestions.

Fortunately, North American students tend to be good writers of dialogue. Ours is such an oral culture that we have an advantage in transcribing the rhythms, oddities, and offhanded nature of real speech. Many students find that dialogue comes as naturally to them as it does to Dorothy Allison: "When I hear a character talking, literally, it's like they are dictating and I'm taking it down."

A good way to develop your inborn gift for dialogue is to sit in a crowded place where you don't know anyone—a coffee shop, say, or a mall—and try to write down what you hear people saying. You will quickly notice that people rarely speak in complete, grammatically perfect sentences. We repeat ourselves. We start sentences that we don't finish, and we interrupt other people to finish their sentences. If Amy Bloom is correct in calling good fictional dialogue "conversation's greatest hits," most conversation by real people consists of outtakes that have no reason to be preserved. Most authors enjoy the process of sifting through the dreck and setting aside the good bits, and writing dialogue can become quite addictive. Once you get the knack for doing it, you will find yourself listening in on all sorts of conversations, extracting those moments that might best serve your creative writing. After all, in many respects, what people say reveals who they are.

If you find that the dialogue on the page doesn't sound the way you imagined it would, that may be because you haven't yet mastered the difference between writing and speaking. The first thing to do is get past the censor in your head telling you that all your characters have to sound as though they just walked out of an English essay, complete with perfect grammar and no contractions. In fact, even highly educated people rarely speak as formally as they write, and our conversations usually sound quite different from written language, especially when we're talking with someone we know well.

What about profanity in dialogue? You should turn to your own instructor for guidelines, but most professors of creative writing would probably agree with Daly Walker that "the language must fit the character. If the character is a soldier likely to speak profanity and harbor prejudice, he must speak and think that way on the page. The reader must understand the author is not condoning profanity or prejudice; he's just trying to bring out the truth in his characters."

One of the most important guidelines to remember is that *context dictates dialogue*. Ask yourself: Who is talking to whom? An older person to a younger person? A more powerful character to someone who is in trouble? And where is their conversation taking place? At a club late Saturday night, or in the pew of a church on Sunday morning? Officer Cook's dialogue in "We're on TV in the Universe," for instance, invariably reflects his personality: he is in charge, and everything he says is gruff and to the point. By contrast, the narrator and the juggler find themselves as equals—having both crashed their cars—so their conversation takes the form of friendly banter. Context is particularly important in "Crossing the River Zbrucz," where the narrator's blunt, rude way of speaking to his hosts would be unthinkable if the conversation were taking place on the veranda of a holiday hotel rather than in the midst of a battlefield.

Once you start writing dialogue, you can easily get carried away. If your story seems bogged down by *too much* dialogue, look for passages to cut as well as places to pause so that we can "listen" to the characters think or see them act.

Even stories with lots of conversation usually provide us with periodic breathers. "We're on TV in the Universe" has the most dialogue of our three model stories, yet the exchanges between characters are usually brief. In between, we have the narrator's internal monologues and her descriptions of the scene and the other characters' actions.

Even in the dialogue-heavy passage when the TV crew from Binghamton descends on the accident, speech alternates with action. The crew questions Officer Cook, but he makes it plain that he doesn't want to talk. He tells them to "get off the road," and emphasizes his order by slamming his car door shut. The reporter turns his attention to the narrator and the juggler, but rather than moving immediately into dialogue, Vaughn shows us the juggler "throwing five snowballs in the air" and lets us hear the narrator's belt buckle playing "Stars and Stripes Forever." After the reporter asks about the accident and senses there isn't enough material for a story, he and the cameraman "jogged to the van" before the reporter tells the cameraman, "I know there's a better wreck somewhere down the road." The juggler has the next line, but before he speaks it, the narrator looks at him, and he drops his hands "and let[s] the balls fall past him like tiny comets." As in real life, we *see* the scene as much as we hear it, and we hear the thoughts in the narrator's head even more than we hear the words the characters speak aloud.

Jerome Stern is right that "what your characters don't say and the way they don't [say it]" is a vital, if often ignored, consideration: "How characters sit or stand is as significant as their spoken sentences. Make your readers hear the pauses between sentences. Let them see characters lean forward, fidget with their cuticles, avert their eyes, uncross their legs." The juggler is a good example of someone who talks with his body. He's always tossing something in the air—possibly because he is somewhat manic, or maybe just because, as the narrator concludes, "he was probably doing a little speed."

Other than the body language just mentioned, we have been focusing on direct dialogue: actual speech. Comparing it with indirect or reported dialogue highlights the power of direct dialogue. "The Baby," for example, contains no direct dialogue; instead, we occasionally hear, secondhand, what has already been said. The narrator tells us:

> My wife said that maybe we were being too rigid and that the baby was losing weight. But I pointed out to her that the baby had a long life to live and had to live in a world with others, had to live in a world where there were many, many rules, and if you couldn't learn to play by the rules you were going to be left out in the cold with no character, shunned and ostracized by everyone.

Reported dialogue is appropriate for this story: the narrator is so disconnected from reality, so unaware of other people, that it makes sense he wouldn't take the time to quote his wife directly. Nevertheless, the dialogue's impact is diminished considerably by being reported. If you really want your readers to experience your characters speaking, you need to use direct dialogue, which means, among other things, following the conventions of printed dialogue.

Dialogue in stories and novels has a special way of appearing on the page. Each time a different speaker begins talking, you indent that person's speech and start a new paragraph. This is an important point, yet one that new writers forget more often than not, so it's worth repeating: each time a new character speaks, that character gets her or his *own paragraph*. This might seem like an unnecessary convention, but it turns out to be a handy one. If there are only two speakers, you don't need to keep tagging them by name once you identify who's who. For instance:

"I've lost him," Carrie said.

Jonathan's throat went dry. "Who?"

"Who do you *think* I'm talking about?"

"You're telling me that you've lost our *son?*"

The dialogue establishes that only Carrie and Jonathan are present, so our minds can easily toggle back and forth between the two, especially since each has a distinct and conflicting point of view. Indeed, many writers would agree with Russell Banks that readers should be able to tell who is speaking even if there are no dialogue tags at all. A good writer can capture the tone of his characters' voices to such an extent that adding "Jonathan said" or Carrie shouted" is unnecessary.

There are a few other points to remember about the conventions of fictional dialogue:

▸ Commas and periods go *inside* the quotation marks when you are punctuating dialogue. Jim said, "Hi." *Or:* "Hi," Jim said.

▸ When one character addresses another, you need a comma before, or after, or before *and* after the name of the character who is being addressed. "What are you doing, Lindy?" *Or:* "Lindy, you're making me sick!" *Or:* "Hey, Lindy, what's up?"

▸ Paragraphs are always indented *five spaces,* and the beginnings of sentences are always *capitalized*.

New fiction writers sometimes get carried away with the verbs associated with speaking. Characters will *exclaim* or *remonstrate* or *expostulate* or *admonish* instead of just *saying* something. Often novice writers choose the fancier tags because they mistakenly believe that their readers will be bored by a steady diet of the same word. In fact, though, the words "said" or "say" quickly disappear for most readers. Chances are you didn't notice that in "We're on TV in the Universe," "said," is the only verb used to indicate that dialogue is being spoken.

Granted, once in a while you might want to make it clear that a character shouts or whispers a remark, but choose your synonyms for "said" judiciously. (Note: You should never use the word "quoted" as a dialogue tag. For example, in the sentence *"I've lost him," Carrie quoted,* the use of "quoted" is incorrect.)

"Dialogue in fiction should be reserved for the culminating moments," Edith Wharton once remarked, and Isaac Babel seems sympathetic to this idea. In "Crossing the River Zbrucz," there is no dialogue during the march into Poland. We begin to hear characters speak only when the officer enters the commandeered house. Even then, dialogue is used sparingly and strategically, and it always conveys information about the character who is speaking. For instance, when the narrator yells, "Clean up this mess! . . . How can you live like this?" at the woman whose home he is occupying, we see that he is insensitive to her plight.

For example, a brief, strong passage of dialogue early in your story can serve as an attention getter. The narrator's conversation with the chicken in "We're on TV in the Universe" is a good example:

"So you don't want to go to a party?" I said. "You want to go home and become drumsticks and Hot Buffalo Wings?"

"Er-err-errr," the chicken said.

"Just kidding," I said.

In only a few lines, we learn that the person telling us her story is whimsical, lonely, and perhaps a tad crazy.

Finally, wherever, whenever, and however you use dialogue, you should manage it with as much care as you do the other elements of fiction, for good dialogue is likely to prove one of your most useful tools as a storyteller.

## CHECKLIST Writing dialogue

- ☐ **Do you have enough dialogue?** Although new writers often have an aptitude for dialogue, they tend to underuse it. Not only is dialogue fun to read, but it generally makes a story move faster. And one of the easiest ways to follow the creative writing mantra of "show, don't tell" is through the use of dialogue. Rather than writing, "Jim was mean," for example, it's much more effective to say, "Jim snarled, 'I'd rather get a root canal than go out on a date with you!'"

- ☐ **Do you have too much dialogue?** A less common problem in short fiction is too much dialogue, but it does happen. Go through your story and look for places where the conversations are not moving your narrative forward or are introducing irrelevant information about your characters.

☐ **Does your dialogue sound like real speech?** One of the quickest ways to lose a reader is to write dialogue that doesn't sound like the speech we hear around us all the time. Unless you're writing a period piece set in a nineteenth-century drawing room, you wouldn't say: "I am unaware of the nature of your question. I have not received your postal communication." Instead, use more realistic dialogue: "What are you talking about? I never got your letter." Read your dialogue aloud. Have someone else read it to you. If something sounds phony, delete it or make it less formal. Use contractions and sentence fragments. Rough it up.

☐ **Have you clearly, and unobtrusively, tagged all speakers of dialogue?** It might be tedious for a reader to be continually reminded which of two people is speaking, but when three or more characters are involved in a conversation, it's possible for the reader (and writer) to get lost. When you have finished your first draft, reread your dialogue and make certain your reader doesn't have to waste time untangling who said what to whom. Also, remember that every time a character "expostulates" or "divulges" something rather than simply "says" it, your reader will focus on how that statement is being said rather than the content of the remark.

# Setting the scene ▶

Novelist Richard Russo says, "In the end, the only compelling reason to pay more attention to place, to exterior setting, is the belief, the faith, that place and its people are intertwined, that place is character, and that to know the rhythms, the textures, the feel of a place is to know more deeply and truly its people." Robin Hemley agrees: "Any description of place should . . . be anchored within a character's consciousness, and say as much about the character as it does about the place."

In other words, although setting is important for conveying the atmosphere of a story, its primary function is to highlight the characters and their conflicts. Setting is the place where your story is set (a high school gymnasium in West Texas) as well as the time (late afternoon in the year 1947). As you begin thinking about the setting for your own story, you'll want to choose a time and place that fit your story's focus. If, for instance, your story involves two brothers who have always despised and resented each other, it makes more sense to put them in an enclosed atmosphere—for example, at midnight in the cold, damp bedroom they shared as boys rather than in a sunny meadow on a summer day. More than likely, as in the scenario just described, your characters will suggest setting rather than the other way around, and in most stories, as Russo and Hemley advise, the focus will remain on people rather than place.

It *is* important, though, for you, the author, to have a strong sense of where and when your story is taking place. Does the brothers' old room still contain their childhood dresser, nicked and scraped from some of their battles? Does their window look out on a dreary field? Or a trailer park in the rain? If your story takes place in one or two main locales, you might even sketch out a map or floor plan. Where is the front door located? How long does it take to get there from the kitchen? This may sound trivial, but if it takes a character half an hour to walk across a room, your reader will begin to doubt not just the reality of the setting but also the "truth" of the rest of your story.

Although you need to have a clear picture of the setting, how much of that information you decide to share with your reader depends on the nature of your story. Some narratives require a great deal of description, while too much setting will grind other stories to a halt. Either way, be wary of piling on any more details than are absolutely necessary for the integrity of your story.

Each of the three model stories uses setting appropriately, although in different ways. An extended description of time and place is crucial to Isaac Babel's "Crossing the River Zbrucz." Babel actually tells us where we are: the border region between Russia and Poland. He doesn't, however, turn the story into a geography lesson. Present-day readers of the story, with no footnotes to rely on, can locate Novograd-Volynsk and Krapivno—the places named in the opening paragraph—with a quick Internet search. Of course, for Babel's first group of readers, Russians in the 1920s, Novograd-Volynsk and Krapivno would have been as familiar as Afghanistan and Baghdad are to Americans early in the twenty-first century. In addition to establishing the locale for those who are interested, the casual way Babel drops place names into the story establishes the narrator's authority. We believe, especially after reading the rest of the story, that this is someone who has been to the area he describes. In any case, even if we have no idea where the road "from Brest to Warsaw" is, we know the important fact that it was "built on the bones of muzhiks," or peasants.

This rather grim bit of information is followed by a sketch of the countryside that initially seems quite romantic: "Fields of purple poppies are blossoming around us, a noon breeze is frolicking in the yellowing rye, virginal buckwheat is standing on the horizon like the wall of a faraway monastery. Silent Volhynia is turning away, Volhynia is leaving, heading into the pearly white fog of the birch groves, creeping through the flowery hillocks, and with weakened arms entangling itself in the underbrush of hops." *Wow,* the reader may be thinking, *even if Volhynia is an impoverished region in the middle of a war, the place certainly is beautiful.* Of course, that's just what Babel wants us to think because in the following sentence he gives us a simile that entirely demolishes the bucolic picture he has just been painting: "The orange sun is rolling across the sky like a severed head."

Babel continues this technique of alternately describing the bleak and the beautiful in the second half of the paragraph. While the "gentle light glimmers in the ravines among the clouds," the "stench of yesterday's blood and slaughtered horses drips into the evening chill." The River Zbrucz is itself both lovely and awful. "The majestic moon lies on the waves" created by "the foaming knots of its rapids," yet all the "bridges are destroyed," and the river seems almost to be attacking the people who are trying to wade across it: "Someone sinks, and loudly curses the Mother of God." When Babel describes the stench coming from the Zbrucz, and later the cold, rushing river, we receive further evidence about the setting from images of smell and touch. Normally we think of imagery as referring to vivid visual descriptions, but if you draw on all five of the senses as you write, you will help your reader fully inhabit a scene.

The tiny world of the second paragraph is created in ten sentences. It's an amazing feat of description, and Babel accomplishes it because he uses *specific details* ("fields of purple poppies" and "yellowing rye, virginal buckwheat") rather than generalities (flowers and crops). We see further examples of his descriptive expertise in his account of the home where the narrator is quartered, which has already been plundered by the Polish army: "I find ransacked closets, torn pieces of women's fur coats on the floor, human excrement, and fragments of the holy Seder plate that the Jews use once a year for Passover." Again, the details bring the scene to life. The torn fur coats suggest that the family had been well-off before the war, yet now their home is covered in excrement. And the detail of the shattered Seder plate is a symbol that indicates something of what has happened to Jewish people in this conflict: they and their religion have come under attack from both sides.

Babel's final descriptive coup comes when he reveals that the man the protagonist thought was sleeping is actually dead: "His gullet has been ripped out, his face hacked in two, and dark blood is clinging to his beard like a clump of lead." It's a gruesome, unforgettable depiction of a brutal murder, one we are unlikely to forget, and it makes a powerful statement: no good can come from war. Yet this sentence of description is far more eloquent and compelling than if the author had come out and baldly declared his opinion. As in poetry, one good image is worth a passel of words.

Donald Barthelme can be quite skilled at describing setting—his well-known story "The Balloon" is just one excellent example—but he apparently decided that emphasizing a specific time and place would distract from the overall effect of "The Baby," so we learn what little we know about the setting of the story through incidental details the narrator lets drop. With no textual assertions in the story to the contrary, a contemporary American audience will probably assume that the time is the present and that the place is somewhere in the United States. The story appears to be set in a home or an apartment, or at least someplace where the baby has a room, but what the place looks like is left mostly to our own imaginations.

The closest thing to a conventional description of setting comes when the narrator tells us why his daughter should be happy spending so many hours in her solitary time-outs: "Her room was very nice, with a nice wooden rocking horse and practically a hundred dolls and stuffed animals. Lots of things to do in that room if you used your time wisely, puzzles and things." Even in this quick sketch, the author provides us with some information about the family's economic status—they must be at least middle class if they are able to afford a wooden rocking horse and all those dolls and stuffed animals for their only child. And while the careless tone of those two sentences may lead us to read through them quickly, they not only give us a glimpse of the baby's room but also tell us a great deal about the narrator's character. For one thing, he doesn't pay much attention to detail. There are "practically a hundred dolls and stuffed animals," but we have no real notion of exactly how many there are or what they look like. His casualness also points to what, in another story, would be an enormous character flaw: he has no idea of how to raise a child. Who could possibly consider locking up his small child an appropriate punishment for tearing out the pages of books? (Incidentally, what in the world is a baby going to do with a puzzle?)

The setting of Stephanie Vaughn's "We're on TV in the Universe" is even more precise than Babel's story. We know that the accident takes place just after the narrator crosses the Susquehanna River on Interstate 17 and that she runs into a Tioga County Sheriff's Department car. A quick look at a map shows that there is only one place in Tioga County, New York, where the highway crosses the river, just east of the town of Waverly.

That level of specificity is matched by the detailed, yet concise, descriptions of various aspects of the accident scene. Her car does "a simple dance down the highway," and we learn quite a bit about the car itself. "Sliding above a thin layer of air and water," it is "four thousand pounds of chrome and steel, bronze metallic paint, power steering, power brakes, AC, AM/FM, good tires, fine upholstery, all the things you like to see in an ad when you're looking for a big, used American car." The sheriff's car is "parked on the road berm just beyond the bridge"; the juggler's car, a red Mustang, "had already hit the ice slick and had departed from the road. It had slid down a steep bank and been caught by the drifts."

Specificity doesn't preclude Vaughn from using fanciful language, of course. The "crazed lights" on the sheriff's car are "slinging snowfish around his head." When the juggler is tossing snowballs into the air, they go "so high that they disappeared into the feathered darkness before they met his lightning hands again." "Crazed lights," "snowfish," "feathered darkness": We might almost be in the realm of poetry, Vaughn's writing is so imaginative.

Her inventiveness becomes even more apparent when she checks into "Koch's Universe Motel, which had a giant neon sign depicting stars and spaceships." After seeing her accident scene on television, the narrator begins imagining the station's satellite signal transmitting her image, along with "everybody who had ever been on TV," out into space. She imagines herself and Officer Cook "moving fast, already on our way to the moon. Pretty soon we'd be passing through the orbit of Mars, then Jupiter, Saturn, Uranus, Neptune and Pluto. We'd be going to Andromeda and who knows where else. What a vacation." Setting, in short, may not only encompass the world in which a story actually takes place, but in imagined realms as well.

## CHECKLIST Setting the scene

☐ **Is the description of place and time appropriate to your particular story?** Some stories, such as "Crossing the River Zbrucz" and "We're on TV in the Universe," require lots of detail. Others, such as "The Baby," work well without those specifics. Check your story for spots that seem blank or blurry (add more details) or cluttered and jumbled (eliminate unnecessary information). Remember that the simple fact of naming or not naming a location—Wal-Mart versus "a large retail store," or Chicago versus "a large city"—may affect the level of detail you need to include in the rest of your story.

☐ **Is your description of real places accurate?** Chicago is a great place in which to set a story, but do you really want to put your story there if you have never been to the city? Be especially wary of using landmarks and details in a way that will strike a false note with people who do know the city. Rather than heading to London, try looking closer to home for your setting. For readers who have lived their entire lives in large metropolitan areas, Chadron, Nebraska, will be as foreign and exotic as Timbuktu.

☐ **If you're certain that your story has to be set in another time or place, have you done sufficient research to make the setting believable?** Novelists usually do a great deal of research when working up background material for their books. Fortunately, as the writer of a short story, your task is considerably easier. What you're looking for is a handful of details that will be accurate, out of the ordinary, and absolutely right.

☐ **If your story is set in an imaginary time and place, are there enough concrete details to make it convincing?** In the introduction to this chapter, we addressed some of the risks of writing genre fiction in a creative writing class; your instructor may have discussed this issue, too. However, if you decide to take the plunge into fantasy or science fiction, remember two words: Harry Potter. If you ask fans of J. K. Rowling's series what they love about her work, they will probably talk about how *real* she has made her imaginary world. The trick, of course, is to borrow concrete details from planet Earth and creatively import them into your made-up universe.

☐ **Do you have too many scenes for a short story?** Some short stories cover a great deal of time and ground, but setting in those pieces tends to be minimal. *Most* stories unfold over the course of a handful of scenes. If you are describing a single unified action but find that you are trying to set it in four or five different places, take another look at the story. Wouldn't it be easier on your reader to have the action occur in fewer locations?

☐ **Is there any description in your story that does not develop character or move the story forward but instead seems to exist chiefly because you enjoyed writing it?** You know you're spending too much time on setting when you're more concerned with how a place looks than with what the characters are doing there. You may have realized you were going overboard even as you were writing that page-long description of your childhood tree house, but you just couldn't stop yourself. That's fine; reliving the past is one of the pleasures of creative writing. However, at the revision stage, as you look coldly at those sentences that have absolutely nothing to do with your story, do the right thing and delete them.

# Deciding on point of view, developing tone and style ▶

Antonya Nelson has a test for deciding on the point of view—the narrative perspective from which to tell a story. She asks herself, "Who should be telling the story and why at this particular moment?" Once Nelson has answered those questions, "which sound like simple decisions—but are not at all simple—the stories tend to have their own tone and setting and sense of movement." In short, choosing your narrator is one of the most important decisions you will make about your story.

If you have already started writing, you may not have consciously realized that you were forced to adopt a point of view the moment you began. Telling your story from one perspective rather than another may seem like a "natural" decision, but it is always worth considering your options, even if you have already completed a draft. Selecting one point of view over another may be the difference between a successful story and a failed one.

There are four main narrative points of view in fiction. The **first-person point of view** is told from the perspective of a character who is participating—sometimes centrally, sometimes more peripherally—in the action of the story: "I get in the car, turn on the ignition, and drive to the end of Mulligan Street." The **first-person plural point of view** turns the narrator into a group of people: "We get in the car, turn on the ignition, and drive to the end of Mulligan Street." The **second-person point of view** requires the reader to become a character in the story: "You get in the car, turn on the ignition, and drive to the end of Mulligan Street." The **third-person limited point of view** looks over the shoulder, and sometimes into the mind, of a single character in the story: "He gets in the car, turns on the ignition, and drives to the end of Mulligan Street, thinking, *I will never come this way again.*" The **third-person omniscient point of view** allows the narrator to enter, godlike, the mind and situation of anyone in the story. "He gets in the car, turns on the ignition, and drives to the end of Mulligan Street, thinking, *I will never come this way again.* Standing in the driveway, remembering their first night together in that motel near Myrtle Beach, she mutters, 'Don't come back.' Meanwhile, on the other side of town, his new lover is watching *American Idol* and wondering if he'll remember to stop for burritos on his way over."

As we will see, each point of view has its advantages and disadvantages, so you might wonder why you can't tell your story from multiple points of view. That is certainly a possibility in longer works of fiction. Novelists often switch from the perspective of one character to another to good effect, and many fine longer stories have more than one point of view. However, trying to tell your story from more than one perspective in a short story is probably a mistake. Simply establishing a single distinctive narrative voice is tricky enough in a couple of thousand words or fewer; trying to create *several* of those voices in the span of a few pages adds considerable pressure on you as the author. Moreover, as Wayne Booth notes in *The Rhetoric of Fiction,* shifting point of view midstory destroys the illusion of a real world and reminds readers that an author is involved in the storytelling process. Once again, while this is a dependable technique in longer fiction, it is less effective in shorter forms. It is far better for beginning writers to focus their efforts on establishing and maintaining a single point of view. No less an authority than Flannery O'Connor tells us: "If you violate the point of view you destroy the sense of reality and louse yourself up generally."

## First-person point of view

Patricia Hampl believes that "the American consciousness is most congenial in the presence of the first-person voice. Not because we're egotistical, but because, for good or ill, we did predicate this nation based on individuality." And Sue Miller says that "the first person is more propulsive, and more immediately seductive to a reader." Both writers suggest one of the main appeals of the first-person point of view: the energy and urgency of the narrator's voice. First-person narrators are part of the action. Being on the scene gives them a special authority to tell the story. "*I* did this . . . ," they can say, or "*I* saw that . . . ," and generally we give credence to such claims.

Of course, not all narrators are reliable. They may declare that they have done or seen something that is a complete fabrication. However, that uncertainty between what's real and what's not sometimes makes first-person narrators all the more interesting. First-person narrators often tell us as much about themselves as they do about the story they are relating, and, like police detectives listening to a potentially biased witness, we must decide just how much to trust the narrator.

All three of our model authors employ first-person narrators whose lives share at least a few similarities with their own. As the biographical note to "Crossing the River Zbrucz" indicates, Babel was Jewish, unlike his pitiless narrator. Yet Babel *did* serve in the Russian army, so he is also drawing on personal experiences to make his story seem authentic. Similarly, Donald Barthelme was the father of a daughter, which means that his story's premise—a child's propensity for tearing up her books—may have come from real life. However, the exaggerated nature of the father's response clearly fictionalizes that real first-person experience. And while Stephanie Vaughn, who has lived for decades in upstate New York, may be referencing an event in "We're on TV in the Universe" that once happened to her younger self, it is difficult to reconcile the unemployed and unsettled narrator with the story's author, an Ivy League professor.

These examples demonstrate that while you may want to draw on your own life for first-person narration, it's important to remember that you are writing a *story*, not an essay. Use what you can from your experience to make your story more convincing, and jettison the rest. Don't waste time trying to justify your narrator's behavior; instead, let him or her act in whatever way your story dictates. Seasoned writers will tell you that even when your narrator is based on someone very much like yourself, you still need the freedom to morph that narrator into someone other than the person you really are. Just about any character you create is bound to have elements of you blended in, but when you're beginning to write fiction, it helps to have the extra perspective that comes from stepping outside yourself. There's something liberating about pretending to be someone else, and often it is through "inhabiting" (to use Sue Miller's word) the lives of other people that we really come to understand ourselves.

Frederick Reiken identifies another potential problem of the first-person point of view: "In crossing the line and having a protagonist act essentially as a stand-in for the author, the reader often winds up being asked to become complicit with whatever the character is involved in." If your narrator is doing something readers find particularly loathsome—selling methamphetamine, say, or beating up little kids—those readers will distance themselves from the story in a way that they would not if they were merely looking over the character's shoulder rather than being, as John Gardner puts it, "locked . . . in one character's mind."

## First-person plural point of view

The problems with using the "we" form for your narration should be immediately apparent. How is it possible for multiple people to be talking simultaneously in a single voice? How are they privy to the information they have? How does it come to pass that I, the reader, am part of the group narration? And who is this group of people telling the story anyway?

Like the second-person, "we" calls attention to itself as a narrative device. Your readers will be conscious that they are reading a story, that someone else is telling them what they have done or what they will do. Still, if you want to startle your audience out of its normal reading habits, the third-person's point of view is worth considering.

One of the most effective practitioners of this unusual perspective is Steven Millhauser, who uses it precisely because so few other writers do. According to Millhauser, "'We' is an adventure. The main use of 'we' is that it represents the voice of a community. The speaker is multiple. This means that you can't tell the usual kind of story, about a favored protagonist. The slant is radically different."

If you like the story you have to tell, but decide that a conventional way of telling it isn't working, it's worth at least redrafting a few paragraphs to see if "the voice of a community" is the best way to approach the material.

## Second-person point of view

The second-person point of view is essentially a "command form" of narrative. The writer tells the reader: "You do this . . ." or "You went there . . ." This point of view is relatively rare in fiction writing; however, because short stories often rely so much on surprise, its unusual perspective is an alternative worth considering.

Lorrie Moore's story "How" in the anthology of stories at the end of this chapter, effectively uses this point of view. Moore calls her version "second-person, mock imperative," and she uses it in part to lampoon self-help books addressed to women. In "How to Be an Other Woman," another story from her collection, *Self-Help*, Moore writes: "After four movies, three concerts, and two-and-a-half museums, you sleep with him. It seems the right number of cultural events." This darkly comic touch can also be found in another second-person work of fiction, Jay McInerney's novel *Bright Lights, Big City*, which begins: "You are not the kind of guy who would be at a place like this at this time of the morning. But here you are, and you cannot say that the terrain is entirely unfamiliar, although the details are fuzzy. You are at a nightclub talking to a girl with a shaved head."

Jim Grimsley argues that the second-person voice "gives you exactly the right distance between the narrator and the point-of-view character." Pam Houston, yet another writer who has successfully used the second-person voice, agrees. She believes this point of view has two advantages. It allows the writer to distance herself from her narrator: "The second person takes this layer of shame and washes it over the story without her having to say 'I am ashamed.' It's kind of a diversion—it's not me, it's you." Houston also believes that the second-person voice mimics the way many of us actually speak: "'So, you know, you're in this bar and this guy comes up to you . . .' It's the rhythm of American storytelling."

Given its advantages, you might wonder why the second-person point of view isn't used more often. The answer is that many readers find it annoying and intrusive; they feel as though they are being bossed around or accused of doing something they didn't do. As is the case with an intensely unlikable first-person narrator, your readers may simply stop reading if they can't sympathize with the second-person character they must become in the story.

## Third-person limited point of view

Monica Wood has a simple trick for identifying the difference between the third-person omniscient and the third-person limited point of view: "Omniscience works from the outside in: Felix looked like a run-over squirrel. Third-person limited works from the inside out: Felix felt like a run-over squirrel."

Carolyn Chute prefers the third-person limited to the first-person voice because "you can do almost the same stuff . . . but you can get a little bit fancier with the language." Chute believes that the first-person point of view "really limits you in that anything a character wouldn't see you can't talk about, or it will sound too contrived."

Because third-person limited allows you to see both inside the character *and* the world around him or her, this narrative strategy lets the reader make connections before the character does. It's much easier to convey irony with third-person than with first-person, to show how your characters' words and actions don't necessarily correspond with their real desires.

However, with the added flexibility of seeing both through your characters' eyes *and* over their shoulders comes increased authorial accountability. A first-person narrator who tells his story in a strange way, or leaves out important information, or gets mixed up about details may be doing so because the writer wants the narrator to come across as flaky and confused. Of course, there's always a chance that the *writer* is flaky and confused, but readers are much more forgiving of the eccentricities of a first-person narrator than they are of someone writing in the third person. The third-person limited point of view has distinct advantages as a narrative approach, but using it will test your skills as a writer.

## Third-person omniscient point of view

The word "omniscient" means "all-knowing," to have infinite awareness of everything. When you write from this point of view, you are able to move, in a godlike fashion, in and out of every character's thoughts. You can jump back and forth in time, and divulge or conceal whatever you please. Sounds tempting, doesn't it?

Unfortunately, if you have divine powers as a storyteller, you also have divine responsibilities. In Gustave Flaubert's words: "The artist must be within his work like God within the Creation; invisible and all-powerful; we feel him throughout, but we do not see him." It's quite a daunting task just to maintain a consistent narrative voice—especially if you are a new writer—much less creating a voice that sounds truly omniscient. Moreover, as Rick DeMarinis warns, the third-person omniscient point of view "is more suited to the novel than it is to the short story."

In a longer story, it is possible to convincingly portray the thought processes of two or three well-developed characters. However, third-person omniscience is very rare in the shortest stories. You don't have the time to go flitting about from one character and scene to another, so it's probably best to avoid this point of view in shorter stories unless you have a truly compelling reason to use it.

## Tense

Like choosing a narrative point of view, selecting the verb tense for your story may seem a casual, relatively unimportant decision. The past tense is by far the most common tense for storytelling, and new writers tend to use it as a matter of course. This makes sense: the stories we tell one another have nearly always happened in the past. For most readers, the past tense is "unmarked"; that is, they don't notice it one way or the other. Even Barthelme's "The Baby," the least conventional of our three model stories, is told in the past tense, which may suggest how widespread its use is.

For better or worse, the present tense is more conspicuous. It draws readers' attention to the fact that the story is happening *now*, as it is being told. Some writers dislike the present tense because they feel it is too noticeable: it alerts readers to the fact that a narrator is very much behind the telling of the story. Yet the immediacy of the present tense is well suited to very short stories, and Babel employs it effectively in "Crossing the River Zbrucz."

The future tense occasionally makes a cameo appearance for a sentence or two in stories told in the past and present tense, but it is rare to see an entire story written using this form. An exception can be found in some of the experimental work of Angus Woodward, where the future tense is used effectively in combination with the second-person point of view. "You will walk down the street and step inside the last phone booth left in the city" is an intriguing way to start a story.

## Tone and style

Discussions of point of view and tense inevitably lead to discussions of tone and style. Generally **tone** refers to the mood or atmosphere of a story. **Style** in fiction refers to the author's selection and placement of words in a sentence, sentences in a paragraph, and paragraphs in a story. Stylistic choices are important in creating the tone, and from a writer's perspective, these two elements of fiction writing are practically inseparable.

Each of our three model authors has commented insightfully on style. As Isaac Babel said, "No iron spike can pierce a human heart as icily as a period in the right place." That's quite a claim, but we see careful attention to every word choice, every mark of punctuation, in "Crossing the River Zbrucz." Donald Barthelme believed that style was "both a response to constraint and a seizing of opportunity. Very often a constraint is an opportunity. . . . Style enables us to speak, to imagine again." We find Barthelme turning a constraint into an opportunity in the way he uses the voice of his narrator. The man is patently unsuitable as a parent, totally unaware of how to care for an infant, yet Barthelme makes the narrator's dim-wittedness the central fun of the story. Stephanie Vaughn values the immediacy of the story form. For her, style is means of a straightaway immersing the reader in the story's world: "The short story can be hot and sweet or hot and fierce. You get it in one sitting or you don't get it. It's like a shore break. It happens quickly, and is right there in front of you, menacing you. First you're looking at the shore break, and then if you don't back up, it's on you."

"It's all about the sentences," says Rick Moody of Amy Hempel, one of the great contemporary practitioners of the short-short story. "It's about the way the sentences move in the paragraphs. It's about rhythm. It's about ambiguity. It's about the way emotion, in difficult circumstances, gets captured in language." Hempel herself agrees that creating style involves writing good sentences: "Though it's unlikely you'll write something nobody has ever *heard* of, the way you have a chance to compete is in the way you say it."

But how do you write these wonderful sentences? How do you create your own style? The nineteenth-century French novelist Stendahl wrote to his contemporary Honoré de Balzac: "I see but one rule: to be clear. If I am not clear, all my world crumbles to nothing." That's one approach to style, to get things down as close as possible to the way you actually see and imagine them. In the poetry chapter, I advised you to write toward clarity and revise toward strangeness. That suggestion applies equally well to all creative writing. Your first drafts should be attempts to understand your subject matter, to know your characters and identify their conflicts, to plainly sketch out the world they inhabit. You may be trying to recreate the mind-set of a drug-addled schizophrenic, but if your writing never penetrates beyond your character's haze, it loses clarity. Most literary fiction employs ambiguity in some way, but there is good ambiguity, intentional on the writer's part, and bad ambiguity, which is caused by careless thinking and sloppy writing. Even in a story swirling with doubt about the nature of reality, there will be certain aspects that you *don't* want your reader to misinterpret: at these points, you must be clear so that your world does not "crumble to nothing."

Charles Baxter has this practical stylistic advice: "Cut the adjectives unless you absolutely have to have them. Make sure the verbs are the very best ones you can find. Make them forceful. Make them direct. Make them to the point." Baxter is not alone in his distrust of adjectives. Many creative writing instructors would endorse Mark Twain's famous admonition: "As to the adjective: when in doubt, strike it out." William Zinsser is even more to the point: "Look for the clutter in your writing and prune it ruthlessly. Be grateful for everything that you can throw away. Re-examine each sentence that you put on paper. Is every word doing new work? Can any thought be expressed with more economy? Is there anything pompous or pretentious or faddish? Are you hanging on to something useless just because you think it's beautiful? Simplify. Simplify."

This need to be precise when revising your work, to evaluate not only every sentence but also every word, is a subject that writers continually return to when discussing their fiction. Annie Proulx is a big fan of the dictionary: "If I feel a section is limp, [I] take a couple of days and just do dictionary work and recast the sentences so that they have more power because their words aren't overused."

Of course, different stories require different styles. As Richard Lanham says, "A style is a response to a situation." In "Crossing the River Zbrucz," Babel's style moves from the lush passage describing the beauty of the countryside to the curt, brutal sentences about the state of the father's corpse. Different moments in the story demand different styles, and Babel is up to the challenge. Barthelme's stylistic emphasis is on the creation of an outrageously memorable narrative voice. Stephanie Vaughn's style is inviting partly because it is deceptively simple: her voice is so funny, familiar, and self-deprecating that we don't necessarily realize the artistry that has gone into her prose until we go back and reread the story.

Most writers begin by imitating the work of writers they admire. If you have caught yourself doing this, you may feel a bit guilty. Isn't it wrong to copy? Not necessarily. You have to start somewhere, so imitating writers who seem to be doing something right is a natural first step. If you keep writing long enough, you will either surmount the influence eventually or incorporate elements of the writer's style into your own style. Remember, though, that developing a distinctive individual style is a process that occurs over a long period of time; it generally doesn't happen during a single creative writing course. Once you do find your voice, you may agree with John Middleton Murry, who says, "The test of a true individuality of style is that we should feel it to be inevitable."

Finally, don't forget that style in fiction means laserlike concentration on every aspect of your writing. "Sloppy style" is an oxymoron, one likely to result in a poor grade for your story. Don't assume that your instructor—or anyone else, for that matter—will do your editing for you. Whether it's your first draft or the finished piece, turn in the very best work you are capable of writing. This means that you must revise, edit, and *proofread*. If you have weak skills in this area, ask a friend who is good at editing to take a look at your story, or consult a tutor in your campus's writing center.

## CHECKLIST Deciding on point of view, developing tone and style

- [ ] **Have you given careful thought to the question: "Who should be telling this story, and why, at this particular moment?"** Figuring out when, where, why, and by whom a story is being told influences the story's ultimate success. Although the first narrative point of view that occurs to you may turn out to be the best for your story, it is possible that an unusual perspective may allow you to do your strongest writing. A story about something painful that actually happened to you might, for instance, be told more easily from the point of view of another character, possibly even set in a different time and place. Similarly, if you find yourself unable to inhabit a story about someone with a very different lifestyle or set of beliefs, it might be useful to try writing in the first person, to "become" the person you are not.

☐ **Have you fully considered which verb tense will most effectively tell your story?** Most stories are told in the past tense, so you will probably want to consider that the "default tense"—one that won't arouse much notice in your readers. The present tense is more arresting: it claims that the story is taking place while the reader is reading. As we noted earlier, because very short fiction relies on immediacy and surprise, the present tense is more prevalent here than elsewhere. The future tense is difficult to sustain in a longer work of fiction, but it might be employed successfully in the more experimental realm of the short story.

☐ **Are the tone and style of your story appropriate to its content?** Obviously a story about a poker game in a logging camp will require a different tone and style from a story about a bridge game set in a nursing home. Especially when revising your work, think carefully about not only the words you choose but also the construction of your sentences and paragraphs. In literature, the quality of your writing ultimately matters at least as much as your subject matter.

# Getting started writing the short story ▶

In the poetry chapter we noted Donald Murray's admonition that "great is the enemy of good," and that advice has equal validity when applied to the efforts of beginning fiction writers. In other words, shoot for something strong but achievable; you can always revise later. In fact, Anne Lamott bluntly advises writers to reconcile themselves to "shitty first drafts." We creative writing instructors assume you will do something about those drafts by the time they reach your final portfolio, but remember that we aren't anticipating a work of genius your first time out. Most of us are more than happy to see good stories rather than fair or bad ones. And as Lamott says, the only way to get started is to jump into the writing process and see what happens: "Very few writers really know what they are doing until they do it."

That's an important point. Throughout this chapter, we have emphasized that you need to make every word count in your finished story, but when you're sitting down to write, you want to shake free of the demon Expectation and just start writing. Don't worry about grammar. Don't worry about punctuation. Tell yourself that if this story stinks, you can throw it away without ever showing it to a single living soul.

By now, you should have a pretty good idea of what a short story is. You have seen some of the ways that different authors structure their pieces, how they create conflict, decide on point of view, set a scene, and shape a character. Ideally, you already have a bit of plot and setting in mind. You know that your opening should make readers want to drop whatever they're doing and read your story instead. You know that something has to change during the course of the story and that there will be a surprise, a *snap,* at the end. You may not know exactly what that snap is yet, but that doesn't matter. Start writing. As long as you have a central character who—to paraphrase both Aristotle and Janet Burroway—wants something and wants it very badly, that character's driving motivation will probably be sufficient to ignite your fiction.

So sit down in front of your computer—or notebook or typewriter or voice recorder—and begin.

## KICK-STARTS Beginning your story

The material for stories is everywhere. From the anecdote about a party you overheard on the bus this morning, to that old family story about your great-aunt Gladys and her ham radio, to the disastrous Thanksgiving dinner you ate at Denny's last year, the world is full of story ideas. However, if you still have no idea what you want to write about—if your fingers are frozen and your mind is blank—here are some exercises to give you that initial push. Over the years, these strategies have worked well for many of my students. At least one of them is likely to work for you, too.

1. Start keeping a journal. Today. Right now. Your journal can be a notebook of lined paper, or a word processing file on your hard drive, or even a blog. Write down every possible story idea you can think of, including ideas other writers have already used (you can always tweak the details). Draw pictures of characters and settings. Make lists. Take your journal to a crowded place—your school's cafeteria at lunchtime or the mall on Saturday. Discreetly listen to several conversations, and jot down the highlights. In short, throw everything into the bag. Then raid your journal for ideas when you're ready to write.

2. Quickly jot down the names of the five to ten most interesting people you know. Then take a closer look at the list. Which *two* people from that list would make the most sparks fly if they were put into a story together? What would be the nature of their conflict? Set them loose on each other and see what happens.

3. In his excellent book *Turning Life into Fiction,* Robin Hemley recommends the time-honored technique of mixing and matching the most intriguing characteristics from different people to create composite characters. Give it a try, and then look for ways to put those characters at odds with one another.

▶ **4.** Brainstorm. This is an activity in which you cut loose with your pen or pencil or computer and let the ideas flow. Linda Flower advises: "The purpose of brainstorming is to stimulate creative thought. . . . When you come up with an idea or a phrase that isn't quite right, resist the temptation to throw it out and start again. Just write it down. . . . Don't stop to perfect spelling, grammar, or even phrasing. Keep working at the level of ideas." Flower notes that brainstorming differs from freewriting in that the latter method encourages the writer to spill out *anything* that occurs to him or her, while brainstorming "is not free association; it is a goal-directed effort to discover ideas relevant to your problem." Your goal is to write a short story, and your method is to open the floodgates and get everything that is even potentially relevant down on paper.

▶ **5.** Because literary writing depends so heavily on images, you might want to focus your story around a specific object. Look slowly around the room you're in now until your eye alights on an object that suggests a story. Is that string of Christmas lights demanding that a story be told about why it was hung above the window? And what about the broken laptop stashed in the corner? Why does your protagonist refuse to throw it away?

▶ **6.** If you have some extra time on your hands, go to a secondhand store. Look around for an object that is begging to be the centerpiece of a story. What is the story behind that peacoat with a big splash of chartreuse paint on the front? Did an artist get in a fight with her lover? Was an elderly man attacked by a paintball gang? Pulitzer Prize–winning novelist Annie Proulx loves poking around among old things and recommends driving down back roads and stopping for yard sales. For Proulx, the attraction is not just the things she buys but also what she hears along the way: "I listen attentively in bars and cafés, while standing in line at the checkout counter, noting particular pronunciations and the rhythms of regional speech, vivid turns of speech and the duller talk of everyday life."

▶ **7.** The smell and texture of an object can be great triggers for writing, but if you're pressed for time, you can use the Internet instead. Type a random noun—for example, "pineapple"—into the Google Image Search and see what turns up. A recent search resulted in plenty of photographs of pineapples, as one might expect. However, the search also showed a bare-chested young man holding two pineapple slices over his nipples. On the next page was a photo of the Pineapple Inn in Newport, Rhode Island. It doesn't take much imagination to realize that combining the young man and the inn could produce quite a story!

▶ **8.** In a single sitting, write three to five openings for three to five different stories. Then put them aside for a day or two. Reread them, and choose the one that is most likely to make a reader want to keep reading.

▶ **9.** The great short story writer John Cheever once said of his own work: "My favorite stories are those that were written in less than a week and were often composed aloud." Take the "Cheever Challenge": Get a digital recorder, or a willing listener, and tell a story aloud. Give yourself less than a week to turn your oral version into a completed story on paper.

10. Write a story in which you reveal a secret about yourself, but have that secret apply to a character who is very much unlike you.

11. Write a story that could get you into trouble. Expose an uncomfortable truth about someone you know, or reveal a secret you promised never to disclose. Then transform your narrative into fiction by changing the setting and altering the characters' names and appearances.

12. "My writing often unfolds like a connect-the-dots exercise," says Lori Ostlund. "Anecdotes and images pop into my head, and my job is to figure out how they all tie together." Make a list of interesting anecdotes and images that may not have an obvious connection with one another. Then connect the dots between apparently disparate material and turn it into a story.

13. Tell the story that only you can tell—the story you have inside that's screaming to get out.

14. If you enrolled in this course with a longer story already in mind, go ahead and write it. Once you're finished, let it sit for a few days. Then go back and revise it, cutting out all the extraneous material. Often that merciless revision will result in a much stronger piece of fiction.

15. Read before you write. If you find yourself blocked, read some of the stories in this book's anthology. The excitement of reading a great piece of fiction can often motivate you to try to create one yourself. There are far too many excellent anthologies of short fiction than we have room to list here; however, if you'd like to see what the finest North American writers are currently writing, a good place to start is *The Best American Short Stories* series, which features a new guest editor each year.

# An Anthology of
# Short Stories

## Lisa Alvarez

## Cielito Lindo

When the twelve-piece mariachi band her uncle had booked to serenade his wife on their fiftieth wedding anniversary started playing and filled up the church's basement room with the blast of five trumpets, Linda decided to sit next to her father after all because she knew they wouldn't be able to speak over the music and so she would get credit, good daughter credit she imagined, but at the same time she wouldn't have to say a thing or listen to what he had to say about her mother (*after all these years still "that crazy woman" if he was sober or "that bitch" if he was drunk*) or her own sorry life (*manless childless pointless in his view*). Linda also imagined that if she, his nearly fifty-year-old daughter, sat next to him, her presence might dissuade him from hitting on the younger female guests. She'd already seen his eyes wander as the generation of family grandchildren, now in their late twenties and early thirties, arrived, accompanied by their friends. The women wore dancing dresses cut just low enough to raise his hopes. He was drinking tonight, she noted, something dark and on the rocks.

Her father was handsome in a kind of craggy roosterlike way. He'd aged well and knew it. Still had all his hair, more than most men forty years younger. Tonight he dressed up in dark jeans and cowboy boots, a fine white shirt unbuttoned to show a puff of chest hair that belied his seventy-plus years. He always did that with his shirts and it embarrassed her, the sight of that patch of burnished skin and curling white hair. Linda wondered if, had she been a boy, the son her mother claimed he always wanted, she would feel different, feel pride, a kind of male camaraderie rooted in perhaps her own hopes as a middle-aged male swimming in the same hairy gene pool.

Linda sat and watched her father move in rather gentlemanly appreciation of the music, his head nodding, his eyes beaming. It was as if he and not his brother-in-law had paid for the band and made the arrangements, a kind of easy but dishonest sense of proprietorship that she often saw him deploy at family dinners and parties. As if he, along with the other *tíos*[1] and *tías*,[2] had helped out or pitched in when, as she well knew, all he'd done again was show up.

When the mariachis launched into the inevitable "Cielito Lindo," her aunt and uncle stood in front of the musicians. They swayed together, which was as close as they would ever get to dancing, and the crowd began to stand too and sing along to the music they had heard their whole lives, in restaurants and on street corners, in movie houses and on car radios. It meant something to them all, if perhaps not the same thing, this song with its *ay ay ay ay*, with its command to sing and not cry. Some people, she noticed, knew all the words, and some knew only the chorus. Linda was one of the chorus singers.

Her father drained his glass, got to his feet, and began to sway, to sing. He knew all the words. He even turned to Linda and smiled as if she too, his daughter, was a lovely woman, worthy of such a song. Her father knew how to look at a woman and make her feel like that, she thought. Pretty. It didn't take much. Something about the full attention of his eyes. He bent down and reached out his hand, the gentleman again, a gallant gesture, to raise her to her feet. And when he did, when her old father leaned toward her, she noticed his white dress shirt was undone one button more than his usual two. And when Linda stood beside him and glanced again, she saw that instead of his usual wife-beater undershirt (*How she hated that name however true it might be for him*), with its white ribbing and scoop neck, it appeared to her that her father was wearing a white camisole with a bouquet of embroidered flowers at its center. She looked away. Linda herself had worn such things as a girl, to dances in this very basement and yes, like her father, had left her blouses unbuttoned to the flowers, hoping perhaps something else would show as well and someone else would notice.

Linda watched as the bows of the violins cut the air with a kind of violence but, unable to help herself, her eyes shifted back to the garland of tightly stitched pink rosebuds with their satin petals and green leaves that adorned her father, his puff of chest hair rising now like a cloud above a garden.

Linda wondered what this girl's undershirt meant, with its tiny flowers: *Where did it come from? Whose was it? Had her father picked it up off the floor of some woman's bedroom and mistaken it for his own? Had he donned it like a strange trophy? Had the shirt made its way into his laundry cycle at his apartment building and gone unnoticed? Did he know? Should she tell him?*

Her father sang now, full-throated, and when she looked at him in profile, Linda saw his strength and handsomeness, perhaps what her mother had seen,

1. **tíos:** uncles
2. **tías:** aunts

yes, over fifty years ago now. But she also saw all those years gone and she knew there were not that many left for him now. Linda could see what her father could not: those flowers, that white hair, the mistakes a person makes. ◀

# Margaret Atwood

# An Angel

know what the angel of suicide looks like. I have seen her several times. She's around.

She's nothing like the pictures of angels you run across here and there, the ones in classical paintings, with their curls and beautiful eyelashes, or the ones on Christmas cards, all cute or white. Much is made, in these pictures, of the feet, which are always bare, I suppose to show that angels do not need shoes: walkers on nails and live coals all of them, aspirin hearts, dandelion-seed heads, air bodies.

Not so the angel of suicide, who is dense, heavy with antimatter, a dark star. But despite the differences, she does have something in common with those others. All angels are messengers, and so is she; which isn't to say that all messages are good. The angels vary according to what they have to say: the angel of blindness, for instance, the angel of lung cancer, the angel of seizures, the destroying angel. The latter is also a mushroom.

(Snow angels, you've seen them: the cold blank shape of yourself, the outline you once filled. They too are messengers, they come from the future. This is what you will be, they say, perhaps what you are: no more than the way light falls across a given space.)

Angels come in two kinds: the others, and those who fell. The angel of suicide is one of those who fell, down through the atmosphere to the earth's surface. Or did she jump? With her you have to ask.

Anyway, it was a long fall. From the friction of the air, her face melted off like the skin of a meteor. That is why the angel of suicide is so smooth. She has no face to speak of. She has the face of a gray egg. Noncommittal; though the shine of the fall still lingers.

They said, the pack of them, I will not serve. The angel of suicide is one of those: a rebellious waitress. Rebellion, that's what she has to offer, to you, when you see her beckoning to you from outside the window, fifty stories up, or the edge of the bridge, or holding something out to you, some emblem of release, soft chemical, quick metal.

Wings, of course. You wouldn't believe a thing she said if it weren't for the wings. ◀

# Aimee Bender

# Loser

Once there was an orphan who had a knack for finding lost things. Both his parents had been killed when he was eight years old—they were swimming in the ocean when it turned wild with waves, and each had tried to save the other from drowning. The boy woke up from a nap, on the sand, alone. After the tragedy, the community adopted and raised him, and a few years after the deaths of his parents, he began to have a sense of objects even when they weren't visible. This ability continued growing in power through his teens and by his twenties, he was able to actually sniff out lost sunglasses, keys, contact lenses and sweaters.

The neighbors discovered his talent accidentally—he was over at Jenny Sugar's house one evening, picking her up for a date, when Jenny's mother misplaced her hairbrush, and was walking around, complaining about this. The young man's nose twitched and he turned slightly toward the kitchen and pointed to the drawer where the spoons and knives were kept. His date burst into laughter. Now that would be quite a silly place to put the brush, she said, among all that silverware! and she opened the drawer to make her point, to wave with a knife or brush her hair with a spoon, but when she did, boom, there was the hairbrush, matted with gray curls, sitting astride the fork pile.

Jenny's mother kissed the young man on the cheek but Jenny herself looked at him suspiciously all night long.

You planned all that, didn't you, she said, over dinner. You were trying to impress my mother. Well you didn't impress me, she said.

He tried to explain himself but she would hear none of it and when he drove his car up to her house, she fled before he could even finish saying he'd had a nice time, which was a lie anyway. He went home to his tiny room and thought about the word lonely and how it sounded and looked so lonely, with those two l's in it, each standing tall by itself.

As news spread around the neighborhood about the young man's skills, people reacted two ways: there were the deeply appreciative and the skeptics. The appreciative ones called up the young man regularly. He'd stop by on his way to school, find their keys, and they'd give him a homemade muffin. The skeptics called him over too, and watched him like a hawk; he'd still find their lost items but they'd insist it was an elaborate scam and he was doing it all to get attention. Maybe, declared one woman, waving her index finger in the air, Maybe, she said, he steals the thing so we think it's lost, moves the item, and then comes over to save it! How do we know it was really lost in the first place? What is going on?

The young man didn't know himself. All he knew was the feeling of a tug, light but insistent, like a child at his sleeve, and that tug would turn him in the right direction and show him where to look. Each object had its own way of inhabiting space, and therefore messaging its location. The young man could sense, could smell, an object's presence—he did not need to see it to feel where it put its gravity down. As would be expected, items that turned out to be miles away took much harder concentration than the ones that were two feet to the left.

When Mrs. Allen's little boy didn't come home one afternoon, that was the most difficult of all. Leonard Allen was eight years old and usually arrived home from school at 3:05. He had allergies and needed a pill before he went back out to play. That day, by 3:45, a lone Mrs. Allen was a wreck. Her boy rarely got lost—only once had that happened in the supermarket but he'd been found quite easily under the produce tables, crying; this walk home from school was a straight line and Leonard was not a wandering kind.

Mrs. Allen was just a regular neighbor except for one extraordinary fact—through an inheritance, she was the owner of a gargantuan emerald she called the Green Star. It sat, glass-cased, in her kitchen, where everyone could see it because she insisted that it be seen. Sometimes, as a party trick, she'd even cut steak with its beveled edge.

On this day, she removed the case off the Green Star and stuck her palms on it. Where is my boy? she cried. The Green Star was cold and flat. She ran, weeping, to her neighbor, who calmly walked her back home; together, they gave the house a thorough search, and then the neighbor, a believer, recommended calling the young man. Although Mrs. Allen was a skeptic, she thought anything was a worthwhile idea, and when the line picked up, she said, in a trembling voice:

You must find my boy.

The young man had been just about to go play basketball with his friends. He'd located the basketball in the bathtub.

You lost him? said the young man.

Mrs. Allen began to explain and then her phone clicked.

One moment please, she said, and the young man held on.

When her voice returned, it was shaking with rage.

He's been kidnapped! she said. And they want the Green Star!

The young man realized then it was Mrs. Allen he was talking to, and nodded. Oh, he said, I see. Everyone in town was familiar with Mrs. Allen's Green Star. I'll be right over, he said.

The woman's voice was too run with tears to respond.

In his basketball shorts and shirt, the young man jogged over to Mrs. Allen's house. He was amazed at how the Green Star was all exactly the same shade of green. He had a desire to lick it.

By then, Mrs. Allen was in hysterics.

They didn't tell me what to do, she sobbed. Where do I bring my emerald? How do I get my boy back?

The young man tried to feel the scent of the boy. He asked for a photograph and stared at it—a brown-haired kid at his kindergarten graduation—but the young man had only found objects before, and lost objects at that. He'd never found anything, or anybody, stolen. He wasn't a policeman.

Mrs. Allen called the police and one officer showed up at the door.

Oh it's the finding guy, the officer said. The young man dipped his head modestly. He turned to his right; to his left; north; south. He got a glimmer of a feeling toward the north and walked out the back door, through the backyard. Night approached and the sky seemed to grow and deepen in the darkness.

What's his name again? he called back to Mrs. Allen.

Leonard, she said. He heard the policeman pull out a pad and begin to ask basic questions.

He couldn't quite feel him. He felt the air and he felt the tug inside of the Green Star, an object displaced from its original home in Asia. He felt the tug of the tree in the front yard which had been uprooted from Virginia to be replanted here, and he felt the tug of his own watch which was from his uncle; in an attempt to be fatherly, his uncle had insisted he take it but they both knew the gesture was false.

Maybe the boy was too far away by now.

He heard the policeman ask: What is he wearing?

Mrs. Allen described a blue shirt, and the young man focused in on the blue shirt; he turned off his distractions and the blue shirt, like a connecting radio station, came calling from the northwest. The young man went walking and walking and about fourteen houses down he felt the blue shirt shrieking at him and he walked right into the backyard, through the back door, and sure enough, there were four people watching TV including the tear-stained boy with a runny nose eating a candy bar. The young man scooped up the boy while the others watched, so surprised they did nothing, and one even muttered: Sorry, man.

For fourteen houses back, the young man held Leonard in his arms like a bride. Leonard stopped crying and looked up at the stars and the young man smelled Leonard's hair, rich with the memory of peanut butter. He hoped Leonard would ask him a question, any question, but Leonard was quiet. The young man answered in his head: Son, he said, and the word rolled around, a marble on a marble floor. Son, he wanted to say.

When he reached Mrs. Allen's door, which was wide open, he walked in with quiet Leonard and Mrs. Allen promptly burst into tears and the policeman slunk out the door.

She thanked the young man a thousand times, even offered him the Green Star, but he refused it. Leonard turned on the TV and curled up on the sofa. The young man walked over and asked him about the program he was watching but Leonard stuck a thumb in his mouth and didn't respond.

Feel better, he said softly. Tucking the basketball beneath his arm, the young man walked home, shoulders low.

In his tiny room, he undressed and lay in bed. Had it been a naked child with nothing on, no shoes, no necklace, no hairbow, no watch, he could not have found it. He lay in bed that night with the trees from other places rustling and he could feel their confusion. No snow here. Not a lot of rain. Where am I? What is wrong with this dirt?

Crossing his hands in front of himself, he held on to his shoulders. Concentrate hard, he thought. Where are you? Everything felt blank and quiet. He couldn't feel a tug. He squeezed his eyes shut and let the question bubble up: Where did you go? Come find me. I'm over here. Come find me.

If he listened hard enough, he thought he could hear the waves hitting. ◄

## T. Coraghessan Boyle

# The Hit Man

### Early Years

The Hit Man's early years are complicated by the black bag that he wears over his head. Teachers correct his pronunciation, the coach criticizes his attitude, the principal dresses him down for branding preschoolers with a lit cigarette. He is a poor student. At lunch he sits alone, feeding bell peppers and salami into the dark slot of his mouth. In the hallways, wiry young athletes snatch at the black hood and slap the back of his head. When he is thirteen he is approached by the captain of the football team, who pins him down and attempts to remove the hood. The Hit Man wastes him. Five years, says the judge.

### Back on the Street

The Hit Man is back on the street in two months.

### First Date

The girl's name is Cynthia. The Hit Man pulls up in front of her apartment in his father's hearse. (The Hit Man's father, whom he loathes and abominates, is a mortician. At breakfast the Hit Man's father had slapped the cornflakes from his son's bowl. The son threatened to waste his father. He did not, restrained no doubt by considerations of filial loyalty and the deep-seated taboos against patricide that permeate the universal unconscious.)

Cynthia's father has silver sideburns and plays tennis. He responds to the Hit Man's knock, expresses surprise at the Hit Man's appearance. The Hit Man takes Cynthia by the elbow, presses a twenty into her father's palm, and disappears into the night.

## Father's Death

At breakfast the Hit Man slaps the cornflakes from his father's bowl. Then wastes him.

## Mother's Death

The Hit Man is in his early twenties. He shoots pool, lifts weights and drinks milk from the carton. His mother is in the hospital, dying of cancer or heart disease. The priest wears black. So does the Hit Man.

## First Job

Porfirio Buñoz, a Cuban financier, invites the Hit Man to lunch. I hear you're looking for work, says Buñoz.

That's right, says the Hit Man.

## Peas

The Hit Man does not like peas. They are too difficult to balance on the fork.

## Talk Show

The Hit Man waits in the wings, the white slash of a cigarette scarring the midnight black of his head and upper torso. The makeup girl has done his mouth and eyes, brushed the nap of his hood. He has been briefed. The guest who precedes him is a pediatrician. A planetary glow washes the stage where the host and the pediatrician, separated by a potted palm, cross their legs and discuss the little disturbances of infants and toddlers.

After the station break the Hit Man finds himself squeezed into a director's chair, white lights in his eyes. The talk-show host is a baby-faced man in his early forties. He smiles like God and all His Angels. Well, he says. So you're a hit man. Tell me—I've always wanted to know—what does it feel like to hit someone?

## Death of Mateo María Buñoz

The body of Mateo María Buñoz, the cousin and business associate of a prominent financier, is discovered down by the docks on a hot summer morning. Mist rises from the water like steam, there is the smell of fish. A large black bird perches on the dead man's forehead.

## Marriage

Cynthia and the Hit Man stand at the altar, side by side. She is wearing a white satin gown and lace veil. The Hit Man has rented a tuxedo, extra-large, and a silk-lined black-velvet hood.

... Till death do you part, says the priest.

## Moods

The Hit Man is moody, unpredictable. Once, in a luncheonette, the waitress brought him the meatloaf special but forgot to eliminate the peas. There was a spot of gravy on the Hit Man's hood, about where his chin should be. He looked up at the waitress, his eyes like pins behind the triangular slots, and wasted her.

Another time he went to the track with $25, came back with $1,800. He stopped at a cigar shop. As he stepped out of the shop a wino tugged at his sleeve and solicited a quarter. The Hit Man reached into his pocket, extracted the $1,800 and handed it to the wino. Then wasted him.

## First Child

A boy. The Hit Man is delighted. He leans over the edge of the playpen and molds the tiny fingers around the grip of a nickel-plated derringer. The gun is loaded with blanks—the Hit Man wants the boy to get used to the noise. By the time he is four the boy has mastered the rudiments of Tae Kwon Do, can stick a knife in the wall from a distance of ten feet and shoot a moving target with either hand. The Hit Man rests his broad palm on the boy's head. You're going to make the Big Leagues, Tiger, he says.

## Work

He flies to Cincinnati. To L.A. To Boston. To London. The stewardesses get to know him.

## Half an Acre and a Garage

The Hit Man is raking leaves, amassing great brittle piles of them. He is wearing a black T-shirt, cut off at the shoulders, and a cotton work hood, also black. Cynthia is edging the flower bed, his son playing in the grass. The Hit Man waves to his neighbors as they drive by. The neighbors wave back.

When he has scoured the lawn to his satisfaction, the Hit Man draws the smaller leaf-hummocks together in a single mound the size of a pickup truck. Then he bends to ignite it with his lighter. Immediately, flames leap back from the leaves, cut channels through the pile, engulf it in a ball of fire. The Hit Man stands back, hands folded beneath the great meaty biceps. At his side is the three-headed dog. He bends to pat each of the heads, smoke and sparks raging against the sky.

## Stalking the Streets of the City

He is stalking the streets of the city, collar up, brim down. It is late at night. He stalks past department stores, small businesses, parks, and gas stations. Past apartments, picket fences, picture windows. Dogs growl in the shadows, then slink away. He could hit any of us.

## Retirement

A group of businessman-types—sixtyish, seventyish, portly, diamond rings, cigars, liver spots—throws him a party. Porfirio Buñoz, now in his eighties, makes a speech and presents the Hit Man with a gilded scythe. The Hit Man thanks him, then retires to the lake, where he can be seen in his speedboat, skating out over the blue, hood rippling in the breeze.

## Death

He is stricken, shrunken, half his former self. He lies propped against the pillows at Mercy Hospital, a bank of gentians drooping round the bed. Tubes run into the hood at the nostril openings, his eyes are clouded and red, sunk deep behind the triangular slots. The priest wears black. So does the Hit Man.

On the other side of town the Hit Man's son is standing before the mirror of a shop that specializes in Hit Man attire. Trying on his first hood. ◀

# Ron Carlson

# A Kind of Flying

By our wedding day, Brady had heard the word *luck* two hundred times. Everybody had advice, especially her sister Linda, who claimed to be "wise to me." Linda had wisdom. She was two years older and had wisely married a serviceman,

Butch Kistleburg, whose status as a GI in the army guaranteed them a life of travel and adventure. They were going to see the world. If Brady married me, Linda told everybody, she would see nothing but the inside of my carpet store.

Linda didn't like my plans for the ceremony. She thought that letting my best man, Bobby Thorson, sing "El Paso" was a diabolical mistake. "'El Paso,'" she said. "Why would you sing that at a wedding in Stevens Point, Wisconsin?" I told her: because I liked the song, I'm a sucker for a story, and because it was a love song, and because there *wasn't* a song called "Stevens Point."

"Well," she said that day so long ago, "that is no way to wedded bliss."

I wasn't used to thinking of things in terms of bliss, and I had no response for her. I had been thinking of the great phrase from the song that goes ". . . maybe tomorrow a bullet may find me . . ." and I was once again recommitted to the musical part of the program.

What raised *all* the stakes was what Brady did with the cake. She was a photographer even then and had had a show that spring in the Stevens Point Art Barn, a hilarious series of eye-tricks that everyone thought were double exposures: toy soldiers patrolling bathroom sinks and cowboys in refrigerators. Her family was pleased by what they saw as a useful hobby, but the exhibition of photographs had generally confused them.

When Brady picked up the wedding cake the morning we were wed, it stunned her, just the size of it made her grab her camera. She and Linda had taken Clover Lane, by the Gee place, and Brady pictured it all: the cake in the foreground and the church in the background, side by side.

When Brady pulled over near the cottonwoods a quarter mile from the church, Linda was not amused. She stayed in the car. Brady set the wedding cake in the middle of the road, backed up forty feet, lay down on the hardtop there, and in the rangefinder she saw the image she wanted: the bride and the groom on top of the three-tiered cake looking like they were about to step over onto the roof of the First Congregational Church. We still have the photograph. And when you see it, you always hear the next part of the story.

Linda screamed. Brady, her eye to the viewfinder, thought a truck was coming, that she was a second away from being run over on her wedding day. But it wasn't a truck. Linda had screamed at two birds. Two crows, who had been browsing the fenceline, wheeled down and fell upon the cake, amazed to find the sweetest thing in the history of Clover Lane, and before Brady could run forward and prevent it, she saw the groom plucked from his footing, ankle deep in frosting, and rise—in the beak of the shiny black bird—up into the June-blue sky.

"Man oh man oh man," Linda said that day to Brady. "That is a bad deal. That," she said, squinting at the two crows, who were drifting across Old Man Gee's alfalfa, one of them with the groom in his beak, "is a definite message." Then Linda, who had no surplus affection for me, went on to say several other things which Brady has been good enough, all these years, to keep to herself.

When Bobby Thorson and I reached the church, Linda came out as we were unloading his guitar and said smugly, "Glen, we're missing the groom."

Someone called the bakery, but it was too late for a replacement, almost one o'clock. I dug through Brady's car and found some of her guys: an Indian from Fort Apache with his hatchet raised in a non-matrimonial gesture; the Mummy, a translucent yellow; a kneeling green soldier, his eye to his rifle; and a little blue frogman with movable arms and legs. I was getting married in fifteen minutes.

The ceremony was rich. Linda read some Emily Dickinson; my brother read some Robert Service; and then Bobby Thorson sang "El Paso," a song about the intensities of love and a song which seemed to bewilder much of the congregation.

When Brady came up the aisle on her father's arm, she looked like an angel, her face blanched by seriousness and—I found out later—fear of evil omens. At the altar she whispered to me, "Do you believe in symbols?" Thinking she was referring to the rings, I said, "Of course, more than ever!" Her face nearly broke. I can still see her mouth quiver.

Linda didn't let up. During the reception when we were cutting the cake, Brady lifted the frogman from the top and Linda grabbed her hand: "Don't you ever lick frosting from any man's feet."

I wanted to say, "They're flippers, Linda," but I held my tongue.

That was twenty years ago this week. So much has happened. I've spent a thousand hours on my knees carpeting the rooms and halls and stairways of Stevens Point. Brady and I now have three boys who are good boys, but who—I expect—will not go into the carpet business. Brady has worked hard at her art. She is finished with her new book, *Obelisks*, which took her around the world twice photographing monuments. She's a wry woman with a sense of humor as long as a country road. Though she's done the traveling and I've stayed at home, whenever she sees any bird winging away, she says to me: *There you go.*

And she may be kind of right with that one. There have been times when I've ached to drop it all and fly away with Brady. I've cursed the sound of airplanes overhead and then when she comes home with her camera case and dirty laundry, I've flown to her—and she to me. You find out day after day in a good life that your family is the journey.

And now Linda's oldest, Trina, is getting married. We're having a big family party here in Stevens Point. Butch and Linda have all come north for a couple of weeks. Butch has done well; he's a lieutenant colonel. He's stationed at Fort Bliss and they all seem to like El Paso.

Trina came into the store yesterday pretending to look at carpet. People find out you're married for twenty years, they ask advice. What would I know? I'm just her uncle and I've done what I could. For years I laid carpet so my wife could be a photographer, and now she'll be a photographer so I can retire and coach baseball. Life lies before us like some new thing.

It's quiet in the store today. I can count sparrows on the wire across the road. My advice! She smiled yesterday when I told her. Just get married. Have a friend sing your favorite song at the wedding. Marriage, she said, what is it? Well, I said, it's not life on a cake. It's a bird taking your head in his beak and you walk the sky. It's marriage. Sometimes it pinches like a bird's mouth, but it's definitely flying, it's definitely a kind of flying. ◀

# Raymond Carver

## Popular Mechanics

Early that day the weather turned and the snow was melting into dirty water. Streaks of it ran down from the little shoulder-high window that faced the backyard. Cars slushed by on the street outside, where it was getting dark. But it was getting dark on the inside too.

He was in the bedroom pushing clothes into a suitcase when she came to the door.

I'm glad you're leaving! I'm glad you're leaving! she said. Do you hear?

He kept on putting his things into the suitcase.

Son of a bitch! I'm so glad you're leaving! She began to cry. You can't even look me in the face, can you?

Then she noticed the baby's picture on the bed and picked it up.

He looked at her and she wiped her eyes and stared at him before turning and going back to the living room.

Bring that back, he said.

Just get your things and get out, she said.

He did not answer. He fastened the suitcase, put on his coat, looked around the bedroom before turning off the light. Then he went out to the living room.

She stood in the doorway of the little kitchen, holding the baby.

I want the baby, he said.

Are you crazy?

No, but I want the baby. I'll get someone to come by for his things.

You're not touching this baby, she said.

The baby had begun to cry and she uncovered the blanket from around his head.

Oh, oh, she said, looking at the baby.

He moved toward her.

For God's sake! she said. She took a step back into the kitchen.

I want the baby.

Get out of here!

She turned and tried to hold the baby over in a corner behind the stove.

But he came up. He reached across the stove and tightened his hands on the baby.

Let go of him, he said.

Get away, get away! she cried.

The baby was red-faced and screaming. In the scuffle they knocked down a flowerpot that hung behind the stove.

He crowded her into the wall then, trying to break her grip. He held on to the baby and pushed with all his weight.

Let go of him, he said.

Don't, she said. You're hurting the baby, she said.

I'm not hurting the baby, he said.

The kitchen window gave no light. In the near-dark he worked on her fisted fingers with one hand and with the other hand he gripped the screaming baby up under an arm near the shoulder.

She felt her fingers being forced open. She felt the baby going from her.

No! she screamed just as her hands came loose.

She would have it, this baby. She grabbed for the baby's other arm. She caught the baby around the wrist and leaned back.

But he would not let go. He felt the baby slipping out of his hands and he pulled back very hard.

In this manner, the issue was decided.  ◄


# Dan Chaon

# St. Dismas

That summer, not long after he turned twenty-three, Pierce kidnapped his ex-girlfriend's son, Jesse. Actually, Pierce thought, it wasn't so much a kidnapping as it was a rescue—Jesse had come with him willingly enough—though there was also, Pierce had to admit, an element of sheer vindictiveness, a desire to wake her up and make her suffer. In any case, after a couple of weeks on the road with Jesse, Pierce had begun to realize that he had probably made a mistake.

They had been traveling west without any real plan in mind, and they had arrived at last at Pierce's father's house in St. Dismas, Nebraska. St. Dismas was one of those old dried-up prairie towns, not even worthy of being called a "town," not even a settlement anymore. There were a few empty old houses and sheds, and a gas station, long closed, and an abandoned grain elevator alongside the railroad tracks, and a few straggling cottonwood trees sending their snowy seeds through the empty streets. Beyond the little cluster of buildings were long stretches of fields—wheat, sunflowers, alfalfa—and a two-lane highway that led off toward the rest of the world.

Pierce was dreaming of St. Dismas when he woke up that morning. He could picture the town as seen from above and the tangle of dirt roads that led away from it, and the highway. He was sleeping in his father's old room, and Jesse was across the hall in the room that Pierce and his brother had once occupied when they were kids. Everything in the house was more or less as it had been since his father died, over a year before—couch and lamp and ashtray, dishes and canned goods in the cupboard and a refrigerator that he didn't dare to open, dressers and pillows and blankets. A. lot of dust and mildew.

Pierce opened his eyes and he could hear Jesse talking to himself.

—All right, he was saying. Thank you, thank you, you're a great audience, he said, and Pierce knew that he was probably hopping around in front of the mirror, "capering," as Pierce's father would have said. Telling himself his little secret jokes, making faces and then laughing at the expressions he created. Pierce and Jesse had shared any number of motel rooms, and Pierce had often opened his eyes from a deep sleep to find Jesse deeply involved in one of these private performances.

In general, Pierce thought, Jesse wasn't a bad kid, and there were a lot of things that he actually really liked about him. He was an entertaining liar and a natural-born thief, which had proved useful, and he was always eager to please. It hadn't taken any persuasion at all to get him to turn on his mom, to show where she'd hidden her money and her drugs, and then he'd cheerfully climbed into the car with Pierce and driven away.

He was an impressive acrobat, too. He could walk on his hands just as naturally as if his palms were the soles of his feet, and he could climb up a tree and in through the window of a house with the ease of a monkey.

But Pierce wasn't sure what to do with him. Jesse had recently taken to calling him "Dad," even though Pierce obviously wasn't his father, Jesse was only twelve years younger than Pierce himself. But what could you do? His mother was a nasty piece of work, very neglectful, a temperamental drug addict with a meth lab in her basement, and Pierce assumed that the kid had never learned right from wrong or good from bad and probably didn't have a clear concept of what the term "Dad" even meant.

Pierce had been mixed up with Jesse's mother for over a year. She had been a regular at the bar where Pierce had worked, and at first, honestly, he had been flattered by the attention of an older woman, he'd been impressed by her apathy and amorality, which had at the time seemed very worldly and cool. She had been a drug addict for as long as he'd known her, but in those last few months she'd somehow tipped over the line that separated an interesting, sexy druggie from a boring, nasty one. Honestly, it seemed like she'd become less and less human—her teeth had begun to fall out and she got these strange, measlelike bumps on her face that she couldn't stop picking at, and the tendons on her neck stood out as if she were always straining to sing a high note. Though she was only twenty-seven, she had begun to look like a little old lady, and he pictured her as a zombie, a dead thing clambering out of a grave with a femur clenched in her teeth, her eyes glazed.

It was almost a joke, by the end. When Pierce and Jesse would see her come stumbling out of the bedroom, hunched and moving her tongue around in her gap-toothed mouth in that slow, lizardy way, the two of them could barely keep from laughing. How repulsive she was, Pierce could hardly believe it, and at first it had made him feel happy to think that not only was he rescuing Jesse from her filthy household, but he was also shafting her at the same time. He loved imagining the tortuous inner debate she must have gone through, trying to decide whether to call the cops out to her house. To go into the police station, maybe. How enraged she must have been! The idea had tickled him.

Still, he hadn't really planned ahead—he certainly hadn't imagined that Jesse would still be with him, his responsibility, all this time later.

But what to do with him? How to dump him? He was a liability, he called attention to himself with his odd, hyperactive behavior, he made people look at them and ask questions. And remember their faces.

Pierce rose up out of bed and padded down the hall. Jesse was there in his old bedroom, facing the full-length mirror that was attached to the door. He was saluting himself and marching in place with a look of fierce triumph, like a soldier tramping through the streets of a smoldering enemy town.

Pierce paused and regarded him for a moment until he stopped moving and put his arms to his sides.

—What's up, Pierce said.

—Nothing.

—Well, you better think about getting packed up, Pierce said. We're going to leave pretty soon.

The boy looked at Pierce in that blank, fake-innocent way that he had, glancing sidelong at the mirror again, as if his reflection were an old pal he shared some little secret with. It had occurred to Pierce recently: Jesse was the kind of person who could betray his own mother.

—Can we steal some stuff? he asked.

Pierce gave him a stare.

—It's my house, Pierce said. You can't really steal from your own house.

—Hmm, he said, and he bent down and picked up a feathered Native American headdress, which Pierce guessed he must have dug out of a closet or a drawer, some old souvenir that Pierce's father had once bought at some long-ago road-side attraction or another. The old room was still full of this kind of stuff from Pierce's childhood, junk, Pierce thought, that his dad hadn't ever bothered to throw away.

—I guess I can keep this, then, Jesse said.

He was a real pack rat, this kid, Pierce thought. Every motel room they stayed in, Jesse made up a collection of the free soaps and shampoos and lotions, and sometimes took along the television remote for good measure. And then there were the houses he and Pierce had broken into.

There was that little place in Champaign-Urbana, the occupants away for the weekend, where Jesse had carefully combed through their CDs for stuff he liked: Creedence Clearwater Revival, The Shins, Young Jeezy. In another place in Wisconsin, a vacation house on a lake, he'd been crazy for the tackle box and the little plastic worms and frogs with hooks in them, the metal spinners with pieces of feather fluff attached, the weights and bobbers. Then there was that farmhouse outside Des Moines, where he'd been so enchanted by the collection of figurines on the shelf in the living room—little china elves and fairies and dwarves and goblins and such—that he hadn't even seemed to notice the fact that the house was occupied. Pierce went into the bedroom, looking for things to steal, and was surprised to discover that there was a little old man asleep in the bed, his gaunt head sticking up out of the covers and his mouth open, drawing small breaths.

*Maybe I should kill him,* Pierce thought, but he wasn't quite ready for that kind of thing yet. He backed out, slowly, closing the door quietly behind him, and Jesse was busily packing the knickknacks into his already overstuffed duffel.

—Let's go, Pierce whispered. I thought I told you to check the bedroom. There's *people* in here, you fuckin' jag-off.

—Wait a minute, Jesse said, in his high, nasal, rat-boy voice. I'm not finished! He spoke stubbornly, loudly, and Pierce couldn't help but think, *Jesus Christ, this kid is going to get me sent to prison.*

—Shh! Pierce said, but Jesse only looked at him, his eyes gleaming. He held up a little knickknack knight, holding its sword aloft.

—This is so awesome! Jesse said. Can you believe this?

Still, all that plunder they'd gathered was as nothing compared to the treasures he was finding in Pierce's old bedroom. Jesse's eyes were wide with excitement and greed. A shoebox full of plastic dinosaurs and farm animals, another of Matchbox cars, yet another with plastic robot dolls that Pierce and his brother had both loved. It was hard to believe that all of it was still here, Pierce thought, untouched for years, and of course he couldn't help but feel kind of sad to see it all spread out once again in the open air.

Back in the day, they had been a pretty nice little family—Pierce, his brother, and his father—and actually, when you thought about it, it didn't make sense that they hadn't turned out better. Pierce's dad had been a housepainter by trade, which meant that he could arrange his schedule to be around whenever they needed him. He was always taking them to school in the morning, or picking them up after basketball practice, or making dinner so they could eat together, the three of them. He didn't make any kind of big mistake that Pierce could remember, he didn't do anything wrong, but the kind of familial attachment that you read about or see on TV, that didn't stick. For whatever reason, they just didn't love him that much. When he had died, Pierce and his brother had both gone on with their lives—Pierce's brother was in Seattle, managing a restaurant, and Pierce himself had quit his job as a bartender to spend more time with Jesse's mother and her meth lab in southern Michigan. It was impossible to take time off for a funeral, too expensive and too far away and so on.

The cremation ashes arrived by parcel service a few weeks after his death, and one Sunday afternoon not long later, stoned and feeling kind of ceremonial, Pierce took them out on a boat and poured them into Lake Erie. He peered down at the surface of the lake as the ashes soaked up the dark-green water and slowly dissolved. That was it. There were a couple of exchanges of emails, but, as it turned out, neither Pierce nor his brother ever managed to get back to St. Dismas to clean out the house and put all their things to rest. There wasn't anything of value in there, and even the property wasn't worth the cost of the upkeep and yearly property taxes.

So mostly their home was still here, just as they left it, a delinquent house that maybe the county owned now—Pierce didn't know for sure. Maybe nobody owned it now, and it was just going to melt into rot and ruin and vanish into the soil.

Out in the garage, Pierce found the shovel neatly stored among the tools where it had always been, and he took it out into the backyard to look for a place where possibly a hole could be dug. The garden was high with weeds, and flocks of grasshoppers flicked themselves ahead of him as he walked through the old plot. When they were growing up, Pierce's father was proud of his tomato plants. They had pumpkins, zucchini, radishes, potatoes. None left, of course, but the soil was still soft enough to dig a hole into.

.

Jesse was still sitting on the floor of Pierce's former bedroom, wearing that crown of Indian feathers, sifting through another box, and he didn't even look up as Pierce stood there in the doorway.

Jesse had found a little trunk under the bed, and Pierce guessed that the kid thought it was going to be something really special—pirate's treasure, gold doubloons and necklaces of jewels; who knows what he imagined. Pierce could picture the greedy look that Jesse's mother would get, hovering over her little Baggie full of clear, chunky meth crystals.

But when Jesse opened his treasure chest, there were only blocks. Wooden building blocks—red rectangles, blue squares, green cylinders, orange triangles. Jesse picked one up out of the trunk and examined it. Smelled it. He began to sift through the wooden pieces, thinking that there was something better underneath.

Pierce shifted a little. Of course, he knew what was in that little trunk, but he was surprised at how vividly a memory arranged itself in his mind.

He had an affection for blocks as a kid—he didn't know why. You have the soul of a carpenter, Pierce's father told him once, but his father was wrong about that, Pierce thought, as he was with most things he imagined he knew about Pierce's soul.

In fact, there hadn't been any particular artfulness or skill in the constructions Pierce made. That didn't really matter to him. Still, standing there at the edge of the room, listening to the xylophone rustle of wood as Jesse sifted his way toward the bottom of the trunk, Pierce could picture the game he used to play with them.

It was something to do with making a city, Pierce remembered. For a moment Pierce could distinctly recall the feeling of being alone in the center of this old room. Stacking blocks into skyscrapers. Clustering the skyscrapers into cities. How good it felt to be alone, stacking blocks. That's what came to him again, a kind of weight solidifying in his chest: how much he had loved to be alone—to be outside of his own life, a giant, sentient cloud looming over his imaginary city, hovering above it. There was a certain kind of blank omniscience that felt like his true self, at last.

But then his father stood in the doorway, peering in at him, and he looked up. The feeling flew up out of him like a startled pigeon.

—What are you making? Pierce's father asked. He was smiling a little, hopefully, imagining his son with the soul of a carpenter, his son the builder, the architect, but Pierce's shoulders tightened and his eyes grew flat, that joy of aloneness ruined.

—Nothing, Pierce said. His hand moved, as if innocently, and the skyscrapers came down easily, spilling over into a scattered pile of disordered shapes.

—Oops, Pierce said.

*I should just kill him*, Pierce thought. *That would be the simplest thing, if I was smart*, he thought. He imagined the gangster-type people you saw on TV; they probably would have put a bullet in the back of Jesse's head right then, while he was kneeling there, pawing through the blocks. It would solve a lot of future complications.

Jesse must have heard the car start, because he came running out of the house just as Pierce was turning out of the driveway. Pierce had nearly forgotten the sort of dust plume that a car pulls up on those old dirt roads, and he could see Jesse in a cloud behind him, waving his arms.

—Hey, Jesse was yelling. Dad! Pierce! Come back!

It was the kind of devotion that Pierce's father would have been moved by. The kind of devotion he had deserved. How Pierce's father's heart would have broken, to see one of his sons wailing with sorrow, tears streaming, calling after him as he drove down the driveway.

There was about five miles of dirt road up ahead before Pierce got to two-lane blacktop, and then another twenty miles or so to the next town, another grain elevator tower rising up out of the prairie, with a little scattering of little houses around it, and then eventually the interstate and some cities and something. He could picture himself from above, from a distance. The landscape a series of geometric blocks. His car no bigger than a flea, and Jesse even smaller, running and shrinking, running and shrinking. ◄

# John Cheever

# Reunion

The last time I saw my father was in Grand Central Station. I was going from my grandmother's in the Adirondacks to a cottage on the Cape that my mother had rented, and I wrote my father that I would be in New York between trains for an hour and a half, and asked if we could have lunch together. His secretary wrote to say that he would meet me at the information booth at noon, and at twelve o'clock sharp I saw him coming through the crowd. He was a stranger to me—my mother divorced him three years ago and I hadn't been with him since—but as soon as I saw him I felt that he was my father, my flesh and blood, my future and my doom. I knew that when I was grown I would be something like him; I would have to plan my campaigns within his limitations. He was a big, good-looking man, and I was terribly happy to see him again. He struck me on the back and shook my hand. "Hi, Charlie," he said. "Hi, boy. I'd like to take you up to my club, but it's in the Sixties, and if you have to catch an early train I guess we'd better get something to eat around here." He put his arm around me, and I smelled my father the way my mother sniffs a rose. It was a rich compound of whiskey, after-shave lotion, shoe polish, woolens, and the rankness of a mature male. I hoped that someone would see us together. I wished that we could be photographed. I wanted some record of our having been together.

We went out of the station and up a side street to a restaurant. It was still early, and the place was empty. The bartender was quarreling with a delivery boy, and there was one very old waiter in a red coat down by the kitchen door. We sat down, and my father hailed the waiter in a loud voice. *"Kellner!"* he shouted. *"Garçon! Cameriere! You!"* His boisterousness in the empty restaurant seemed out of place. "Could we have a little service here!" he shouted. "Chop-chop." Then he clapped his hands. This caught the waiter's attention, and he shuffled over to our table.

"Were you clapping your hands at me?" he asked.

"Calm down, calm down, *sommelier*," my father said. "If it isn't too much to ask of you—if it wouldn't be too much above and beyond the call of duty, we would like a couple of Beefeater Gibsons."

"I don't like to be clapped at," the waiter said.

"I should have brought my whistle," my father said. "I have a whistle that is audible only to the ears of old waiters. Now, take out your little pad and your little pencil and see if you can get this straight: two Beefeater Gibsons. Repeat after me: two Beefeater Gibsons."

"I think you'd better go somewhere else," the waiter said quietly,

"That," said my father, "is one of the most brilliant suggestions I have ever heard. Come on, Charlie, let's get the hell out of here."

I followed my father out of that restaurant into another. He was not so boisterous this time. Our drinks came, and he cross-questioned me about the baseball season. He then struck the edge of his empty glass with his knife and began shouting again. *"Garçon! Kellner! Cameriere! You!* Could we trouble you to bring us two more of the same."

"How old is the boy?" the waiter asked.

"That," my father said, "is none of your God-damned business."

"I'm sorry, sir," the waiter said, "but I won't serve the boy another drink."

"Well, I have some news for you," my father said. "I have some very interesting news for you. This doesn't happen to be the only restaurant in New York. They've opened another on the corner. Come on, Charlie."

He paid the bill, and I followed him out of that restaurant into another. Here the waiters wore pink jackets like hunting coats, and there was a lot of horse tack on the walls. We sat down, and my father began to shout again. "Master of the hounds! Tallyhoo and all that sort of thing. We'd like a little something in the way of a stirrup cup. Namely, two Bibson Geefeaters."

"Two Bibson Geefeaters?" the waiter asked, smiling.

"You know damned well what I want," my father said angrily. "I want two Beefeater Gibsons, and make it snappy. Things have changed in jolly old England. So my friend the duke tells me. Let's see what England can produce in the way of a cocktail."

"This isn't England," the waiter said.

"Don't argue with me," my father said. "Just do as you're told."

"I just thought you might like to know where you are," the waiter said.

"If there is one thing I cannot tolerate," my father said, "it is an impudent domestic. Come on, Charlie."

The fourth place we went to was Italian. *"Buon giorno,"* my father said. *"Per favore, possiamo avere due cocktail americani, forti, forti. Molto gin, poco vermut."*

"I don't understand Italian," the waiter said.

"Oh, come off it," my father said. "You understand Italian, and you know damned well you do. *Vogliamo due cocktail americani. Subito."*

The waiter left us and spoke with the captain, who came over to our table and said, "I'm sorry, sir, but this table is reserved."

"All right," my father said. "Get us another table."

"All the tables are reserved," the captain said.

"I get it," my father said. "You don't desire our patronage. Is that it? Well, the hell with you. *Vada all' inferno.* Let's go, Charlie."

"I have to get my train," I said.

"I'm sorry, sonny," my father said. "I'm terribly sorry." He put his arm around me and pressed me against him. "I'll walk you back to the station. If there had only been time to go up to my club."

"That's all right, Daddy," I said.

"I'll get you a paper," he said. "I'll get you a paper to read on the train."

Then he went up to a newsstand and said, "Kind sir, will you be good enough to favor me with one of your God-damned, no-good, ten-cent afternoon papers?" The clerk turned away from him and stared at a magazine cover. "Is it asking too much, kind sir," my father said, "is it asking too much for you to sell me one of your disgusting specimens of yellow journalism?"

"I have to go, Daddy," I said. "It's late."

"Now, just wait a second, sonny," he said. "Just wait a second. I want to get a rise out of this chap."

"Goodbye, Daddy," I said, and I went down the stairs and got my train, and that was the last time I saw my father. ◀

# Allegra Goodman

# La Vita Nuova

The day her fiancé left, Amanda went walking in the Colonial cemetery off Garden Street. The gravestones were so worn that she could hardly read them. They were melting away into the weedy grass. You are a very dark person, her fiancé had said.

She walked home and sat in her half-empty closet. Her vintage nineteen-fifties wedding dress hung in clear asphyxiating plastic printed "NOT A TOY."

She took the dress to work. She hooked the hanger onto a grab bar on the T and the dress rustled and swayed. When she got out at Harvard Square, the guy who played guitar near the turnstiles called, "Congratulations."

Work was at the Garden School, where Amanda taught art, including theatre, puppets, storytelling, drumming, dance, and now fabric painting, She spread the white satin gown on the art-room floor. Two girls glued pink feathers all along the hem. Others brushed the skirt with green and purple. A boy named Nathaniel dipped his hand in red paint and left his little handprint on the bodice as though the dress were an Indian pony. At lunchtime, the principal asked Amanda to step into her office.

You are like living with a dark cloud, Amanda's fiancé had told her when he left. You're always sad.

I'm sad now, Amanda had said.

The principal told Amanda that, for an educator, boundaries were an issue. "Your personal life," said the principal, "is not an appropriate art project for first grade. Your classroom," said the principal, "is not an appropriate forum for your relationships. Let's pack up the wedding dress."

"It's still wet," Amanda said.

Her mother could not believe it. She had just sent out all the invitations. Her father swore he'd kill the son of a bitch. They both asked how this could have happened, but they remembered that they had had doubts all along. Her sister Lissa said she could not imagine what Amanda was going through. She must feel so terrible. Was Amanda going to have to write to everyone on the guest list? Like a card or something? She'd have to tell everybody, wouldn't she?

I waited all this time because I didn't want to hurt you, Amanda's fiancé had said.

After school, she went for a drink with the old blond gym teacher, Patsy. They went to a bar called Cambridge Common and ordered gin-and-tonics. Patsy said, "Eventually, you're going to realize that this is a blessing in disguise."

"We had too many differences," said Amanda.

Patsy lifted her glass. "There you go."

"For example, I loved him and he didn't love me."

"Don't be surprised," said Patsy, "if he immediately marries someone else. Guys like that immediately marry someone else."

"Why?" Amanda asked.

Patsy sighed. "If I knew that, I'd be teaching at Harvard, not teaching the professors' kids."

Amanda tried writing a card or something. She wrote that she and her fiancé had decided not to marry. Then she wrote that her fiancé had decided not to marry her. She said that she was sorry for any inconvenience. She added that she would appreciate gifts anyway.

Her parents told her not to send the card. They said that they were coming up for a week. She said that they couldn't come, because she was painting her apartment. She did not paint the apartment.

In the winter, Amanda cut her hair short like a boy's.

"Oh, your hair," said Patsy. "Your beautiful curls."

In the spring, the principal told Amanda that, regretfully, she was not being renewed for the following year, because the art program at the Garden School was moving in a different direction.

In the summer, Amanda's fiancé married someone else.

When school ended, Amanda took a job babysitting Nathaniel, the boy with the red handprint. Nathaniel's mother asked for stimulating activities, projects, science. No TV. Nathaniel's father didn't ask for anything.

Their first day together, Amanda asked Nathaniel, "What do you want to do?"

"Nothing."

She said, "You read my mind."

They ate chocolate mice at Burdick's and then they stood in front of the Harvard Coop and listened to Peruvian musicians. They explored the cemetery, and Amanda told Nathaniel that the gravestones were dragons' teeth. They walked down to the river and she said, "If you trace the river all the way to the beginning, you'll find a magic cave." They took the T to Boston and stood in line for the swan boats in the Public Garden. She said, "At night, these boats turn into real swans."

Nathaniel said, "You have a great imagination."

His mother lived in a Victorian house on Buckingham Street. She worked at the Media Lab at M.I.T. and she had deadlines. The house had a garden full of flowers, but Nathaniel didn't play there, because you couldn't really dig.

His father lived in an upside-down town house on Chauncy Street. The bedrooms were on the bottom floors, and the kitchen and living room on top. His father was writing a book and he came home late.

Amanda and Nathaniel had pizza delivered to Chauncy Street and watched Charlie Chaplin movies from Hollywood Express. Sometimes they spread a sheet over the couch and ate a big bowl of popcorn.

It's hard to be with you, her fiancé had said. I feel like I'm suffocating.

Open a window, Amanda had said.

When the movie was done, Amanda gathered the sheet and stepped onto the balcony, where she shook out the crumbs.

Amanda and Nathaniel had playdates with his friends at Walden Pond. They went canoeing on the Charles, and Nathaniel dropped his paddle in the water. Amanda almost tipped the boat, trying to fish it out. They wrote a book about pirates. Nathaniel told the stories and Amanda typed them on the computer in his father's study. "Aarrr, matey," she typed, "I'm stuck on a ship."

When his father stayed out past Nathaniel's bedtime, Amanda tucked Nathaniel in, and then she read books in the study. The books were about American history. She read only a few pages of each, so she didn't learn anything.

If you ever stopped to listen, her fiancé had said, then you would understand.

She stood on a chair and pulled out some small paperbacks from the top shelf. Dante, *The Divine Comedy*, in a new translation. Boccaccio, *The Decameron*, Chaucer's *Canterbury Tales*, complete and unabridged. Dante again, *La Vita Nuova*.

"La Vita Nuova" explained how to become a great poet. The secret was to fall in love with a perfect girl but never speak to her. You should weep instead. You should pretend that you love someone else. You should write sonnets in three parts. Your perfect girl should die.

Amanda's mother said, "You have your whole life ahead of you."

She fell asleep on the couch waiting for Nathaniel's father to come home. When she woke up, she saw him kneeling in front of her. She said, "What's wrong?"

He said, "Nothing's wrong. I'm sorry. I didn't want to wake you."

But he did wake her. She went home and stayed awake all night.

"Let's go somewhere," she told Nathaniel the next day.

"Where?"

"Far away."

They took the T to Ashmont, at the end of the Red Line. They sat together in the rattling car and talked about doughnuts.

"I like cinnamon doughnuts, but they make me cough," Nathaniel said.

She slept lightly. She dreamed she was walking with Nathaniel in a pine forest. She was telling him not to step on the dead hummingbirds. The birds were sapphire-throated, brilliant blue. She stole *La Vita Nuova*. It was just a paperback.

Her sister called to check in. Her friend Jamie said she knew someone she'd like Amanda to meet. Amanda said, "Soon."

Jamie said, "What exactly are you waiting for?"

Nathaniel's father pretended not to look at her. Amanda pretended not to notice his dark eyes.

"The question is what you're going to do in September," Amanda's mother told her on the phone.

"The question is what you're going to do with your life," her father said.

Dante wrote, "O you who on the road of Love pass by, / Attend and see / If any grief there be as heavy as mine."

"When was the last time you painted anything?" her mother asked. "Apart from your apartment?"

Her father said, "I paid for Yale."

All day, Amanda and Nathaniel studied the red ants of Buckingham Street. They experimented with cake crumbs and observed the ants change course to eat them. Nathaniel considered becoming an entomologist when he grew up.

The next day, he decided to open his own ice-cream store.

They biked to Christina's, in Inman Square. Nathaniel pedalled in front on his little bike. Amanda pedalled behind on her big bike and watched for cars.

At Christina's, Nathaniel could read almost all the flavors on the board: adzuki bean, black raspberry, burnt sugar, chocolate banana, chocolate orange, cardamom. Nathaniel said, "I'll have vanilla." They sat in front near the bulletin board with ads for guitar lessons, tutoring, transcendental meditation.

"What's an egg donor?" Nathaniel said.

I want to be with you for the rest of my life, her fiancé had told her once. You are my best friend, he had written on her birthday card. You make me smile, you make me laugh. "Love weeps," Dante wrote.

"Could I have a quarter for a gumball?" Nathaniel asked Amanda.

"You just had ice cream," she said.

"Please."

"No! You just had ice cream. You don't need candy."

"Please, please, please," he said.

"You're lovely," Nathaniel's father whispered to Amanda late that night. She was just leaving, and he'd opened the door for her.

"You're not supposed to say that," Amanda whispered back. "You're supposed to write a sonnet."

Nathaniel said that he knew what to do when you were upset. She said, "Tell me, Nathaniel."

He said, "Go to the zoo."

Nathaniel studied the train schedule. They took the Orange Line to Ruggles Station and then the No. 22 bus to the Franklin Park Zoo. They watched orangutans sitting on their haunches, shredding newspapers, one page at a time. They climbed up on viewing platforms to observe the giraffes. They ran down every path. They looked at snakes. They went to the little barnyard and a goat frightened Nathaniel. Amanda said the goat was just curious. She said, "Goats wouldn't eat you."

Nathaniel fell asleep on the T on the way home. He leaned against Amanda and closed his eyes. The woman sitting next to Amanda said, "He's beautiful."

Amanda's friend Jamie had a party in Somerville. The wine was terrible. The friend that Jamie wanted Amanda to meet was drunk. Amanda got drunk, too, but it didn't help.

She was late to work the next day. She found Nathaniel waiting on his mother's porch. "I thought you were sick," he said.

"I was," she told him.

They walked to Harvard Square and watched the street magicians. They went to Le's and shared vegetarian summer rolls and Thai iced tea.

"This tastes like orange chalk," Nathaniel said.

They went to a store called Little Russia and looked at the lacquered dolls there. "See, they come apart," Amanda told Nathaniel. "You pop open this lady, and inside there's another, and another, and another."

"Do not touch, please," the saleslady told them.

They walked down to the river and sat on the grass under a tree and talked about their favorite dogs.

"Labradoodle," Amanda said.

Nathaniel giggled. "No, Schnoodle."

"Golden Strudel."

Nathaniel said, "Is that the kind you had when you were young?"

She dreamed that she was a Russian doll. Inside her was a smaller version of herself, and inside that an even smaller version.

She ordered a set of blank wooden dolls online and began painting them. She covered the dolls with white primer. Then she painted them with acrylics and her finest brushes.

First, a toddler only an inch high, in a gingham bathing suit.

Second, a fingerling schoolgirl, wearing glasses.

Third, an art student, with a portfolio under her arm.

Fourth, a bride in white with long flowing hair.

Fifth, a babysitter in sandals and sundress. She painted Nathaniel standing in front of her in his gecko T-shirt and blue shorts. He stood waist high, with her painted hands on his shoulders.

When the paint was dry, she covered each doll with clear gloss. After that coat dried, she glossed each doll again until the reds were as bright as candy apples, the blues sparkled, and every color looked good enough to eat.

She bought another set of blanks and began all over. She stayed up late each night painting.

"Why are you so sleepy?" Nathaniel asked her in the afternoons.

In the mornings, his mother asked her, "Why are you always late?"

She fell asleep with Nathaniel at eight o'clock. She curled up next to him in his captain's bed and woke when his father came in and touched her cheek.

"I was wondering if you could come to the Cape with us," Nathaniel's father said as they tiptoed out into the hall.

She shook her head.

"Just for a few days in August."

His voice was low. His eyes were almost pleading. You are so beautiful, her fiancé had said.

She painted Nathaniel's father on a set of Russian dolls.

First, she painted a toddler in a romper.

Second, she painted a boy in a little Catholic-school uniform with short pants and a tie.

Third, she painted a bridegroom, dashing in a dark suit with white stephanotis for his boutonnière.

Fourth, she painted a new father, with a baby Nathaniel in his arms.

Fifth, she painted a gray-haired man in reading glasses. She painted Nathaniel's father older than he was, and stouter. Not handsome, as he was in real life, but grandfatherly, with a belly following the contours of the bell-shaped doll.

As before, she coated each painted doll with clear gloss until the colors gleamed. As before, she made each doll a perfect jewel-like object, but she spent the most time on the biggest, oldest doll.

After that, she bought more blanks and painted more sets: people she knew, people she didn't know. People she met. Portraits in series, five dolls each. She painted Patsy, blonder and blonder in each incarnation. She painted her fiancé as a boy, as an athlete, as a law student, as a paunchy bald guy, as a decrepit old man. She didn't kill him, but she aged him.

She lined up the dolls and photographed them. She thought about fellowships. She imagined group shows, solo shows. Refusing interviews.

She took Nathaniel to swimming lessons. She went down to the harbor with him and they threw popcorn to seagulls that caught the kernels in midair.

Nathaniel had his seventh-birthday party on Castle Island. He and his friends built a walled city of sandcastles with a moat. Nathaniel was the architect. Amanda was his assistant. His father was the photographer. His mother served the cake.

At the end of the party, Amanda gathered the presents. Nathaniel was leaving for the Cape with his father, and then his mother was going to take him to the Vineyard for Labor Day weekend. Nathaniel said, "When we come back, it will be September."

She said, "You're right."

He said, "Could you come with me?"

Amanda said, "I can't. I'm painting my apartment."

He said, "What color?"

She said, "Actually, I'm moving."

"Moving away?"

She told him, "You can talk to me on the phone."

Nathaniel started to cry.

His mother said, "Honey!"

He held on to Amanda and cried. "Why can't you be my babysitter anymore?"

"I'm going to New York," she said.

"Why?"

Because your mother doesn't like me, she told him silently. Because your father wants to sleep with me. Because the only reason I came to Boston was my fiancé. Because the question is what I'm going to do with my life. But all she said aloud was "That's where I'm from."

She knelt down and gave him a map she'd drawn. She'd singed the edges of the parchment to make it look old.

The map showed the cave at the source of the Charles River, the swan boats flying away, the chocolate mice at Burdick's. Christina's Ice Cream, Ashmont, the cemetery with dragons' teeth.

Nathaniel's mother said, "This is gorgeous."

Nathaniel's father said, "You're really very talented."

Nathaniel said that he didn't want a map. He said that he would rip it up.

His mother said, "Nathaniel, is that any way to treat a gift?"

His father said, "Come here."

Nathaniel tore a big piece out of the map. He screamed at his parents, "I don't want you!"

"He's tired," Nathaniel's mother told Amanda. "He's exhausted. Too much excitement in one day."

"I'm not tired!" Nathaniel screamed, and he wouldn't let go of Amanda. He held on to her, half strangling her with his arms around her neck.

"Look, Nathaniel—" his father began.

His mother interrupted. "You're making it worse!"

Nathaniel was crying harder. He cried with his whole body. No one could get him to stop.

Amanda closed her eyes. She said she was sorry. She said, "Please stop." Finally, she rocked him in her arms and said, "I know. I know." ◄

## Ursula Hegi

# Doves

Francine is having a shy day, the kind of day that makes you feel sad when the elevator man says good afternoon, the kind of day that makes you want to buy two doves.

Her raincoat pulled close around herself, Francine walks the twelve blocks to Portland Pet And Plant. She heads past the African violets, past the jade plants and fig trees, past the schnauzers and poodles, past the hamsters and turtles, past the gaudy parrot in the center cage who shrieks: "Oh amigo, oh amigo . . ."

What Francine wants are doves of such a smooth gray that they don't hurt your eyes. With doves like that you don't have to worry about being too quiet.

They make soft clucking sounds deep inside their throats and wait for you to notice them instead of clamoring for your attention.

Six of them perch on the bars in the tall cage near the wall, two white with brownish speckles, the others a deep gray tinged with purple. Above the cage hangs a sign: Ring Neck Doves $7.99. Doves like that won't need much; they'll turn their heads toward the door when you push the key into the lock late in the afternoon and wait for you to notice them instead of clamoring for your attention.

"Oh amigo, oh amigo . . . ," screeches the parrot. Francine chooses the two smallest gray doves and carries them from the store in white cardboard boxes that look like Chinese takeout containers with air holes. The afternoon has the texture of damp newspaper, but Francine feels light as she walks back to her apartment.

In her kitchen she sets the boxes on top of her counter, opens the tops, and waits for the doves to fly out and roost on the plastic bar where she hangs her kitchen towels. But they crouch inside the white cardboard as if waiting for her to lift them out.

She switches on the radio to the station where she always keeps it, public radio, but instead of Tuesday night opera, a man is asking for donations. Francine has already sent in her contribution, and she doesn't like it when the man says, "None of you would think of going into a store and taking something off the shelves, but you listen to public radio without paying . . ." The doves move their wing feathers forward and pull their heads into their necks as if trying to shield themselves from the fund-raising voice.

Francine turns the dial past rock stations and commercials. At the gaudy twang of a country-western song, the doves raise their heads and peer from the boxes. Their beaks turn to one side, then to the other, completing a nearly full circle. Low velvet sounds rise from their throats. Francine has never listened to country-westerns; she's considered them tacky, but when the husky voice of a woman sings of wanting back the lover who hurt her so, she tilts her head to the side and croons along with the doves.

Before she leaves for her job at K-Mart the next morning, Francine pulls the radio next to the kitchen sink and turns it on for the doves. They sit in the left side of her double sink which she has lined with yellow towels, their claws curved around folds of fabric, their eyes on the flickering light of the tuner that still glows on the country-western station. When she returns after working all day in the footwear department, they swivel their heads toward her and then back to the radio as if they'd been practicing that movement all day.

At K-Mart she finds that more people leave their shoes. It used to be just once or twice a week that she'd discover a worn pair of shoes half pushed under the racks by someone who's walked from the store with stolen footwear. But now she sees them almost every day—sneakers with torn insoles, pumps with imitation leather peeling from the high heels, work shoes with busted seams—as if a legion of shoe thieves had descended on Portland.

Francine keeps the discarded shoes in the store's lost and found crate out back, though no one has ever tried to claim them. But some are still good enough to donate to Goodwill. She murmurs to the doves about the shoes while she refills their water and sprinkles birdseed into the porcelain soap dish. Coming home to them has become familiar. So have the songs of lost love that welcome her every evening. A few times she tried to return to her old station, but as soon as the doves grew listless, she moved the tuner back. And lately she hasn't felt like changing it at all. She knows some of the lines now, knows how the songs end.

Francine has a subscription to the opera, and after feeding the doves, she takes a bubble bath and puts on her black dress. In the back of the cab, she holds her purse with both hands in her lap. Sitting in the darkened balcony, she feels invisible as she listens to *La Traviata*, one of her favorite operas. For the first time it comes to her that it, too, is about lost love and broken hearts.

In the swell of bodies that shifts from the opera house, Francine walks into the mild November night, leaving behind the string of waiting taxicabs, the expensive restaurants across from the opera house, the stores and the bus station, the fast-food places and bars.

A young couple saunters from the Blue Moon Tavern hand in hand, steeped in amber light and the sad lyrics of a slow-moving song for that instant before the door closes again. Francine curves her fingers around the doorhandle, pulls it open, and steps into the smoky light as if she were a woman with red boots who had someone waiting for her. Below the Michelob clock, on the platform, two men play guitars and sing of betrayed love.

On the bar stool, her black dress rides up to her knees. She draws her shoulders around herself and orders a fuzzy navel, a drink she remembers from a late night movie. The summer taste of apricots and oranges soothes her limbs and makes her ease into the space her body fills.

A lean-hipped man with a cowboy hat asks Francine to dance, and as she sways in his arms on the floor that's spun of sawdust and boot prints, she becomes the woman in all the songs that the men on the platform sing about, the woman who leaves them, the woman who keeps breaking their hearts. ◀

## Pam Houston

# Symphony

Sometimes life is ridiculously simple. I lost fifteen pounds and the men want me again. I can see it in the way they follow my movements, not just with their eyes but with their whole bodies, the way they lean into me until they almost topple over, the way they always seem to have itches on the back of their necks. And I'll admit this: I am collecting them like gold-plated sugar spoons, one from every state.

This is a difficult story to tell because what's right about what I have to say is only as wide as a tightrope, and what's wrong about it yawns wide, beckoning, on either side. I have always said I have no narcotic, smiling sadly at stories of ruined lives, safely remote from the twelve-step program and little red leather booklets that say "One Day at a Time." But there is something so sweet about the first kiss, the first surrender that, like the words "I want you," can never mean precisely the same thing again. It is delicious and addicting. It is, I'm guessing, the most delicious thing of all.

There are a few men who matter, and by writing them down in this story I can make them seem like they have an order, or a sequence, or a priority, because those are the kinds of choices that language forces upon us, but language can't touch the joyful and slightly disconcerting feeling of being very much in love, but not knowing exactly with whom.

First I will tell you about Phillip, who is vast and dangerous, his desires uncontainable and huge. He is far too talented, a grown-up tragedy of a gifted child, massively in demand. He dances, he weaves, he writes a letter that could wring light from a black hole. He has mined gold in the Yukon, bonefished in Belize. He has crossed Iceland on a dogsled, he is the smartest man that all his friends know. His apartment smells like wheat bread, cooling. His body smells like spice. Sensitive and scared scared scared of never becoming a father, he lives in New York City and is very careful about his space. It is easy to confuse what he has learned to do in bed for love or passion or art, but he is simply a master craftsman, and very proud of his good work.

Christopher is innocent. Very young and wide-open. He's had good mothering and no father to make him afraid to talk about his heart. In Nevada he holds hands with middle-aged women while the underground tests explode beneath them. He studies marine biology, acting, and poetry, and is not yet quite aware of his classic good looks. Soon someone will tell him, but it won't be me. A few years ago he said in a few more years he'd be old enough for me, and in a few more years, it will be true. For now we are friends and I tell him my system, how I have learned to get what I want from many sources, and none. He says this: You are a complicated woman. Even when you say you don't want anything, you want more than that.

I have a dream in which a man becomes a wolf. He is sleeping, cocooned, and when he stretches and breaks the parchment there are tufts of hair across his back and shoulders, and on the backs of his hands. It is Christopher, I suspect, though I can't see his face. When I wake up I am in Phillip's bed. My back is to his side and yet we are touching at all the pressure points. In the predawn I can see the line of electricity we make, a glow like neon, the curve of a wooden instrument. As I wake, "Symphony" is the first word that forms in my head.

Jonathan came here from the Okavango Delta in Botswana; he's tall and hairy and clever and strong. In my living room I watch him reach inside his shirt and scratch his shoulder. It is a savage movement, rangy and impatient, lazy too, and without a bit of self-consciousness. He is not altogether human. He has spent the last three years in the bush. I cook him T-bone steaks because he says he won't eat complicated food. He is skeptical of the hibachi, of the barely glowing coals. Where he comes from, they cook everything with fire. He says things against my ear, the names of places: Makgadikgadi Pans, Nxamaseri, Mpandamatenga, Gabarone. Say these words out loud and see what happens to you. Mosi-oa-Toenja, "The Smoke That Thunders." Look at the pictures: a rank of impalas slaking their thirst, giraffes, their necks entwined, a young bull elephant rising from the Chobe River. When I am with Jonathan I have this thought which delights and frightens me: It has been the animals that have attracted me all along. Not the cowboys, but the horses that carried them. Not the hunters, but the caribou and the bighorn. Not Jonathan, in his infinite loveliness, but the hippos, the kudu, and the big African cats. You fall in love with a man's animal spirit, Jonathan tells me, and then when he speaks like a human being, you don't know who he is.

There's one man I won't talk about, not because he is married, but because he is sacred. When he writes love letters to me he addresses them "my dear" and signs them with the first letter of his first name and one long black line. We have only made love one time. I will tell you only the one thing that must be told: After the only part of him I will ever hold collapsed inside me he said, "You are so incredibly gentle." It was the closest I have ever come to touching true love.

Another dream: I am in the house of my childhood, and I see myself, at age five, at the breakfast table; pancakes and sausage, my father in his tennis whites. The me that is dreaming, the older me, kneels down and holds out her arms waiting for the younger me to come and be embraced. Jonathan's arms twitch around me and I am suddenly awake inside a body, inside a world where it has become impossible to kneel down and hold out my arms. Still sleeping, Jonathan pulls my hand across his shoulder, and presses it hard against his face.

I'm afraid of what you might be thinking. That I am a certain kind of person, and that you are the kind of person who knows more about my story than me. But you should know this: I could love any one of them, in an instant and with every piece of my heart, but none of them nor the world will allow it, and so I move between them, on snowy highways and crowded airplanes. I was in New York this morning. I woke up in Phillip's bed. Come here, he's in my hair. You can smell him. ◀

# Jamaica Kincaid

## Girl

Wash the white clothes on Monday and put them on the stone heap; wash the color clothes on Tuesday and put them on the clothesline to dry; don't walk barehead in the hot sun; cook pumpkin fritters in very hot sweet oil; soak your little cloths right after you take them off; when buying cotton to make yourself a nice blouse, be sure that it doesn't have gum on it, because that way it won't hold up well after a wash; soak salt fish overnight before you cook it; is it true that you sing benna[1] in Sunday school?; always eat your food in such a way that it won't turn someone else's stomach; on Sundays try to walk like a lady and not like the slut you are so bent on becoming; don't sing benna in Sunday school; you mustn't speak to wharf-rat boys, not even to give directions; don't eat fruits on the street—flies will follow you; *but I don't sing benna on Sundays at all and never in Sunday school;* this is how to sew on a button; this is how to make a button-hole for the button you have just sewed on; this is how to hem a dress when you see the hem coming down and so to prevent yourself from looking like the slut I know you are so bent on becoming; this is how you iron your father's khaki shirt so that it doesn't have a crease; this is how you iron your father's khaki pants so that they don't have a crease; this is how you grow okra—far from the house, because okra tree harbors red ants; when you are growing dasheen[2], make sure it gets plenty of water or else it makes your throat itch when you are eating it; this is how you sweep a corner; this is how you sweep a whole house; this is how you sweep a yard; this is how you smile to someone you don't like too much; this is how you smile to someone you don't like at all; this is how you smile to someone you like completely; this is how you set a table for tea; this is how you set a table for dinner; this is how you set a table for dinner with an important guest; this is how you set a table for lunch; this is how you set a table for breakfast; this is how to behave in the presence of men who don't know you very well, and this way they won't recognize immediately the slut I have warned you against becoming; be sure to wash every day, even if it is with your own spit; don't squat down to play marbles—you are not a boy, you know; don't pick people's flowers—you might catch something; don't throw stones at blackbirds, because it might not be a blackbird at all; this is how to make a bread pudding; this is how to make doukona[3]; this is how to make pepper pot; this is how to make a good medicine for a cold; this is how to make a good medicine to throw away a child before

---

1. **benna:** Calypso music
2. **dasheen:** an edible root
3. **doukona:** a sweet and spicy pudding

it even becomes a child; this is how to catch a fish; this is how to throw back a fish you don't like, and that way something bad won't fall on you; this is how to bully a man; this is how a man bullies you; this is how to love a man, and if this doesn't work there are other ways, and if they don't work don't feel too bad about giving up; this is how to spit up in the air if you feel like it, and this is how to move quick so that it doesn't fall on you; this is how to make ends meet; always squeeze bread to make sure it's fresh; *but what if the baker won't let me feel the bread?;* you mean to say that after all you are really going to be the kind of woman who the baker won't let near the bread? ◀

# Lorrie Moore

# How

*So all things limp together for the only possible.*
*—Beckett*
Murphy

Begin by meeting him in a class, in a bar, at a rummage sale. Maybe he teaches sixth grade. Manages a hardware store. Foreman at a carton factory. He will be a good dancer. He will have perfectly cut hair. He will laugh at your jokes.

A week, a month, a year. Feel discovered, comforted, needed loved, and start sometimes, somehow, to feel bored. When sad or confused, walk uptown to the movies. Buy popcorn. These things come and go. A week, a month, a year.

Make attempts at a less restrictive arrangement. Watch them sputter and deflate like balloons. He will ask you to move in. Do so hesitantly, with ambivalence. Clarify: rents are high, nothing long-range, love and all that, hon, but it's footloose. Lay out the rules with much elocution. Stress openness, non-exclusivity. Make room in his closet, but don't rearrange the furniture.

And yet from time to time you will gaze at his face or his hands and want nothing but him. You will feel passing waves of dependency, devotion, and sentimentality. A week, a month, a year, and he has become your family. Let's say your real mother is a witch. Your father a warlock. Your brothers twin hunchbacks of Notre Dame. They all live in a cave together somewhere.

His name means savior. He rolls into your arms like Ozzie and Harriet, the whole Nelson genealogy. He is living rooms and turkey and mantels and Vicks, a nip at the collarbone and you do a slow syrup sink into those arms like a hearth, into those living rooms, well hello Mary Lou.

Say you work in an office but you have bigger plans. He wants to go with you. He wants to be what it is that you want to be. Say you're an aspiring architect. Playwright. Painter. He shows you his sketches. They are awful. What do you think?

Put on some jazz. Take off your clothes. Carefully. It is a craft. He will lie on the floor naked, watching, his arms crossed behind his head. Shirt: brush on snare, steady. Skirt: the desultory talk of piano keys, rocking slow, rambling. Dance together in the dark though it is only afternoon.

Go to a wedding. His relatives. Everyone will compare weight losses and gains. Maiden cousins will be said to have fattened embarrassingly. His mother will be a bookkeeper or a dental hygienist. She will introduce you as his *girl*. Try not to protest. They will have heard a lot about you. Uncles will take him aside and query, What is keeping you, boy? Uncomfortable, everywhere, women in stiff blue taffeta will eye you pitifully, then look quickly away. Everyone will polka. Someone will flash a fifty to dance with the bride and she will hike up her gown and flash back: freshly shaven legs, a wide rolled-out-barrel of a grin. Feel spared. Thought you two'd be doing this by now, you will hear again. Smile. Shrug. Shuffle back for more potato salad.

It hits you more insistently. A restlessness. A virus of discontent. When you pass other men in the street, smile and stare them straight in the eye, straight in the belt buckle.

Somehow—in a restaurant or a store—meet an actor. From Vassar or Yale. He can quote Coriolanus's mother. This will seem good. Sleep with him once and ride home at 5 A.M. crying in a taxicab. Or: don't sleep with him. Kiss him good night at Union Square and run for your life.

Back at home, days later, feel cranky and tired. Sit on the couch and tell him he's stupid. That you bet he doesn't know who Coriolanus is. That since you moved in you've noticed he rarely reads. He will give you a hurt, hungry-to-learn look, with his James Cagney eyes. He will try to kiss you. Turn your head. Feel suffocated.

When he climbs onto the covers, naked and hot for you, unleash your irritation in short staccato blasts. Show him your book. Your aspirin. Your clock on the table reading 12:45. He will flop back over to his side of the bed, exasperated. Maybe he'll say something like: Christ, what's wrong? Maybe he won't. If he spends too long in the bathroom, don't ask questions.

The touchiest point will always be this: he craves a family, a neat nest of human bowls; he wants to have your children. On the street he pats their heads. In the supermarket they gather around him by the produce. They form a tight little cluster of cheeks and smiles and hopes. They look like grapes.

It will all be for you, baby; reel, sway backward into the frozen foods. An unwitting sigh will escape from your lips like gas. He will begin to talk about a movie camera and children's encyclopedias, picking up size-one shoes in department stores and marveling in one high, amazed whistle. Avoid shopping together.

He will have a nephew named Bradley Bob. Or perhaps a niece named Emily who is always dressed in pink and smells of milk and powder and dirty diapers, although she is already three. At visits she will prance and squeal. She will grab his left leg like a tree trunk and not let go. She will call him nunko. He will know tricks: pulling dimes from her nose, quarters from her ears. She will shriek with glee, flapping her hands in front of her. Leg released, he will pick her up, carry her around like a prize. He is the best nunko in town.

Think about leaving. About packing a bag and slithering off, out the door.

But it is hot out there. And dry. And he can look somehow good to you, like Robert Goulet in a bathing suit.

No, it wouldn't be in summer.

Escape into books. When he asks what you're reading, hold it up without comment. The next day look across to the brown chair and you will see him reading it too. A copy from the library that morning. He has seven days. He will look over the top and wink, saying: Beat you.

He will seem to be listening to the classical music station, glancing quickly at you for approval.

At the theater he will chomp Necco wafers loudly and complain about the head in front of him.

He will ask you what *supercilious* means.

He will ask you who Coriolanus is.

He might want to know where Sardinia is located.

What's a *croissant*?

Begin to plot your getaway. Envision possibilities for civility. These are only possibilities.

A week, a month, a year: Tell him you've changed. You no longer like the same music, eat the same food. You dress differently. The two of you are incongruous together. When he tells you that he is changing too, that he loves your records, your teas, your falafel, your shoes, tell him: See, that's the problem. Endeavor to baffle.

Pace around in the kitchen and say that you are unhappy.

But I love you, he will say in his soft, bewildered way, stirring the spaghetti sauce but not you, staring into the pan as if waiting for something, a magic fish, to rise from it and say: That is always enough, why is that not always enough?

You will forget whoever it was that said never trust a thought that doesn't come while walking. But clutch at it. Apartments can shrink inward like drying ponds. You will gasp. Say: I am going for a walk. When he follows you to the door, buzzing at your side like a fly by a bleeding woman, add: *alone*. He will look surprised and hurt and you will hate him. Slam the door, out, down, hurry, it will be colder than you thought, but not far away will be a bar, smoky and dark and sticky with spilled sours. The bartender will be named Rusty or Max and he will know you. A flashy jukebox will blare Jimmy Webb. A balding, purple-shirted man to your left will try to get your attention, mouthing, singing drunkenly. Someone to your right will sniffle to the music. Blink into your drink. Hide behind your hair. Sweet green icing will be flowing down. Flowing, baby, like the Mississippi.

Next: there are medical unpleasantries. Kidneys. He will pee blood. Say you can't believe it. When he shows you later, it will be dark, the color of meat drippings. A huge invisible fist will torpedo through your gut, your face, your pounding heart.

This is no time to leave.

There will be doctor's appointments, various opinions. There is nothing conclusive, just an endless series of tests. He will have jarred urine specimens in the refrigerator among the eggs and peanut butter. Some will be in salad dressing bottles. They will be different colors: some green, some purple, some brown. Ask which is the real salad dressing. He will point it out and smile helplessly. Smile back. He will begin to laugh and so will you. Collapse. Roll. Roar together on the floor until you cannot laugh anymore. Bury your face in the crook of his neck. There will be nothing else in the world you can do. That night lie next to each other, silent, stiff, silvery-white in bed. Lie like sewing needles.

Continue to doctor-hop. Await the reports. Look at your watch. If ever you would leave him. Look at your calendar. It wouldn't be in autumn.

There is never anything conclusive, just an endless series of tests.

Once a week you will feel in love with him again. Massage his lower back when it is aching. Lay your cheek against him, feeling, listening for his kidneys. Stay like that all night, never quite falling asleep, never quite wanting to.

The thought will occur to you that you are waiting for him to die.

You will meet another actor. Or maybe it's the same one. Begin to have an affair. Begin to lie. Have dinner with him and his Modigliani-necked mother.

She will smoke cigars, play with the fondue, discuss the fallacy of feminine maternal instinct. Afterward, you will all get high.

There is never anything conclusive, just an endless series of tests.

———

And could you leave him tripping merrily through the snow?

You will fantasize about a funeral. At that you could cry. It would be a study in post-romantic excess, something vaguely Wagnerian. You would be comforted by his lugubrious sisters and his dental hygienist mom. The four of you in the cemetery would throw yourselves at his grave's edge, heaving and sobbing like old Israeli women. You, in particular, would shout, bare your wrists, shake them at the sky, foam at the mouth. There would be no shame, no dignity. You would fly immediately to Acapulco and lounge drunk and malodorous in the casinos until three.

After dinners with the actor: creep home. Your stomach will get fluttery, your steps smaller as you approach the door. Neighbors will be playing music you recall from your childhood—an opera about a pretty lady who was bad and cut a man's hair in his sleep. You recall, recall your grandfather playing it with a sort of wrath, his visage laminated with Old Testament righteousness, the violins warming, the scenario unfolding now as you stand outside the door. Ray pawned off my ten dresses: it cascades like a waterfall. Dolly-la, Dolly-la: it is the wail, the next to the last good solo of a doomed man.

Tiptoe. It won't matter. He will be sitting up in bed looking empty. Kiss him, cajole him. Make love to him like never before. At four in the morning you will still be awake, staring at the ceiling. You will horrify yourself.

Thoughts of leaving will move in, bivouac throughout the living room; they will have eyes like rodents and peer out at you from under the sofa, in the dark, from under the sink, luminous glass beads positioned in twos. The houseplants will appear to have chosen sides. Some will thrust stems at you like angry limbs. They will seem to caw like crows. Others will simply sag.

When you go out, leave him with a sinkful of dirty dishes. He will slowly dry them with paper towels, his skin scalded red beneath the wet, flattened hair of his forearms. You will be tempted to tell him to leave them, or to use the terrycloth in the drawer. But you won't. You will put on your coat and hurry away.

When you return, the bathroom light will be on. You will see blouses of yours that he has washed by hand. They will hang in perfect half-inches, dripping, scolding from the shower curtain rod. They will be buttoned with his Cagney eyes, faintly hooded, the twinkle sad and dulled.

Slip quietly under the covers; hold his sleeping hand.

There is never anything conclusive.

At work you will be lachrymose and distracted. You will shamble through the hall like a legume with feet. People will notice.

Nightmares have seasons like hurricanes. Be prepared. You will dream that someone with a violin case is trailing you through the city. Little children come at you with grins and grenades. You may bolt awake with a spasm, reach for him, and find he is not there, but lost in his own sleep, somnambulant, is roaming through the apartment like an old man, babbling gibberish, bumping into tables and lamps, a blanket he has torn from the bed wrapped clumsily around him, toga-style. Get up. Go to him. Touch him. At first he will look at you, wide-eyed, and not see. Put your arms around his waist. He will wake and gasp and cry into your hair. In a minute he will know where he is.

———

Dream about rainbows, about escapes, about wizards. Your past will fly by you, event by event, like Dorothy's tornadoed neighborhood, past the blown-out window. Airborne. One by one. Wave hello, good-bye. Practice.

Begin to call in sick. Make sure it is after he has already left for work. Sit in a rocking chair. Stare around at the apartment. It will be mid-morning and flooded in a hush of sunlight. You rarely see it like this. It will seem strangely deserted, premonitory. There will be apricots shrunk to buttons on the windowsill. A fly will bang stupidly against the panes. The bed will lie open, revealed, like something festering, the wrinkles in the sheets marking time, marking territory like the capillaries of a map. Rock. Hush. Breathe.

On the night you finally tell him, take him out to dinner. Translate the entrees for him. When you are home, lying in bed together, tell him that you are going to leave. He will look panicked, but not surprised. Perhaps he will say, Look, I don't care who else you're seeing or anything: what is your reason?

Do not attempt to bandy words. Tell him you do not love him anymore. It will make him cry, rivulets wending their way into his ears. You will start to feel sick. He will say something like: Well, you lose some, you lose some. You are supposed to laugh. Exhale. Blow your nose. Flick off the light. Have a sense of humor, he will whisper into the black. Have a heart.

Make him breakfast. He will want to know where you will go. Reply: To the actor. Or: To the hunchbacks. He will not eat your breakfast. He will glare at it, stir it around the plate with a fork, and then hurl it against the wall.

When you walk up Third Avenue toward the IRT, do it quickly. You will have a full bag. People will seem to know what you have done, where you are going.

They will have his eyes, the same pair, passed along on the street from face to face, like secrets, like glasses at the opera.

This is what you are.
Rushing downstairs into the steamy burn of the subway.
Unable to look a panhandler in the pan.

You will never see him again. Or perhaps you will be sitting in Central Park one April eating your lunch and he will trundle by on roller skates. You will greet him with a wave and a mouth full of sandwich. He will nod, but he will not stop.

There will be an endless series of tests.

A week, a month, a year. The sadness will die like an old dog. You will feel nothing but indifference. The logy whine of a cowboy harmonica, plaintive, weary, it will fade into the hills slow as slow Hank Williams. One of those endings. ◀

# Joyce Carol Oates

# Wolf's Head Lake

It's an early dusk at the lake because the sky's marbled with clouds and some of them are dark, heavy, tumescent as skins of flesh ready to burst. It's an early dusk because there's been thunder all afternoon, that laughing-rippling sound at the base of the spine. And heat lightning, quick spasms of nerves, forking in the sky then gone before you can exactly see. Only a few motorboats out on the lake, men fishing, nobody's swimming any longer, this is a day in summer ending early. In my damp puckered two-piece bathing suit I'm leaning in the doorway of the wood-frame cottage, #11, straining the spring of the rusted screen door. You don't realize the screen is rusted until you feel the grit on your fingers, and you touch your face, your lips, needing to feel *I'm here! Alive* and you taste the rust, and the slapping of waves against the pebbled beach is mixed with it, that taste. Along Wolf's Head Lake in the foothills of the Chautauqua Mountains the small cottages of memory, crowded together in a grid of scrupulous plotted rows at the southern edge of the lake that's said to be shaped like a giant wolf's head, sandy rutted driveways and grassless lots and towels and bathing suits hanging on clotheslines chalk-white in the gathering dusk. And radios turned up high. And kids' raised voices, shouting in play. He's driving a car just that color of the storm clouds. He's driving slowly, you could say aimlessly. He's in no hurry to switch on his headlights. Just cruising. On Route 23 the two-lane blacktop highway, cruising down from Port Oriskany maybe, where maybe he lives, or has been living, but he's checked out now, or if he's left some clothes and things behind in the rented room he won't be back to claim them. You have an uncle who'd gotten shot up as he speaks of it, not bitterly, nor even ironically, in the War, and all he's good for now, he says, is managing a cheap hotel in Port Oriskany, and he tells stories of guys like this how they appear, and then they disappear. And no trace unless the cops are looking for them and even then, much of the time, no trace. *Where do they come from, it's like maple seeds blowing.* And you think *What's a maple seed want but to populate the world with its kind.* He's wearing dark glasses, as dark comes on. Circling the cottages hearing kids' shouts, barking dogs. He might have a companion. In the rooms-by-the-week hotel in Port Oriskany, these guys have companions, and the companion is a woman. This is strange to me, yet I begin to see her. She's a hefty big-breasted woman like my mother's older sister. Her hair is bleached, but growing out. She's got a quick wide smile like a knife cutting through something soft. She's the one who'll speak first. Asking if you know where somebody's cottage is, and you don't; or, say you're headed for the lake, in the thundery dusk, or sitting on the steps at the dock where older kids are drinking from beer cans, tossing cigarette butts into the lake, and it's later, and darker, and the air tastes of rain though it hasn't started yet to rain, and she's asking would you like to come for a ride, to Olcott where there's the carnival, the Ferris wheel, it's only a few miles away. Asking what's your name, and you're too shy not to tell. Beneath the front seat of the car, the passenger's seat, there's a length of clothesline. You would never imagine clothesline is so strong. Each of them has a knife. The kind that fold up. From the army-navy supply store. For hunting, fishing. Something they do with these knives, and each other, drawing thin trickles of blood, but I'm not too sure of this, I've never seen it exactly. I'm leaning in the doorway, the spring of the screen door is strained almost to breaking. Mosquitoes are drawn to my hot skin, out of the shadows. I see the headlights on Route 23 above the lake, a mile away. I see the slow passage, he's patient, circling the cottages, looking for the way in. ◀

# Ron Rash

## Into the Gorge

His great-aunt had been born on this land, lived on it eight decades and knew it as well as she knew her husband and children. That was what she'd always claimed, and could tell you to the week when the first dogwood blossom would brighten the ridge, the first blackberry darken and swell enough to harvest.

Then her mind had wandered into a place she could not follow, taking with it all the people she knew, their names and connections, whether they still lived or whether they'd died. But her body lingered, shed of an inner being, empty as a cicada husk.

Knowledge of the land was the one memory that refused to dissolve. During her last year, Jesse would step off the school bus and see his great-aunt hoeing a field behind her farmhouse, breaking ground for a crop she never sowed, but the rows were always straight, right-depthed. Her nephew, Jesse's father, worked in an adjoining field. The first few times, he had taken the hoe from her hands and led her back to her house, but she'd soon be back in the field. After a while neighbors and kin just let her hoe. They brought meals and checked on her as often as they could. Jesse always walked rapidly past her field. His great-aunt never looked up, her gaze fixed on the hoe blade and the dark soil it churned, but he had always feared she'd raise her eyes and acknowledge him, though what she might want to convey Jesse could not say.

Then one March day she disappeared. The men in the community searched all afternoon and into evening as the temperature dropped, sleet crackled and hissed like static. The men rippled outward as they lit lanterns and moved into the gorge. Jesse watched from his family's pasture as the held flames grew smaller, soon disappearing and reappearing like foxfire, crossing the creek and then on past the ginseng patch Jesse helped his father harvest. Going deeper into land that had been in the family almost two hundred years, toward the original homestead, the place she'd been born.

They found his great-aunt at dawn, her back against a tree as if waiting for the searchers to arrive. But that was not the strangest thing. She'd taken off her shoes, her dress, and her underclothes. Years later Jesse read in a magazine that people dying of hypothermia did such a thing believing that heat, not cold, was killing them. Back then the woods had been communal, NO TRESPASSING signs an affront, but after her death neighbors soon found places other than the gorge to hunt and fish, gather blackberries and galax. Her ghost was still down there, many believed, including Jesse's own father, who never returned to harvest the ginseng he'd planted. When the Park Service made an offer on the homestead, Jesse's father and aunts sold. That was in 1959, and the government paid sixty dollars an acre. Now, five decades later, Jesse stood on his porch and looked east toward Sampson Ridge, where bulldozers razed woods and pastureland for another gated community. He wondered how much those sixty acres were worth today. Easily a million dollars.

Not that he needed that much money. His house and twenty acres were paid for, as was his truck. The tobacco allotment earned less each year but still enough for a widower with grown children. Enough as long as he didn't have to go to the hospital or his truck didn't throw a rod. He needed some extra money put away for that. Not a million, but some.

So two autumns ago Jesse had gone into the gorge, following the creek to the old homestead, then up the ridge's shadowy north face where his father had seeded and harvested his ginseng patch. The crop was there, evidently untouched for half a century. Some of the plants rose above Jesse's kneecaps, and there was more ginseng than his father could have dreamed of, a hillside spangled with bright yellow leaves, enough roots to bulge Jesse's knapsack. Afterward, he'd carefully replanted the seeds, done it just as his father had done, then walked out of the gorge, past the iron gate that kept vehicles off the logging road. A yellow tin marker nailed to a nearby tree said U.S PARK SERVICE.

Now another autumn had come. A wet autumn, which was good for the plants, as Jesse had verified three days ago when he'd checked them. Once again he gathered the knapsack and trowel from the woodshed. He also took the .32-20 Colt from his bedroom drawer. Late in the year for snakes, but after days of rain the afternoon was warm enough to bring a rattler or copperhead out to sun.

He followed the old logging road, the green backpack slung over his shoulder and the pistol in the outside pouch. Jesse's arthritic knees ached as he made the descent. They would ache more that night, even after rubbing liniment on them. He wondered how many more autumns he'd be able to make this trip. Till I'm seventy, Jesse figured, giving himself two more years. The ground was slippery from all the rain, and he walked slowly. A broken ankle or leg would be a serious thing this far from help, but it was more than that. He wanted to enter the gorge respectfully.

When he got in sight of the homestead, the land leveled out, but the ground grew soggier, especially where the creek ran close to the logging road. Jesse saw boot prints from three days earlier. Then he saw another set, coming up the logging road from the other direction. Boot prints as well, but smaller. Jesse looked down the logging road but saw no hiker or fisherman. He kneeled, his joints creaking.

The prints appeared at least a day old, maybe more. They stopped on the road when they met Jesse's, then also veered toward the homestead. Jesse got up and looked around again before walking through the withered broom sedge and joe-pye weed. He passed a cairn of stones that once had been a chimney, a dry well covered with a slab of tin so rusty it served as more warning than safeguard. The boot prints were no longer discernible but he knew where they'd end. Led the son of a bitch right to it, he told himself, and wondered how he could have been stupid enough to walk the road on a rainy morning. But when he got to the ridge, the plants were still there, the soil around them undisturbed. Probably just a hiker, or a bird watcher, Jesse figured, that or some punk kid looking to poach someone's marijuana, not knowing the ginseng was worth even more. Either way, he'd been damn lucky.

Jesse lifted the trowel from the backpack and got on his knees. He smelled the rich dark earth that always reminded him of coffee. The plants had more color than three days ago, the berries a deeper red, the leaves bright as polished gold. It always amazed him that such radiance could grow in soil the sun rarely touched, like finding rubies and sapphires on the gloamy walls of a cave. He worked with care but also haste. The first time he'd returned here, two years earlier, he'd felt a sudden coolness, a slight lessening of light, as if a cloud had passed over the sun. Imagination, he'd told himself then, but it had made him work faster, with no pauses to rest.

Jesse jabbed the trowel into the loamy soil, probing inward with care so as not to cut the root, slowly bringing it to light. The root was a big one, six inches long, tendrils sprouting from the core like clay renderings of human limbs. Jesse scraped away the dirt and placed the root in the backpack, just as carefully buried the seeds to ensure another harvest. As he crawled a few feet left to unearth another plant, he felt the moist dirt seeping its way through the knees of his blue jeans. He liked being this close to the earth, smelling it, feeling it on his hands and under his nails, the same as when he planted tobacco sprigs in the spring. A song he'd heard on the radio drifted into his head, a woman wanting to burn down a whole town. He let the tune play in his head and tried to fill in the refrain as he pressed the trowel into the earth.

"You can lay that trowel down," a voice behind Jesse said. "Then raise your hands."

Jesse turned and saw a man in a gray shirt and green khakis, a gold badge on his chest and a U.S. Park Service patch on his shoulder. Short blond hair, dark eyes. A young man, probably not even thirty. A pistol was holstered on his right hip, the safety strap off.

"Don't get up," the younger man said again, louder this time.

Jesse did as he was told. The park ranger came closer, picked up the backpack, and stepped away. Jesse watched as he opened the compartment with the ginseng root, then the smaller pouch. The ranger took out the .32-20 and held it in his palm. The gun had belonged to Jesse's grandfather and father before being passed on to Jesse. The ranger inspected it as he might an arrowhead or spear point he'd found.

"That's just for the snakes," Jesse said.

"Possession of a firearm is illegal in the park," the ranger said. "You've broken two laws, federal laws. You'll be getting some jail time for this."

The younger man looked like he might say more, then seemed to decide against it

"This ain't right," Jesse said. "My daddy planted the seeds for this patch. That ginseng wouldn't even be here if it wasn't for him. And that gun, if I was poaching I'd have a rifle or shotgun."

What was happening didn't seem quite real. The world, the very ground he stood on, felt like it was evaporating beneath him. Jesse almost expected somebody, though he couldn't say who, to come out of the woods laughing about the joke just played on him. The ranger placed the pistol in the backpack. He unclipped the walkie-talkie from his belt, pressed a button, and spoke.

"He did come back and I've got him."

A staticky voice responded, the words indiscernible to Jesse.

"No, he's too old to be much trouble. We'll be waiting on the logging road."

The ranger pressed a button and placed the walkie-talkie back on his belt. Jesse read the name on the silver nametag. *Barry Wilson.*

"You any kin to the Wilsons over on Balsam Mountain?"

"No," the younger man said. "I grew up in Charlotte."

The walkie-talkie crackled and the ranger picked it up, said okay, and clipped it back on his belt.

"Call Sheriff Arrowood," Jesse said. "He'll tell you I've never been in any trouble before. Never, not even a speeding ticket."

"Let's go."

"Can't you just forget this?" Jesse said. "It ain't like I was growing marijuana. There's plenty that do in this park. I know that for a fact. That's worse than what I done."

The ranger smiled.

"We'll get them eventually, old fellow, but their bulbs burn brighter than yours. They're not big enough fools to leave us footprints to follow."

The ranger slung the backpack over his shoulder.

"You've got no right to talk to me like that," Jesse said.

There was still plenty of distance between them, but the ranger looked like he contemplated another step back.

"If you're going to give me trouble, I'll just go ahead and cuff you now."

Jesse almost told the younger man to come on and try, but he made himself look at the ground, get himself under control before he spoke.

"No, I ain't going to give you any trouble," he finally said, raising his eyes.

The ranger nodded toward the logging road.

"After you, then."

Jesse moved past the ranger, stepping through the broom sedge and past the ruined chimney, the ranger to his right, two steps behind. Jesse veered slightly to his left, moving so he'd pass close to the old well. He paused and glanced back at the ranger.

"That trowel of mine, I ought to get it."

The ranger paused too and was about to reply when Jesse took a quick step and shoved the ranger with two hands toward the well. The ranger didn't fall until one foot went through the rotten tin, then the other. As he did, the backpack dropped from his hand. He didn't go all the way through, just up to his arms, his fingernails scraping the tin for leverage, looking like a man caught in muddy ice. The ranger's hands found purchase, one on a hank of broom sedge, the other on the metal's firmer edging. He began pulling himself out, wincing as the rusty tin tore cloth and skin. He looked at Jesse, who stood above him.

"You've really screwed up now," the ranger gasped.

Jesse bent down and reached not for the younger man's hand but for his shoulder. He pushed hard, the ranger's hands clutching only air as he fell through the rotten metal, a thump and simultaneous snap of bone as he hit the well's dry floor. Seconds passed but no other sound rose from the darkness.

The backpack lay at the edge and Jesse snatched it up. He ran, not toward his farmhouse but into the woods. He didn't look back again but bear-crawled through the ginseng patch and up the ridge, his breaths loud pants. Trees thickened around him, oaks and poplars, some hemlocks. The soil was thin and moist, and he slipped several times. Halfway up the ridge he paused, his heart battering his chest. When it finally calmed, Jesse heard a vehicle coming up the logging road and saw a pale-green Park Service jeep. A man and a woman got out.

Jesse went on, passing through another patch of ginseng, probable descendants from his father's original seedlings. The sooner he got to the ridge crest, the sooner he could make his way across it toward the gorge head. His legs were leaden now, and he couldn't catch his breath. The extra pounds he'd put on the last few years draped over his belt, gave him more to haul. His mind went dizzy and he slipped and skidded a few yards downhill. For a while he lay still, his body sprawled on the slanted earth, arms and legs flung outward. Jesse felt the leaves cushioning the back of his head, an acorn nudged against a shoulder blade. Above him, oak branches pierced a darkening sky. He remembered the fairy tale about a giant beanstalk and imagined how convenient it would be simply to climb off into the clouds.

Jesse shifted his body so his face turned downhill, one ear to the ground as if listening for the faintest footfall. It seemed so wrong to be sixty-eight years old and running from someone. Old age was supposed to give a person dignity, respect. He remembered the night the searchers brought his great-aunt out of the gorge. The men had stripped off their heavy coats to cover her body and had taken turns carrying her. They had been silent and somber as they came into the yard. Even after the women had taken the corpse into the farmhouse to be washed and dressed, the men had stayed on his great-aunt's porch. Some had smoked hand-rolled cigarettes, others had bulged their jaws with tobacco. Jesse had sat on the lowest porch step and listened, knowing the men had quickly forgotten he was there. They did not talk of how they'd found his great-aunt or the times she'd wandered from her house to the garden. Instead, the men spoke of a woman who could tell you tomorrow's weather by looking at the evening sky, a godly woman who'd taught Sunday school into her seventies. They told stories about her, and every story was spoken in a reverent way, as if now that his great-aunt was dead, she'd once more been transformed back to her true self.

Jesse rose slowly. He hadn't twisted an ankle or broken an arm, and that seemed his first bit of luck since walking into the gorge. When Jesse reached the crest, his legs were so weak he clutched a maple sapling to ease himself to the ground. He looked down through the cascading trees. An orange-and-white rescue squad van had now arrived. Workers huddled around the well, and Jesse couldn't see much of what they were doing, but before long a stretcher was carried to the van. He was too far away to tell the ranger's condition, even if the man was alive.

At the least a broken arm or leg, Jesse knew, and tried to think of an injury that would make things all right, like a concussion to make the ranger forget what had happened, or the ranger hurting bad enough that shock made him forget. Jesse tried not to think about the snapped bone being in the back or neck.

The van's back doors closed from within, and the vehicle turned onto the logging road. The siren was off but the beacon drenched the woods red. The woman ranger scoured the hillside with binoculars, sweeping without pause over where Jesse sat. Another green Park Service truck drove up, two more rangers spilling out. Then Sheriff Arrowood's car, silent as the ambulance.

The sun lay behind Clingman's Dome now, and Jesse knew waiting any longer would only make it harder. He moved in a stupor of exhaustion, feet stumbling over roots and rocks, swaying like a drunk. When he got far enough, he'd be able to come down the ridge, ascend the narrow gorge mouth. But Jesse was so tired he didn't know how he could go any farther without resting. His knees grated bone on bone, popping and crackling each time they bent or twisted. He panted and wheezed and imagined his lungs an accordion that never unfolded enough.

*Old* and a *fool*. That's what the ranger had called Jesse. An old man no doubt. His body told him so every morning when he awoke. The liniment he applied to his joints and muscles each morning and night made him think of himself as a creaky rust-corroded machine that must be oiled and warmed up before it could sputter to life. Maybe a fool as well, he acknowledged, for who other than a fool could have gotten into such a fix?

Jesse found a felled oak and sat down, a mistake, because he couldn't imagine summoning the energy to rise. He looked through the trees. Sheriff Arrowood's car was gone, but the truck and jeep were still there. He didn't see but one person and knew the others searched the woods for him. A crow cawed once farther up the ridge. Then no other sound, not even the wind. Jesse took the backpack and pitched it into the thick woods below, watched it tumble out of sight. A waste, but he couldn't risk their searching his house. He thought about tossing the pistol as well, but the gun had belonged to his father, his father's father before that. Besides, if they found it in his house, that was no proof it was the pistol the ranger had seen. They had no proof of anything, really. Even his being in the gorge was just the ranger's word against his. If he could get back to the house.

Night fell fast now, darkness webbing the gaps between tree trunks and branches. Below, high-beam flashlights flickered on. Jesse remembered two weeks after his great-aunt's burial. Graham Sutherland had come out of the gorge shaking and chalk-faced, not able to tell what had happened until Jesse's father gave him a draft of whiskey. Graham had been fishing near the old homestead and glimpsed something on the far bank, there for just a moment. Though a sunny spring afternoon, the weather in the gorge had suddenly turned cold and damp. Graham had seen her then, moving through the trees toward him, her arms outstretched. *Beseeching me to come to her,* Graham had told them. *Not speaking, but letting that cold and damp touch my very bones so I'd feel what she felt. She didn't say it out loud, maybe couldn't, but she wanted me to stay down there with her. She didn't want to be alone.*

Jesse walked on, not stopping until he found a place where he could make his descent. A flashlight moved below him, its holder merged with the dark. The light bobbed as if on a river's current, a river running uphill all the way to the iron gate that marked the end of Park Service land. Then the light swung around, made its swaying way back down the logging road. Someone shouted and the disparate lights gathered like sparks returning to their source. Headlights and engines came to life, and two sets of red taillights dimmed and soon disappeared.

Jesse made his way down the slope, his body slantways, one hand close to the ground in case he slipped. Low branches slapped his face. Once on level land he let minutes pass, listening for footsteps or a cough on the logging road, someone left behind to trick him into coming out. No moon shone but a few stars had settled overhead, enough light for him to make out a human form.

Jesse moved quietly up the logging road. Get back in the house and you'll be all right, he told himself. He came to the iron gate and slipped under. It struck him only then that someone might be waiting at his house. He went to the left and stopped where a barbed-wire fence marked the pasture edge. The house lights were still off, the way he'd left them. Jesse's hand touched a strand of sagging barbed wire and he felt a vague reassurance in its being there, its familiarity. He was about to move closer when he heard a truck, soon saw its yellow beams crossing Sampson Ridge. As soon as the pickup pulled into the driveway, the porch light came on. Sheriff Arrowood appeared on the porch, one of Jesse's shirts in his hand. Two men got out of the pickup and opened the tailgate. Bloodhounds leaped and tumbled from the truck bed, whining as the men gathered their leashes. He had to get back into the gorge, and quick, but his legs were suddenly stiff and unyielding as iron stobs. It's just the fear, Jesse told himself. He clasped one of the fence's rusty barbs and squeezed until pain reconnected his mind and body.

Jesse followed the land's downward tilt, crossed back under the gate. The logging road leveled out and Jesse saw the outline of the homestead's ruined chimney. As he came closer, the chimney solidified, grew darker than the dark around it, as if an unlit passageway into some greater darkness.

Jesse took the .32-20 from his pocket and let the pistol's weight settle in his hand. If they caught him with it, that was just more trouble. Throw it so far they won't find it, he told himself, because there's prints on it. He turned toward the woods and heaved the pistol, almost falling with the effort. The gun went only a few feet before thunking solidly against a tree, landing close to the logging road, if not on it. There was no time to find the pistol, because the hounds were at the gorge head now, flashlights dipping and rising behind them. He could tell by the hounds' cries that they were already on his trail.

Jesse stepped into the creek, hoping that doing so might cause the dogs to lose his scent. If it worked, he could circle back and find the gun. What sparse light the stars had offered was snuffed out as the creek left the road and entered the woods. Jesse bumped against the banks, stumbled into deeper pockets of water that drenched his pants as well as his boots and socks. He fell and something tore in his shoulder.

But it worked. There was soon a confusion of barks and howls, the flashlights no longer following him but instead sweeping the woods from one still point.

Jesse stepped out of the creek and sat down. He was shivering, his mind off plumb, every thought tilting toward panic. As he poured water from the boots, Jesse remembered that his boot prints led directly from his house to the ginseng patch. They had ways of matching boots and their prints, and not just a certain foot size and make. He'd seen on a TV show how they could even match the worn part of the sole to a print. Jesse stuffed the socks inside the boots and threw them at the dark. Like the pistol, they didn't go far before hitting something solid.

It took him a long time to find the old logging road, and even when he was finally on it he was so disoriented that he wasn't sure which direction to go in. Jesse walked a while and came to a park campground, which meant he'd guessed wrong. He turned around and walked the other way. It felt like years had passed before he finally made it back to the homestead. A campfire now glowed and sparked between the homestead and the iron gate, the men hunting Jesse huddled around it. The pistol lay somewhere near the men, perhaps found already. Several of the hounds barked, impatient to get back onto the trail, but the searchers had evidently decided to wait till morning to continue. Though Jesse was too far away to hear them, he knew they talked to help pass the time. They probably had food with them, perhaps coffee as well. Jesse realized he was thirsty and thought about going back to the creek for some water, but he was too tired.

Dew wet his bare feet as he passed the far edge of the homestead and then to the woods' edge where the ginseng was. He sat down and in a few minutes felt the night's chill envelop him. A frost warning, the radio had said. He thought of how his great-aunt had taken off her clothes and how, despite the scientific explanation, it seemed to Jesse a final abdication of everything she had once been.

He looked toward the eastern sky. It seemed he'd been running a week's worth of nights, but he saw the stars hadn't begun to pale. The first pink smudges on the far ridge line were a while away, perhaps hours. The night would linger long enough for what would or would not come. He waited. ◄

# Lynne Tillman

# The Recipe

—Sadness, that's normal, it goes with the territory, but becoming bitter, bitterness is to be avoided, he said.

—Be a saint instead, she said.

Instead, he'd live from the largesse of a common madness, not just his own, not just from his sadness, he'd lament and move on, lament and move on.

My lament, can't do it, my way.

Clay wouldn't ever want to relinquish internal rhyme, rhyming was a mnemonic device, too, and venerable for a reason, and, along with that, he relied on the beautiful histories meshed inside the roots of words.

—We don't determine what words mean, they determine what we mean, Clay said, later. We don't determine much.

Cornelia was a film editor and also translated documents and titles for a movie company, she also plied her insightful eye as a photo researcher and archivist for a wealthy eccentric, who never left his house and liked to know what was going on, but only in pictures. The eccentric hated to read.

—It would be great if pictures told a story, Cornelia said, but they don't. They tell too many, or they don't tell any.

—Words, also, he said.

—Images are easier to misread, she said.

—I don't know.

Subtitles crowded the image, she explained more than once, they changed the picture, even dominated it, and besides, reading words on a screen disrupted the cinematic flow. He wasn't sure that was all bad, but then he was suspicious of images, which he didn't make. He was wary of words, too, which he used and tried to remake, so he had reason for anxiety. In her business, they talked about "getting a read on" a script, on meaning, sort of instantaneously.

A place for words, orphaned, wayward, no words,
no images, what then.

The lovers argued about the small things, about cleaning up after themselves in their apartment, as responsible adults do, supposedly, and petty problems, at work and with relative strangers, and also the large things, love, politics, history, friendship, art, poetry, which he wrote, when inevitably inconsiderate matter that had earlier settled in words and sentences extruded layers of their pasts, lived together and separately.

> Code, just for now, when you mean its opposite,
> bright lust of sullen night.

He'd been stunned by an obituary: "To my dear friends and chums, It has been wonderful and at times it had been grand and for me, now, it has been enough." The man—it was signed "Michael"—had had the presence of mind to write and place his own death notice, it resonated a unique thoughtfulness, sad and mad, was he a suicide? And, on TV, a Fuji commercial declaimed a new longing for the fast-escaping present: "Because life won't stay still while you go home and get your camera."

> Writing death, perpetual, language like a
> house, an asylum, an orphanage. In a dream I
> wasn't, argued with someone or myself, so lost.
> Perpetual death of words, writing.

He wasn't his dream's hero, but there are no heroes, just cops. Clay stopped to watch two beat cops, surreptitiously he hoped, while they canvassed the street for errant civilians, ordinary or unusual, and the cops, they're ordinary and they're not, and out of uniform they're nothing, or they're nothing just like him, dumb mortals compelled by ignorant, invisible forces, which happened to be, in their case, part of the job. A police car sped by, like a siren, in time or too late to stop it, the robbery, murder, the robber, murderer. He asked the butcher for stew meat but studied another butcher at the bloodstained chopping block who expertly sliced off a layer of fat, thick and marbled, from a porterhouse. Fat enriches the meat's taste, his mother taught him, and also she warned, it's better to be dead and buried than frank and honest. She said she knew things he didn't that she hoped he'd never know, it was the part of her past she wouldn't tell him.

—At the end of the day, everyone wants someone to cook for them, a woman, who was probably waiting for the porterhouse, announced to a man by her side.

The man appeared to understand and nodded his head, a gesture that presumed a semblance of understanding. Clay wondered if giving the appearance of understanding was actually understanding, in some sense, and if duplicity of this sort was necessary for a society's existence, maybe even at its basis or center, and not the ancient totem Émile Durkheim theorized. People regularly don't understand each other, but if that were constantly apparent, rather than gestures of tacit agreement and recognition, a stasis, punctuated by violent acts everywhere, would stall everyone for eternity.

"Security has now been doubled at the stadium, but people's enjoyment won't be hampered, officials say." The radio announcer's voice sounded out of place in the warm, yeasty bakery, where he now was, doing errands like a responsible mate. The baker tuned the radio to a station that gave bulletins every few minutes, which some people listened to all day long, so they knew the news word by word, and Clay imagined they could recite it like a poem.

An epic, way to remember. A gesture, song, war,
a homecoming. Fighting writing my death,
persistent oxymoron. Perpetrator. Victim.
Terror to fight terror. Fire or an argument with
fire. Firefight. Spitfire. Lawless, Eliot Ness,
childhood. Fighting against or for terror, lies
in mouth. Can't leave home without it. Get a
horse instead.

People expected the unexpected, unnatural and natural disasters, a jet crashing in the ocean, all lost, hurricanes beating down towns, all lost, bombs doing their dirty work, lives lost and shattered, houses destroyed, and attentive listeners needed to know, instantly, for a sense of control or protection, and for the inevitable shock of recognition: I'm still alive.

The baker's son Joey, dressed in white like a surgeon, the skin on his florid cheeks dusted with flour, asked him what he wanted, then bantered with him as he always did.

—Sun, Clay, ever see it? You're pasty-faced.

—You're flour-faced. I want a sourdough loaf, and the recipe.

—Forget about it, Joey the baker's son said. Family secret for five generations.

—I'll get it.

—You're just like your mother, Joey said.

His mother had played the violin, and when he couldn't sleep at night, to quiet him after a bad dream, she'd stand in the doorway to his bedroom and pluck each string with adoring concentration. A lullaby, maybe, some song that consoled him for having to leave consciousness at all. He was attached to her concentration, like the strings to her instrument, and this specific image of her, mother violinist bent and absorbed, resisted passing time's arbitrariness, its uneven dissipations. Her face, for a long time now, rested only against walls or stood upright on tables in framed photographs, and he scarcely remembered a conversation they had, just a sentence or two.

Here, waiting. Can't leave home, without a
horse. Get a read on. Long ago, here, a drama
with teeth reneging, nagging. Cracked plates,
baseball bats, stains on home room floor, same
as before, stains like Shroud of Turin.
Jesus bled, writing death fighting terror.

He hadn't moved away from the old neighborhood, waiting for something, teaching English and American literature at the high school he attended, while he grew older in the same place, without stopping time, though he found his illusions encouraged and indemnified by traces of the past, like the indentations in the gym's floor, and, more than traces, bodies, like the baker's and the butcher's, and their children, who would replace them, and stand in their places, in a continuity Clay wouldn't keep up, even by staying in the neighborhood.

Cornelia believed the cult around the Shroud of Turin demonstrated that people do appreciate abstraction, an image instead of a body, though it wasn't exactly an abstraction but close enough. Even if the cloth had once rested on a body, theirs was a reverence for an impression, drawn from but not the same as the body—even if the body wasn't Christ's, since scientists carbon-dated the cloth much later than his death. The cloth was just matter, material separate from and attached to history.

> Not the thing, the stain, palimpsest of pain.
> Life served with death a sanction.

Sometimes Joey the baker's son let him go into the back of the store to watch other white-coated men knead dough, their faces also dusted in white, their concentration, like his mother's on her violin, complete, and he viewed them as content, absorbed in good work. Their hands knew exactly how much to slap and pound, when to stop—every movement was essential. Then Clay ruminated, the way he always did in the bakery, about being a baker; in the butcher shop, he thought about being a butcher. He wanted to be like Joey, they'd gone to school together. If he were, he'd know simple limits, why an action was right or wrong, because the consequences would be immediate, and as usual he rebuked himself for romanticizing their labor and imagining an idyllic life for, say, the old baker and the baker's son he'd known since he was a child, with a life better than his, because, he told Cornelia that night, their work was what it was, nothing else, its routine might be comforting, his wasn't. In the moment, as he watched their hands and smelled baking bread's inimitable aroma, he also felt that the bakers dwelled, as he did, in fantasy, that it enveloped them daily, and that what they did might be something else for them, too. Joey thought he was funny, but Clay loved the way Joey treated him, he felt Joey appreciated him in ways no one else did.

—The butcher, the baker, the candlestick maker, Cornelia teased.

—Cut it out, Clay said.

—Your heroes might surprise you someday, she said.

—I'd like that, Clay said.

—I bet you wouldn't, Cornelia said.

He told her about a distressed woman in the news who had found out she'd been adopted when she was twenty-one, which made sense to her, she was even glad, because she had never felt close to her parents, who were like aliens to her, and then the woman spent years searching for her birth parents. When she was fifty, she found her mother, who'd given her up for adoption because she'd been unmarried and only fifteen. But the mother she unearthed wasn't the mother she expected or wanted, so the woman was very disappointed. Also, her birth father was disreputable and long dead.

—Do you think people have the right to know? Clay asked.

—A constitutional right, Cornelia said.

—Okay.

—What about the right to privacy?

—Maybe some rights kill others.

If Clay turned violent, deranged, on the street, the cops would subdue and cuff him, take him in, interrogate him, or they might just shoot him on the spot, if he charged them menacingly, resisted them, or appeared to be carrying. The cops waited to arrest him and others from doing things they didn't know they could do or felt they had to do or did because inside them lurked instinctual monsters. He didn't know what he had in him, but he knew restraint, and he recognized, as Max Weber wrote early in the twentieth century, that only the state had the right to kill, no one else, and that fact alone defined the state. But where he lived everyone had the right to bear arms, to answer and resist the state's monopoly on power. That was the original idea, anyway, but if Clay carried a gun, he might use it, because he didn't know what he had in him.

Better to be dead and buried than frank and honest, his mother had said. His father ghosted their dining room table, his tales gone to the grave with him and now to his wife's grave also. One night his father hadn't come home from work the way he always did, Clay was seven, and his mother's face never regained its usual smile. She smiled, but not the way she once had. When little Clay walked into the butcher shop or the bakery, he felt the white-clothed men looking sympathetically at him, prying into him for feelings he hadn't yet experienced. The fatherly baker gave him an extra cookie or two, and in school, even on the baseball field, Joey the baker's son didn't call him names anymore, even when he struck out. But his mother clutched his little hand more tightly on the streets, and he learned there was something to fear about just being alive. He learned his father was dead, but it didn't mean much to him, death didn't then, and soon it became everything.

—It's why you're a depressive, Cornelia said. Losing a parent at that age.

—I guess, he said.

—It's why you hold on to everything.

Clay didn't throw out much, like matchbooks and coasters from old restaurants and bars that had closed, outdated business cards, and with this ephemera he first kept his father with him. There was dust at the back of his father's big desk that he let stay there. There was hair in his father's comb, which had been pushed to the back of the bathroom cabinet, so Clay collected the evidence in an envelope, and wondered later if he should have the DNA tested. What if his father wasn't his father? Maybe there was someone alive out there for him, a father, but his mother disabused him of the possibility, and played the violin so consolingly that Morpheus himself bothered to carry him off to a better life. Now, scratches on a mahogany table that once nestled close to his father's side of the bed and his mother's yellowing music books, her sewing cushion with its needles tidily stuck where she'd pushed them last, marked matter-of-fact episodes and incidents in their lives, when accidents occurred or things happened haphazardly, causing nicks and dents, before death recast them as shrines.

How long has this scrap been in the corner of a bureau drawer, he might ask himself, did it have a history? He could read clues incorrectly, though it didn't matter to him if his interpretations were wrong, because there was no way to know, and it wasn't a crime, he wasn't killing anyone. Cornelia's habits were different, heuristically trained and developed in the editing room, where she let go of dialogue and images, thousands of words and pictures every day, where she abandoned, shaped, or controlled objects more than he felt he could, ever.

> At last. To last. Last remains. What lasts
> remains. What, last. Shroud of Turin, Torino
> mio, home to Primo, Levi knew the shroud.

In Clay's sophomore English classes, in which the students read George Eliot's *Mill on the Floss* and Edith Wharton's *Ethan Frome*, his charges contested the rules for punctuation and grammar and argued for spellings and neologisms they used on the Internet and in text messaging. They preferred shorthand, acronyms, to regular English, they wanted speed. He argued for communication, commonality, and clarity, the three C's, for knowing rules and then breaking them consciously, even conscientiously. He attempted to engage them, as he was engaged, in the beauties and mysteries of the history that lives in all languages. It's present, it's still available, he'd say. And, by tracing the root of a word and finding its origin in Latin, Greek, or Sanskrit, and then by delving into its etymology, they could find how meanings had shifted over the years through usage. A few students caught his fervor, he thought, and who knew what would happen to them as they grew up, maybe they'd discover that love, that attachment. Curiously, there were many more new words each year, an explosion added to recent editions of dictionaries, more proportionately than had previously entered editions of the tomes he revered, and yet he remembered, always, what the words once meant, their first meanings. Cornelia told him it was another way he hung on to the past, and grammar countered his internal mess.

The problem is proportion, Clay thought, how to live proportionately. He passed the bakery on his way home, maybe he'd buy cinnamon buns for him and Cornelia for breakfast, and with an image of the pastries and her at the table, so that he could already taste morning in his mouth, he entered the store. It was busy as usual, and Clay waited on line, listening for the casual banter of the bakers, and when he drew nearer to the long counter, he overheard Joey the baker's son.

—I'd kill all of them, nuke 'em, torture's too good for them.

Clay continued to wait, suspended in place, breathing in the bakery's perfume, when finally he reached the front of the line, where the baker's son smiled warmly, the way he always did.

—I got you the recipe, you pasty-faced poet, Joey said.

He always teased him, ever since they were kids. Clay thanked him, smiled, and asked for two cinnamon buns, and then Joey handed him the famous recipe for sourdough bread, which in their family's version was littered with salty olive pieces. The cinnamon buns were still hot, fragrant. Fresh, Clay thought, fresh is a hard word to use, fresh or refreshed. There were suggestions, associations, and connotations always to words, he should stress this more to his students, because the connotations of a word often meant as much as its denotation, sometimes more, and there was ambiguity, ambiguity thrives, because words were the same as life.

> Traces, stains, call it noir, in the shadows,
> torture for us. And the child, the hooded
> childhood. Fresh ambiguity to contradict
> contradictions, refresh
> what remains somewhere else.

The beat cops stationed themselves on the same corner, at the same time, so in a way they made themselves targets or spectacles, Clay thought, or even, by their presence, drew enraged, desperate civilians to them, like a recipe for disaster.

Walking home, mostly oblivious to the familiar streets, Clay looked over the ingredients. A teaspoon of balsamic vinegar, that may have been the secret the baker's family treasured for generations. Or the molasses and tablespoon of rum, that might have been their innovation. Cornelia wasn't in the apartment when he arrived home, she was the one who wanted the recipe, and the rooms felt emptier than usual.

He boiled water, brewed tea, opened the newspaper, couldn't look at the pictures or read the words, stared at the cabinets, they needed fresh paint. He'd cook tonight, a beef stew, because at the end of the day, he remembered the woman saying, everyone wants someone to cook for them. He stood up and, without really thinking, opened a kitchen drawer and tossed the recipe in the back. ◀

# John Edgar Wideman

# Rock River

Main Street out of Rock River narrows abruptly into a two-lane and in twenty-five minutes you are in the middle of nowhere. Past a couple clumps of buildings that used to be towns and one that might still be, then a railroad embankment's on your left for a while till it veers off over the plains, a spine of mountains to the right, blue in the distance, miles of weather-cracked wasteland stretching to foothills hunkered like a pack of gray dogs at the base of the mountains. Moonscape till you turn off at the Bar-H gate on the dirt track under the power line and follow it through a pass, along a ridge and then things get brown, green some, not exactly a welcome mat rolled out but country you could deal with, as long as you don't decide to stay. Trees can tunnel out of thickets of boulders, grass can root in sand and shale, the river you can't find most summers in its seamed bed manages to irrigate a row of dwarf cottonwoods whose tops, situated as they are, higher than anything else around, black-green silhouettes orderly on the horizon, remind you that even the huge sky gives way to something, sometimes, that its weight can be accommodated by this hard ground, that the rooster tail of dust behind your pickup will dissipate, rise and settle.

The road twists and bumps and climbs, curves back on itself, almost disappears totally in a circus of ruts, gouges and tire-size stones, dropping steadily while it does whatever else it's doing, shaking the pickup to pieces, steering it, tossing it up and catching it like a kid warming up a baseball. No seat belt and your head would squash on the roof of the cab. Last few miles the steepest. Then this fold of land levels, meadows and thick, pine woods, sudden outcroppings of aspen, hillocks, mini-ravines, deer country, a greenness and sweet smell of water cutting the sage, a place nothing most of the trip here would have suggested you'd find.

I am alone. My job is to clean up Rick's truck, get it ready to bring back to town. They said that would be all right now. The police have finished their investigation. Tomorrow I'll come back with Stevenson. He can drive my truck and I'll drive Rick's. But today I want to do what I have to do by myself. I expect it will be a mess. He stood outside, but the blast carried backwards to the open window of the truck. They warned me, then they said the gas is OK. Better take jumper cables, though, Quinson said. As if any fool wouldn't know that. Cops were making arrangements to tow it to town. I thought I'd rather drive it. Clean it up first. Then me and Stevenson come out and I'll bring it in.

I have old towels. Two five-gallon cans of water. Upholstery cleaner. Brillo. Spot remover. Mr. Clean, sponges, rags, Windex, all the tools on my knife, heavier gear like shovel, ax and rope that's always stowed in the truck box. I think I have enough. Mary Ellen said, Take this, holding out a can of Pine Sol spray deodor-ant. I hadn't thought of that and was surprised she did and didn't know what to say when she held it out to me.

I shook my head no, but she didn't take it back. Didn't push it on me but she didn't pull it away either.

I think to myself. Can't hurt, can it? There's room. So I took it.

She nodded. Rick got on her nerves. He liked her. He reminded her of her father. Hopeless. Hopeless. Hopeless. You had to smile and be nice to him he was so hopeless. She'd never neglect the small kindnesses to him she said because you'd never want him to feel you'd given up on him. But he could try your patience. Try a saint's. He couldn't count the times she'd said in private she'd given up on Rick. Don't bring him around here anymore, she'd say. I'm sick and tired of that man, she'd say. But then she'd always hug Rick or cry on his shoulder or say something awful and provoking to let him know she was very well aware of how hopeless he was, and let him know he'd never force her to give up on him.

Mary Ellen.

It's been a week. They probably locked it and shut the windows to keep out the rain. They'd want to protect a brand-new vehicle like that.

Almost new.

Looked new. He was so cockeyed proud of it.

I doubt Sarah will want to keep it. Either way if it's cleaned up, that's one thing she won't have to bother with.

Will you be all right?

There's room. Won't hurt to take it. They probably did close up the windows.

I have Rick's extra set of keys. Went by his house to get them. Here's what I saw.

A tall woman. Sarah, Rick's wife. In blue jeans sitting at a table with a look I'd seen somewhere before, a picture of a Sioux Indian in a long line of Indians staring at the camera and it was hard to tell whether male or female, the photo was old and brown, the face I remembered round and the hood of dark hair could be a woman or a long-haired Indian man.

Sarah never wore blue jeans. Dresses almost always. If pants, they were slacks with sewn-in creases. You could never guess what she might say or do but her clothes wasn't the place that she showed she was different. I liked her a whole lot less than I liked Rick. Nobody talked more than Rick once he'd had his few drinks but you knew Rick didn't mean anything by it. When Rick talked you could tell he was talking just to keep himself from sinking down. If he stopped talking, he'd be in trouble, worse trouble than anything he might say would get him in. He needed to keep talking so he could sit there with you and play liar's poker or watch a campfire burn or just drink on Friday afternoon at the Redbird where we all did to forget the week that was. He'd make people mad who didn't know him because he was subject to say anything about anybody, but after a while, if you were around Rick any amount of time at all you knew it was foolish to take what he said seriously, personally. Rick was just riding along on this stream of words, merrily, merrily riding along and you could ride it too or pay it no mind, cause he wasn't really either.

Sarah on the other hand couldn't be any way but personal. She couldn't say Howdy-do without an edge to it. Like she's reminding you she had spoke first, giving you a lesson in manners and too bad you weren't raised right. I think the woman just couldn't help it. Something about growing up in too holy a house. Like the best anybody could do would never be good enough. And somebody had to take the job of reminding people of that fact. So here's Sarah. Eagle eyed and cat quick to pounce on universal slovenliness and your particular personal peccadilloes any hour of night or day. In blue jeans. Looking, as you might suspect, as if she's sleeping poorly or not at all, on the losing side force-marched by cavalry back to the reservation and mug shot. A drink on the kitchen table and offering me one even though we both know it's barely ten o'clock in the morning and that's not what I came for, reminding me, her lips pursed tight, that I'm in no position to judge her, in fact just the opposite case, because when she stares up at me red eyed there's just a little silliness, a little judgmentalness, a little I-know-better-than-you this is not the right thing to be doing but we've both started drinking earlier of a morning, you many more mornings than I, and you with Rick nonstop so morning, afternoon or night left far behind.

I better not stop now.

Didn't think you would.

Better get this done while I'm feeling up to it.

Why don't you let the police handle it?

It's just something I thought I could do. Ease a little of the burden.

You've done enough already. We're all grateful for what you've done for us.

They were going to tow it. Makes more sense to drive it. They said if it was all right with you, it was all right with them. I'm happy to help out if it's OK with you.

There the keys are on the table.

I won't be bringing it back today. Thought I'd just go up today and see what had to be done. Get it ready and tomorrow Stevenson said he would ride up with me and drive my truck back.

Don't bring it here.

You want me to park it at my place?

I don't care where you park it. It's Rick's truck. He won't be needing it. His brains were all over the seat. He drove away from us in that cute little shiny red truck and I don't care if I never see it again.

It's almost new. Rick talked himself up on a real bargain. Probably get most of what he paid if you sell it.

You've been a great help. Keep the truck. He'd want you to have it.

I couldn't do that.

I have some other stuff of his you might want as well. To remember him by. You can have his shotgun if the cops return it.

If you want me to take care of selling the truck I'd be happy to try. I'm sure it will bring a good price. From the outside it seemed in decent shape. Police sealed it and roped off the clearing where it was parked but as far as I could tell from where they kept us standing, everything was fine. Quinson told me it has plenty of gas, that I should bring cables just in case. I guess he thought I was born yesterday.

Simon?

Yes.

Do you miss him?

I'm real sorry. My heart goes out to you and your fine boys.

I can't miss him. He was gone too long.

Still in a state of shock, I guess. I sat there at the funeral still hoping Rick would change his mind.

He left while I was sleeping. I didn't get worried till the third day. I woke up early, early that morning and decided I'd call you. Ask if you'd seen him. Begin the whole humiliating routine. Has anybody seen my husband wandering around town? Blue eyes, blond, slightly balding, eyeglasses, middle-aged but boyish face, till he's acutely sloshed, then he resembles his grandfather's corpse. Tame when sober, answers to the name Rick. Please call 545-6217 if you've seen this individual. No reward. Except knowing you've saved a happy home. I'd made up my mind to begin phoning around and you of course were at the top of the list, but the cops called me first.

What I saw was she looked like parts of this town, skimpy as it is, I haven't seen for years. Below Second Street, near the railroad tracks where there are storage bins for rent. It's a ragtag, helter-skelter whole lot of nothing dead end. Nobody lives there. Nobody's ever going to or ever has. You can hear sixteen-wheelers humping on the interstate, trains rattle across the overpass. It's the kind of hardscrabble little patch of concrete and gravel and cinders and corrugated tin-roofed sheds that will always be at the edge of towns on the prairie and outlast the rest—downtown, the nice neighborhoods—be here when no one's left to listen to coyotes howling, the sage running, wind at night screaming in as many voices as there's stars.

What I saw was her eyes on a level only slightly below mine, fixing me, daring me to ignore them. The last party at their house is what I saw. Rick was chef. Spaghetti sauce from ground antelope. Elk liver pâté. Neatly wrapped packages from his game locker that I'd seen thawing, blooding in his refrigerator when I'd popped in for a Bud the afternoon before. Sarah's eyes told me Rick probably hadn't been to bed or stopped drinking before he started up for this party. He'd been telling the story of how he'd tracked the wily elk whose liver was being nibbled as an hors d'oeuvre on Ritz crackers. No one was listening so Rick was telling it softly, slouched down in an armchair, telling again what he'd related at least three times to every single one of us that evening, mumbled quietly, one more time, his gestures slow motion as somebody underwater, his eyes invisible behind his bifocals, his drink glass abiding on the chair's mashed-potato arm, sunken as deeply, as permanent as Rick is in its lap. You pass by and think that man's not moving soon, nor his drink, and wonder how they ended up that way and wonder if they'd ever get unstuck from the tacky fruit-and-flower print slip-cover that couldn't hide the fact that easy chair had seen better days.

Eye to eye with Sarah and she winks at me, even though both of us long past having fun at this party. But she's sloshed and I'm two sheets and that's why we both came so I wink back and hear the banjo and fiddle and whiny hill voices from the next room, the slapping of knees, whooping and stomping. It's getting good to itself in there. Dancing usually means wee hours before you can squeeze everybody out the door. It's what we've come for. To stay late. To holler a little bit and grab ass and thump a little on one another. I look back but Sarah's gray eyes are gone in the direction of the music, but music's not what's in them. I know by the set of her jaw what's in them. If I was close enough so her breath would ripple my lashes, that close but invisible so I wouldn't spoil her view, what I'd see would be two little Ricks, one in each gray globe of her eyes, two Ricks the stereo in her brain turns to one in three dimensions, real as things get in a kitchen at 11:00 P.M. when a full-scale party's raging.

Sure enough what I see is him stumbling into the kitchen this morning, hitting both sides of the doorframe before he gets through. He tries one more step. More lurch than step. As if his dancing partner has fooled him. He reaches for her hand and she whirls away laughing and he's caught with his weight on the wrong foot and almost falls on his nose after her. But he respects the quickness, the cunning, the spinning sexy grace in her, and forgives and catches himself with a little clumsy half skip, half shuffle, do-si-do, it's just a thing that happens. Hi. Hi. Hi. All. He catches me red-handed sliding the keys off the vinyl tablecloth. There are too many to close in my fist. She didn't separate the truck keys from the rest, twelve, thirteen, fifteen keys in my fist. I could shake them and make a mighty noise, shake them to the beat of that dancing music from the next room.

Where you going with ma keys, Simon? Simon-Simon. What you doing wit ma fucking keys, boyo? Ho. Ho. Don't touch that dial.

He glides in slow. The tempo has changed. He clamps one hand on Sarah's shoulder. Twirls her so she lands smack up against his chest. Then they are both gliding cheek to cheek and the song is waltz time, but they two-step it, hitch around the kitchen graceful as Arthur Murray and Ginger Rogers on stilts. Don't stop when Rick's elbow chops a whole row of empty beer bottles off the counter and they tumble and break and scatter and the worst godawful racket in the world does not attract one interested or curious face from the party in the other room. ◄

# Tobias Wolff

# A White Bible

It was dark when Maureen left the Hundred Club. She stopped just outside the door, a little thrown by the sudden cold, the change from daylight to night. A gusting breeze chilled her face. Lights burned over the storefronts, gleaming in patches of ice along the sidewalk. She reached in her pockets for her gloves, then hopelessly searched her purse. She'd left them in the club. If she went back for them, she knew she'd end up staying—and so much for all her good intentions. Theresa or one of the others would pick up the gloves and bring them to school on Monday. Still, she stood there. Someone came out the door behind her, and Maureen heard music, and voices raised over the music. Then the door swung shut, and she tightened her scarf and turned down the sidewalk toward the lot where she'd left her car.

She had gone almost a block when she realized that she was walking in the wrong direction. Easy mistake—the lot where she and the others usually parked had been full. She headed back, crossing the street to avoid the club. Her fingers had gone stiff. She put her hands in her coat pockets, but then yanked them out when her right foot took a skid on the ice. After that she kept them poised at her sides.

Head bent, she shuffled in tender steps from one safe spot to the next—for all the world like her own worn-out, balding, arthritic mother. Maureen allowed herself this thought in self-mockery, to make herself feel young, but it did not have this effect. The lot was farther than she'd been aware of as she strolled to the club with Molly and Jane and Evan, laughing at Evan's story about his manic Swedish girlfriend. She'd had an awful day at school and was happy to let the week go, to lose herself in jokes and gossip and feel the pale late sunshine almost warm on her face. Now her face was numb, and she was tense with the care of simply walking.

She passed a hunched, foot-stamping crowd waiting to get into Harrigan's, where she herself had once gone to hear the local bands. It had been called Far Horizon then. Or Lost Horizon. *Lost* Horizon, it was.

She scanned the faces as she walked by, helplessly on the watch for her daughter. She hadn't seen her in almost two years now, since Grace walked away from a full scholarship at Ithaca College to come back and live with one of Maureen's fellow English teachers from Saint Ignatius. It turned out they'd been going at it since Grace's senior year at SI—and him a married man with a young daughter. Maureen had always tried to see Grace's willfulness as backbone, but this she could not accept. She had said some unforgivable things, according to Grace. Since when, Maureen wanted to know, had a few home truths become unforgivable?

She was still trying to bring Grace around when Father Crespi got wind of the whole business and fired the teacher. Maureen had not been Father Crespi's source, but Grace wouldn't believe it. She declared things at an end between them, and so far she had kept that vow, though she dumped the luckless fool within a few weeks of his leaving his wife.

Grace was still close to Maureen's mother. From her, Maureen had learned that Grace was doing temp work and keeping house with another man. Maureen couldn't get her mother to say more—she'd given her word! But the old bird clearly enjoyed not saying more, being in the know, being part of Maureen's punishment for driving Grace away, as she judged the matter.

Maureen crossed the street again and turned into the parking lot—an unpaved corner tract surrounded by a chain-link fence. The attendant's shack was dark. She picked her way over ridges of frozen mud toward her car. Last summer's special-offer paint job was already dull, bleached out by road salt. Through a scrim of dried slush on the window, Maureen could see the stack of student blue books on the passenger seat—a weekend's worth of grading. She fished the keys from her purse, but her hand was dead with cold and she fumbled them when she tried to unlock the door. They hit the ground with a merry tinkle. She flexed her fingers and bent down for the keys. As she pushed herself back up, a pain shot through her bad knee. "Goddammit!" she said.

"Don't curse!" The voice came from behind Maureen, a man's voice, but high, almost shrill.

She closed her eyes.

He said something she couldn't make out; he had some sort of accent. He said it again, then added, "Now!"

"What?"

"The *keys*. Give them to me."

Maureen held the keys out behind her, eyes pressed shut. She had just one thought: Do not see him. The keys were taken from her hand, and she heard the door being unlocked.

"Open it," the man said. "Open the door. Yes, now get in."

"Just take it," Maureen said. "Please."

*"Please,* you will get *in*. Please." He took her arm and half pushed, half lifted her into the car and slammed the door shut. She sat behind the steering wheel with her head bent, eyes closed, hands folded over her purse. The passenger door opened. "Compositions," the man muttered.

"Exams," she said, and cringed at her stupidity in correcting him.

Maureen heard the blue books thud onto the floor in back. Then he was on the seat beside her. He sat there a moment, breathing quick shallow breaths. "Open your eyes. Open! Yes, now drive." He jingled the keys.

Looking straight ahead over the wheel, she said, "I don't think I can."

She sensed a movement toward her and flinched. He jingled the keys beside her ear and dropped them in her lap. "Drive."

Maureen had once taken a class in self-defense. That was five years ago, after her marriage ended and left her alone with a teenage daughter—as if the dangers were outside somewhere and not already in the house, between them. She'd forgotten all the fancy moves, but not her determination to fight, for Grace or for herself—to go on the attack, kick the bastard in the balls, scream and kick and hit and bite, fight to the very death. She hadn't forgotten any of this, even now, watching herself do nothing. She was aware of what she was failing to do—was unable to do—and the shock of understanding that she could not depend on herself produced a sense of resignation, an empty echoing calm. With steady hands she started the car and pulled out of the lot and turned left as the man directed, away from the lights of the commercial zone, toward the river.

"Not so slow," he said.

She sped up.

"Slower!"

She slowed down.

"You are trying to be arrested," he said.

"No."

He made a mirthless laughing sound. "Do I look like a fool?"

"No . . . I don't know. I haven't seen you."

"I am not a fool. Turn right."

They were on Frontage Road now, heading upriver. The night was clear, and the almost-full moon hung just above the old tanneries on the far bank. The moon made a broad silver path on the smooth water in the middle of the river, glimmered dully on the slabs of ice jammed up along the sides. The moonlight on Maureen's bare hands turned them ghostly white on the steering wheel. They looked cold; they *were* cold. She felt chilled through. She turned up the heater, and within moments the car was filled with the man's smell—ripe, loamy, not unpleasant.

"You were using alcohol," the man said.

She waited for him to say more. His knees were angled toward her, pressed together against the console. "A little," she said.

He was silent. His breathing slowed, deepened, and Maureen felt obscurely grateful for this. She could feel him watching her.

"Over $70 is in my purse," she said. "Please just take it."

"Seventy dollars? That is your offer?" He laughed the unreal laugh.

"I can get more," she said. Her voice was small and flat—not her voice at all. She hesitated, then said, "We'll have to go to an ATM."

"This is not about money. Drive. Please."

And so she did. This was something she could do, drive a car on Frontage Road, as she'd done for almost 30 years now. She drove past the Toll House Inn, past the bankrupt development with its unfinished, skeletal houses open to the weather, past the road to the bridge that would take her home, past the burned-out house with the trailer beside it, on past the brickworks and the quarry and a line of dairy farms and the farm her grandparents had worked as tenants to escape the tannery, where, after several years of learning the hard way, the owner sold out and a new owner found more experienced hands and sent them packing, back across the river. When she was young, Maureen and her sisters had picked strawberries with their mother on different farms, and Maureen had marveled at how her mother could chat with a woman in the next row or just look dully into the distance while her fingers briskly ransacked the plants for ripe berries, as if possessed of their own eyes and purpose. At the end of a day she'd look over Maureen's card (punched for a fraction of the flats she herself had picked), then hand it back and say, "At least that mouth of yours works."

Maureen drove on past the harshly lit 7-Eleven and the Christmas-tree farm and the old ferry pier where she and Francis, her ex-husband, then a sweet, shy boy, had parked after high school dances to drink and make out; on through pale fields and brief stands of bare black trees that in summer made a green roof overhead. She knew every rise and turn, and the car took them easily, and Maureen surrendered to the comfort of her mastery of the road. The silent man beside her seemed to feel it too; it seemed to be holding him in a trance.

Then he shifted, leaned forward. "Turn right up there," he said in a low voice. "On that road, you see? That one up there, after the sign."

Maureen made the turn almost languidly. The side road was unplowed, covered with crusty snow that scraped against the undercarriage of the car. She hit a deep dip; the front end clanged, the wheels spun wild for a moment, then they caught and the car shot forward again, headlights jumping giddily. The road bent once and ended in a clearing surrounded by tall pines.

"You drive too fast," the man said.

She waited, engine running, hands still on the wheel, headlights ablaze on a Park Service sign picturing animals and plants to be seen hereabouts. The peaked roof over the sign wore a hat of snow. It came to Maureen that she'd been to this place before—a trailhead, unfamiliar at first in its winter bleakness. She had come here with Grace's scout troop to hike up to the palisades overlooking the river. The trail was historic, a route of attack for some battle in the Revolutionary War.

The man sniffed, sniffed again. "Beer," he said.

"I was having a drink with friends."

"A *drink*. You stink of it. The great lady teacher!"

That he knew she was a teacher, that he knew anything about her, snapped the almost serene numbness that had overtaken Maureen. She thought of his seeing the essays. That could explain his knowledge of her work, but not his tone—the personal scorn and triumph in his discovery of her weakness, as he clearly saw it.

A small dull pain pulsed behind her eyes, all that was left of the drink she'd had. The heat blowing in the car was making her contacts dry and scratchy. She reached over to turn it down, but he seized her wrist and pulled it back. His fingers were thin and damp. He turned the heat up again. "Leave it like this—warm," he said, and dropped her hand.

She almost looked at him then, but stopped herself. "Please," she said. "What do you want?"

"This is not about sex," he said. "That is what you are thinking, of course. That is the American answer to everything."

Maureen looked ahead and said nothing. She could see the lights of cars on Frontage Road flickering between the tree trunks. She wasn't very far from the road, but the idea of running for it appeared to her a demeaning absurdity, herself flailing through the drifts like some weeping, dopey, sacrificial extra in a horror movie.

"You know nothing about our life," he said. "Who we are. What we have had to do in this country. I was a doctor! But OK, so they won't let me be a doctor here. I give that up. I give up the old life so my family will have this new life. My son will be a doctor, not me! OK, I accept, that's how it is."

"Where are you from?" Maureen asked, and then said, "Never mind," hoping he wouldn't answer. It seemed to her that the loamy smell was stronger, more sour. She kept her eyes on the Park Service sign in the headlights, but she was aware of the man's knees knocking rapidly and soundlessly together.

"*Never mind,*" he said. "Yes, that is exactly your way of thinking. That is exactly how the great lady teacher destroys a family. Without a thought. Never mind!"

"But I don't know your family." She waited. "I don't know what you're talking about."

"No, you don't know what I'm talking about. You have already forgotten. Never mind!"

"You have the wrong person," Maureen said.

"Have you told a lie, lady teacher?"

"Please. You must have the wrong person. What you're saying—none of it makes sense." And because this was certainly true, because nothing he'd said had anything to do with her, Maureen felt compelled—as prelude to a serious sorting-out of this whole mess—to turn and look at him. He was leaning back into the corner, hunched into a puffy coat of the vivid orange color worn by highway crews. In the reflected glare of the headlights, his dark eyes had a blurred, liquid brightness. Above the straight line of his eyebrows the bald dome of his head gleamed dully. He wore a short beard. A few thin patches of it grew high on his cheeks, to just below his eyes.

"I have the right person," he said. "Now you will please answer me."

She was confused; she shook her head as if to clear it.

"No?" he said. "The great lady teacher has never told a lie?"

"What are you talking about? What lie?"

A sudden glint of teeth behind the beard. "You tell me."

"Any lie? Ever?"

"Ever. Any lie or cheat."

"This is ridiculous. Of course I have. Who hasn't, for God's sake?"

He rocked forward and jabbed his head at her. "Don't curse! No more cursing!"

Maureen could see his face clearly now, the full, finely molded, almost feminine lips, the long thin nose, the dark unexpected freckles across the bridge of his nose and under his eyes, vanishing into the beard. She turned away and leaned her throbbing head against the steering wheel.

"You can lie and cheat," he said. "That's OK, no problem. Who hasn't? Never mind! But for others—poof! No faults allowed!"

"This is crazy," she murmured.

"No, Mrs. Casey. What is crazy is to destroy a good boy's life for nothing."

Her breath caught. She raised her head and looked at him.

"Hassan makes one mistake—one mistake—and you destroy him," he said. "Understand this, most esteemed lady teacher, I will not allow it."

"Hassan? Hassan is your son?"

He leaned back again, lips pursed, cheeks working out and back, out and back like a fish's.

Hassan. She liked him, too much. He was tall and graceful and broodingly, soulfully handsome. Not very bright, Hassan, and bone idle, but with a sudden offhand charm that amused her and had distracted her from dealing firmly with him, as he well knew. He'd been getting away with murder all year, fudging on his homework, handing in essays he obviously hadn't written, and Maureen had done nothing but warn him. She hated calling people on their offenses; her own raised voice and shaking hands, her heart pumping out righteousness, all the rituals of grievance and reproach were distasteful to her, and had always held her back, up to a point. Beyond that point she did not spare the lash. But she was slow to get there. Her sisters had pushed her around, she'd spoiled her daughter. Her husband's gambling had brought them to the point of ruin before her cowardice became too shameful to bear and she began to challenge his excuses and evasions, and finally faced him down—"ran him off," as Grace liked to say when she wanted to cut deep.

A similar self-disgust had caught up with Maureen this morning. After months of letting Hassan slide, she'd seen him blatantly cheating during an exam, and she'd blown—really blown, surprising even herself. She'd pulled him out of class and told him in some detail how little she thought of him, then sent him home with a promise—shouted at his back—to report his cheating to Father Crespi, who would certainly expel him. Hassan had turned then and said, evenly, "Stupid cow." And now, remembering that betrayal, the advantage he'd taken, his insulting confidence that he could cheat in front of her with impunity, she felt her fingers tighten on the steering wheel and she stared fixedly in front of her, seeing nothing.

"Hassan!" she said.

"I will not allow it," he repeated.

"Hassan has been cheating all year," she said. "I warned him. This was the last straw."

"*Warnings.* You should give him help, not warnings. It's hard for Hassan. He wasn't born here, his English is not good."

"Hassan's English is fine. He's lazy and dishonest, that's his problem. He'd rather cheat than do the work."

"Hassan is going to be a doctor."

"Sure."

"He will be a doctor! He will. And you won't stop him—you, a drunken woman."

"Oh," she said. "Of course. Of course. *Women.* All our fault, right? Bunch of stupid cows messing things up for the bulls."

"No! I bow before woman. Woman is the hand, the heart, the soul of her home, set there by God himself. All comes from her. All is owed to her."

"Now you're quoting," Maureen said. "Who's your source?"

"The *home,*" he said. "Not the army. Not the surgery. Not the judge's chair, giving laws. Not the discotheque."

"Who's your source?" Maureen repeated. "God, is it?"

The man drew back. "Have some care," he said. "God is not mocked."

Maureen rubbed her scratchy eyes and one of her contacts drifted out of focus. She blinked furiously until it slipped back into place. "I'm turning the heat off," she said.

"No. Leave it warm."

But she turned it off anyway, and he made no move to stop her. He looked wary, watching her from his place against the door; he looked cornered, as if *she* had seized *him* and forced him to this lonely place. The car engine was doing something strange, surging, then almost dying, then surging again. The noise of the blower had masked it. Piece of shit. Another paycheck down the drain.

"OK, doctor," she said. "You've got your parent-teacher conference. What do you want?"

"You will not report Hassan to Mr. Crespi."

"Father Crespi, you mean."

"I call no man father but one."

"Wonderful. So you choose a school called Saint Ignatius."

"I understand. This would not happen if Hassan were Catholic."

"Oh, *please.* Hassan can't speak English, Hassan needs help, Hassan isn't Catholic. Jesus! *I'm* not even Catholic."

He made his laughing sound. "So you choose a school called Saint Ignatius. With your Jesus on the cross behind your desk—have seen it myself at the open house. I was there! I was there. But no, she is not Catholic, not Mrs. Maureen Casey."

Even with the heat off, the air in the car was stale and close. Maureen opened her window halfway and leaned back, bathing her face in the cold draft of air. "That's right," she said. "I've had it with clueless men passing on orders from God."

"Without God, there is no foundation," he said. "Without God, we stand on nothing."

"Anyway, you're too late. I've already reported him."

"You have not. Mr. Crespi is out of town until Monday."

"Father Crespi. Well, I'm impressed. At least *you've* done your homework."

"Hassan is going to be a doctor," he said, rubbing his hands together, gazing down at them as if expecting some visible result.

"Look at me. *Look at me.* Now listen." She held the man's liquid eyes, held the moment, not at all displeased that what she was about to say, though true, would give him pain. "Hassan is not going to be a doctor," she said. "Wait—just listen. Honestly, now, can you picture Hassan in medical school? Even supposing he could get in? Even supposing he can get through college at all? Think about it—Hassan in medical school. What an idea! You could make a comedy—*Hassan Goes to Medical School.* No. Hassan will not be a doctor. And you know it. You have always known it." She gave that thought some room to breathe. Then she said, "So it doesn't really matter if I report him or not, does it?"

Still she held his eyes. His lips were working, he seemed about to say something, but no sound emerged.

She said, "So. Let's say I don't play along. Let's say I'm going to report him, which I am. What are you going to do about it? I mean, what were you thinking tonight?"

He looked away, back down at his hands.

"You followed me from school, right? You waited for me. You had this spot picked out. What were you going to do if I didn't play along?"

He shook his head.

"Well, what? Kill me?"

He didn't answer.

"You were going to kill me? Too much! Have you got a gun?"

"No! I own no guns."

"A knife?"

"No."

"What, then?"

Head bent, he resumed rubbing his hands together as if over a fire.

"Stop that. What, then?"

He took a deep breath. "Please," he said.

"Strangle me? With those? Stop that!" She reached over and seized his wrists. They were thin, bony. "Hey," she said, then again, "Hey!" When at last he raised his eyes to her, she lifted his hands and pressed the palms to her neck. They were cold, colder than the air on her face. She dropped her own hands. "Go on," she said.

She felt his fingers icy against her neck. His eyes, dark and sad, searched hers.

"Go on," she said, softly.

The engine surged, and he blinked as if in surprise and pulled his hands away. He rested them in his lap, looked at them unhappily, then put them between his knees.

"No?" she said.

"Mrs. Casey . . ."

She waited, but that was all he said. "Tell me something," she said. "What did your wife think of this brainstorm? Did you tell her?"

"My wife is dead."

"I didn't know that."

He shrugged.

"I'm sorry."

"Mrs. Casey . . .

Again she waited, then said, "What?"

"The window? It is very cold."

Maureen had a mind to say no to him, let him freeze, but she was getting pretty numb herself. She rolled the window up.

"And please? The heater?"

Maureen drove back down Frontage Road. He kept his face to the other window, his back to her. Now and then she saw his shoulders moving but he didn't make a sound. She had planned to put him out by the turnoff for her bridge, let him find his own way from there, but as she approached the exit she couldn't help asking where he'd left his car. He said it was in the same lot where she'd parked hers. Ah, yes. That made sense. She drove on.

They didn't speak again until she had stopped just up from the parking lot, under a streetlight, in plain view of the drunks walking past. Even here, cocooned in the car, engine surging, Maureen could feel the heavy bass thump of the music coming from Harrigan's.

"Hassan will be dismissed from school?" he asked.

"Probably. He's spoiled, it'll do him good in the long run. You're the one I haven't made up my mind about. You're the one on the hot seat. Do you understand?"

He bowed his head.

"I don't think you do. Forget the prison time you're looking at—you haven't even said you're sorry. I said it, about your wife, which makes me the only one who's used that word tonight. Which strikes me as pretty damned ridiculous, given the circumstances."

"But I am. I am sorry."

"Yeah—we'll see. One thing, though. Suppose I'd promised not to report Hassan. Whatever made you think I'd keep my word?"

He reached into the breast pocket of his coat and took out a white book and laid it on the dashboard. Maureen picked it up. It was a Bible, a girl's Bible bound in imitation leather with gilt lettering on the cover, the pages edged in gilt. "You would swear," he said. "Like in court, to the judge."

Maureen opened it, riffled the thin, filmy pages. "Where did you get this?"

"Goodwill."

"My dear," she said. "You really thought you could save him."

He pushed the door open. "I am sorry, Mrs. Casey."

"Here." Maureen held out the Bible, but he put up the palms of his hands and backed out of the car. She watched him make his way down the street, a short man, hatless, his bright, puffy coat billowing with the gusts. She saw him turn into the parking lot but forgot to observe his leaving, as she'd intended, because she got caught up leafing through the Bible. Her father had given her one just like it after her confirmation; she still kept it on her bedside table.

This Bible had belonged to Clara Gutierrez. Below her name, someone had written an inscription in Spanish; Maureen couldn't make it out in the dim light, only the day, large and underlined—*Pascua 1980.* Where was she now, this Clara? What had become of her, this ardent, hopeful girl in her white dress, surrounded by her family, godparents, friends, that her Bible should end up in a Goodwill bin? Even if she no longer read it, or believed it, she wouldn't have thrown it away, would she? Had something happened? Ah, girl, where were you? ◀

# A Few Words about Getting Your Work Published

Chances are, sooner or later—and often after much frustration and revision—you are going to feel as though you've written something that deserves a wider audience than your teacher and classmates, your family and friends. If the time comes when you want to share your work with the world, you'll be looking to get published, either in print or online.

If you have a strong poem or story and your school has a literary magazine, that's often a good place for a first publication. Many school literary journals and online magazines have high production values, and obviously the competition among potential contributors is much less than if you were competing against writers from all over the country.

While you may think the logical first step on the road to publication is securing the services of a literary agent, that's not the case. Unless you have an incredibly sensational story to tell or you've secretly been honing your craft for a long time, most agents will want you to have a track record of publication before they even think of representing you. They get paid a percentage of the money their writers make, and they will be uninterested in taking on clients who are likely to be minimal earners in their early years.

Instead, if you decide to go beyond the boundaries of your institution of higher learning, you'll want to start by consulting a directory of literary journal listings to find out which magazines print creative writing. In the long-ago days before the Internet, writers turned to print sources like *Poet's Market* and the *Novel and Short Story Writer's Market* (Writers Digest Books) and *The International Directory of Little Magazines and Small Presses* (Dustbooks). These books provide solid and detailed advice about the process of submitting literary work, and they remain valid ways of checking out potential markets. The listings explain editorial biases, describe the physical appearance of a journal, provide circulation numbers and reporting times, and let the writer know the percentage of manuscripts accepted each year.

Online listings have made these books less necessary than they once were. Obviously, Web sites may change radically or disappear overnight, but among the most reliable online directories of publishing venues are the "Literary Magazines" listings in *Poets & Writers Magazine* (pw.org/literary_magazines), New Pages (newpages.com), and the Council of Literary Magazines and Presses (clmp.org/directory). The advantages of Web-based directories are their cost (free), the currency of their listings, and the immediate access they provide through hyperlinks to the publishers' Web sites.

One question you're likely to ask early on is whether to seek online or print publication, but there's no need to stick to just one, and literary writers often submit to a combination of Web and paper journals.

Of course, each format has advantages and disadvantages. Producing a good-looking digital journal is far cheaper than printing a comparable hard copy issue, and the best Webzines often have a polished appearance that their print counterparts can only envy. Online journals are also available to everyone with an Internet connection, so the potential audience for your writing is much greater than it would be in even a large-circulation print magazine. That said, most online literary journals aren't read any more widely than their print counterparts. Moreover, the ephemeral nature of online publishing means that a publisher may decide to close up shop without notice, with the result that everything published in the e-zine suddenly vanishes. When that happens, writers sometimes wonder if they can still consider themselves "published" now that their work no longer appears on the Internet.

That problem doesn't exist with print magazines. Your poem or story may appear in an edition of just 500 copies, but those copies aren't going to disappear if the publisher goes out of business. You'll always have a paper souvenir of your publication. And because even a small run of a print journal generally costs at least a few thousand dollars to produce, there is a certain prestige attached to print publication that may still be lacking from online sources. Most print journals now have a Web site, which—in addition to providing current submission guidelines—typically also posts at least a few sample pieces from the current and past issues of the journal, one of which may be yours.

Fortunately for beginning writers, there are literally thousands of places to publish work. Indeed, the sheer number of venues may initially appear overwhelming. Don't let that scare you off. Once you've found a directory that suits you, take your time and browse. Not every magazine is for every writer, and you'll soon discover that there are some very specialized publishers, from those that want work from writers only in a certain region of the country, to others that focus solely on writing about specific subject matter, to magazines that specialize in particular literary forms. This market research is especially important for beginning writers, although, as George Core, the editor of *The Sewanee Review*, acknowledges, "Anything good enough is likely to be accepted, even if it should violate various sacred guidelines."

As you decide whether to submit to a journal, look for the percentage of submitted manuscripts that are actually published. The editors of long-established magazines such as *The New Yorker* and *The Atlantic*, for example, accept only a fraction of

1 percent of the poems and stories sent to them. If you were to send your work only to these first-tier journals, you would probably be in for a world of discouragement. Granted, an acceptance by an exclusive magazine would represent a phenomenal start to your career. However, when you are starting out, you shouldn't expect to become famous overnight. Choose newer journals that indicate they are actively seeking to publish new writers and don't receive a flood of submissions.

The process of submission varies from journal to journal—one more reason to pay careful attention to the listings for the magazines to which you are submitting. Generally, though, you will write a *short* cover letter introducing yourself and stating that the work you are enclosing has not been published before. The work itself should include your name and address in a prominent place on the first page of a story and on every individual poem. Many writers also include their phone numbers and e-mail addresses. Nearly all magazines provide a maximum number of poems—usually three to six—that can be submitted or a maximum word or page count for prose. Pay attention to this number if you want your submission to be taken seriously.

If the journal asks for a print submission, you usually need to include a self-addressed, stamped envelope (called an SASE), which is folded and slipped inside the original envelope. Be aware of how much a postal submission weighs. You can usually mail a cover letter, a SASE, and two or three poems for the price of a first-class stamp. After that, you'll need to pay more. If your submission arrives with insufficient postage, chances are strong that it will never be read at all.

Editors requesting e-mail submissions typically indicate whether they prefer the work to be sent as an attachment or pasted into the body of the message. Editors can be quite exacting about such things, so, again, it is essential that you read the journal's listing carefully before submitting.

One way of maximizing your chances of publication is to simultaneously submit the same piece to a number of journals. If you do this, however, make certain that the publisher condones this practice—nearly always this will be stated explicitly in the submission guidelines—and if you have a piece accepted by one journal, be sure to contact the others immediately by e-mail to withdraw that piece. Publishing the same work in two different journals is considered a serious breach of trust by most editors; there are even rumors of a "blacklist" circulating among editors with the names of writers who have tried to double up on a publication without the editors' permission. If a magazine refuses to accept simultaneous submissions, honor that policy.

Recently, both electronic and print journals have begun turning to online submission managers. These managers allow writers to post their work on a Web site, where it is evaluated by the journal's editors. Usually you will be required to register for each new journal, although once you are registered, subsequent submissions to that journal are much quicker. One of these online managers,

Submittable, requires you to register only once; then all submissions to journals subscribing to this service access the same personal information.

Some journals charge for the convenience of online submissions, but many writers and teachers of writing, including this author of this textbook, maintain that writers should not have to pay to have the editor of a magazine consider their work. Most print journals pay only with contributors' copies of the issue in which an author's work has appeared. Cash payment at the beginning level—whether in print or online—is rare. Why should writers pay for the chance to be published when they won't be compensated themselves if they are?

That said, journals nearly always operate on a shoestring budget, and you should do what you can to support them. Editors of print journals often ask that potential contributors purchase a sample copy before submitting. This serves the dual purpose of boosting the magazine's sales and giving the submitter an idea of the type of work the magazine publishes. Online journals naturally want you to read through a few of their recent issues to be certain your aesthetic matches theirs.

After you've taken the time and trouble to submit your thoroughly revised and carefully proofread work, you'll inevitably want an immediate response. Regrettably, that rarely happens. The best literary magazines receive thousands of submissions a month, and it takes even a large and dedicated staff a good deal of time to read through all that work. Be patient, and *don't* pester publishers with questions about how soon they'll be making a decision on your work. Remember that most of them are working for free and are doing the best they can; they resent if you imply otherwise.

When you finally do hear back from a journal, you'll need to be prepared for the most likely outcome of any submission: rejection. Often that takes the form of a brief e-mail or a generic photocopied note on a small slip of paper informing you that while the editors appreciate your submission, they cannot use it at this time. There may be no indication that your work has been read by a living human being other than the word "Sorry" someone has scribbled at the bottom of a note or typed at the end of an e-mail.

Don't let rejection get you down. Every writer gets rejected, and every writer who believes in himself or herself turns around and submits again. Quitting isn't an option if you want to be published.

Indeed, rejection is the dark door at the center of creative writing through which all who hope to survive must pass. Even the most successful writers have been rejected many times, and developing a healthy attitude toward rejection is essential to every writer. "Success is distant and illusory," Joyce Carol Oates points out, "failure one's loyal companion, one's stimulus for imagining the next book will be better, for, otherwise, why write?"

Rejection notices run the gamut from the very brief to elaborate apologies and explanations about why, this time, the writer's piece could not be printed.

Interestingly, many letters of rejection are longer than letters of acceptance, and if you receive the former, think about how much time an editor has invested in commenting on your work. Often these encouraging letters of rejection ask you to submit again and mark the beginning of a writer-editor relationship that ultimately leads to publication. Some writers save their rejection letters in a box, some burn them, and some even paper their walls with them. This last act, a fascinating combination of despair (Everyone hates me!) and chutzpah (But I don't care!), suggests something of the difficult balance a working writer must adopt toward publication. At one time there was even a literary journal that accepted only manuscripts that had already been rejected (a rejection notice had to accompany all submissions).

The lesson here is that there are different levels of rejection, and experienced writers come to distinguish among them. They learn to recognize the important fact that not everyone will be a fan of their work, that race, class, gender, artistic predilections, and whether an editor is having a bad day all affect the likelihood of publication. As writer Sue Lick puts it: "I try to tell myself manuscripts are like shoes. If I were selling shoes, I would expect a lot of people to walk by without buying them or even trying them on. Writing is the same way. It usually takes more than one submission to find the publication for which the manuscript fits perfectly." The smartest writers also use rejection letters as an opportunity to meditate on their writing. Does a pattern of editorial commentary emerge over time? Perhaps editors keep remarking, *Your characters are unconvincing*, or, *You need to tighten the lines of your poems*. If so, how much of this commentary is the editors' inability to recognize your individual style, and how much does the criticism reflect real problems you need to address?

Ultimately it is how one handles rejection that determines whether one will continue as a creative writer. The initial impulse may be to retreat. However, experienced writers learn to disconnect criticism of the work from criticism of the writer: rejection of the work is not equivalent to rejection of one*self*. Poet Michael Dennis Browne lauds the work of psychotherapist Thomas Moore in helping writers overcome their sense of failure. Moore writes:

> Ordinary failures in work are an inevitable part of the descent of the spirit into human limitation. Failure is a mystery, not a problem. Of course this means not that we should try to fail, or to take masochistic delight in mistakes, but that we should see the mystery of incarnation at play whenever our work doesn't measure up to our expectations. If we could understand the feelings of inferiority and humbling occasioned by failure as meaningful in their own right, then we might incorporate failure into our work so that it doesn't literally devastate us.

Learning to handle rejection gracefully, to *learn* from it, makes us more human. And since all writers get rejected, at least in this one instance we're all in it together.

# A Few Words of Farewell

Coming to the end of an introductory creative writing class is a bittersweet time. Students are gratified to finish a job well done, but they also sense that there is much more for them to discover. Still, most students will have learned a great deal—from their instructor and their classmates, from their readings in the genre, and, I hope, from their textbook as well. As I noted in the introduction to this book, *Creative Writing: An Introduction to Poetry and Fiction* is meant to supplement, but never replace, what happens in the classroom, and most of what you take away from your class will be memories of your fellow writers.

Nevertheless, it has been my pleasure to pass on in print what I have learned over the years, not only from my own teachers and the writers I have admired but also from the thousands of creative writing students I have taught, all of them—like you—bringing a fresh perspective and boundless energy to the world of literature.

So let me offer a few final words of advice:

▸ **Keep in touch with the friends you have made.** Look for opportunities outside class to share work with people who have offered constructive criticism. Talk about recent books you have read and loved. Start a writing group. Hang out.

▸ **Keep in touch with your instructor.** Drop by next term and say thanks. Take the time to write an e-mail recalling the highlights of your class. Especially if you have had a literary success, she or he will be glad to know about it.

▸ **Take another creative writing class.** Most colleges and universities have single-genre courses: try an advanced poetry or fiction class, ideally with a different instructor who will offer a new perspective. Attend a writers' conference (many of them are listed on the Association of Writers and Writing Programs' Web site). Learn more about the world of creative writing by reading journals such as *Poets & Writers Magazine* and *The Writer's Chronicle* or books such as *Keywords in Creative Writing.*

▸ **When you feel confident enough to do so, submit your work for publication.** There is nothing quite like the thrill of your first publication, but you cannot win, as the carnival barkers say, if you do not play.

▸ **Most important, keep writing.** Even if you never publish a word, the ability to animate the creatures of your imagination is a special gift, one you should cherish all your life.

# Glossary

**aesthetic** A theory or conception of beauty and taste in art.

**alliteration** The repetition of initial consonant sounds.

**allusion** A reference to a specific person, place, or thing; literary allusions refer to incidents, images, or passages in previous works of literature.

**anapest** A metrical foot consisting of two unstressed syllables followed by one stressed syllable.

**antagonist** A character who serves as another character's opponent or adversary.

**archaic language** Language that evokes an earlier place and time and is now obsolete.

**assonance** The repetition of vowel sounds without the repetition of similar end consonants.

**backstory** The narrative of events leading up to the current moment in a work of fiction; also called exposition.

**ballad** A narrative poem in quatrains rhyming *abcb*, with alternating lines of four and three metrical feet.

**beat** A distinct movement, whether of action, dialogue, or conflict, in a play. Also refers to the pause following the end of that movement.

**chapbook** A short book of poetry, usually fewer than thirty-two pages.

**characters** The people in a work of creative writing.

**chronology** An account of the way time actually moves, from past to present to future.

**cinquain** A poetic form named after the French word *cinq*, meaning "five." In the broadest sense, a cinquain is simply a five-line stanza, although it now usually refers to a five-line form with a specific syllable count in each line.

**cliché** A trite, overused expression.

**climax** The turning point in a narrative; the point of maximum dramatic attention.

**connotation** The meanings a word *suggests* rather than what it specifically names or describes.

**consonance** The recurrence of consonant sounds, especially at the end of stressed syllables, but without similar-sounding vowels.

**couplet** Two consecutive lines of verse that are connected in some significant way.

**creative nonfiction** Literary writing that claims to be true.

**dactyl** A metrical foot consisting of one stressed syllable followed by two unstressed syllables.

**denouement** The French word for "untying," in this case referring to untying the knot of a narrative plot.

**dialect** Nonstandard language associated with a particular group, culture, or region.

**dialogue** Conversation between characters.

**diction** A writer's or speaker's choice of words.

**dimeter** A poetic line consisting of two feet.

**double rhyme** Words with the same vowel sound in the final two syllables.

**dramatic monologue** A literary work (usually a poem) in which the author adopts a persona and writes as if speaking to another character.